RESHAPING YOUR BUSINESS with WEB 2.0

Using the New Collaborative Technologies to Lead Business Transformation

Vince Casarez

Billy Cripe

Jean Sini

Philipp Weckerle

McGraw Hill

New York   Chicago   San Francisco   Lisbon   London   Madrid   Mexico City
Milan   New Delhi   San Juan   Seoul   Singapore   Sydney   Toronto

The McGraw·Hill Companies

Cataloging-in-Publication Data is on file with the Library of Congress

McGraw-Hill books are available at special quantity discounts to use as premiums and sales promotions, or for use in corporate training programs. To contact a special sales representative, please visit the Contact Us page at www.mhprofessional.com.

Reshaping Your Business with Web 2.0: Using the New Collaborative Technologies to Lead Business Transformation

1 2 3 4 5 6 7 8 9 0 FGR FGR 0 1 9 8

ISBN 978-0-07-160078-1
MHID   0-07-160078-7

Sponsoring Editor:	Roger Stewart
Editorial Supervisor:	Jody McKenzie
Project Manager:	Patricia Wallenburg
Acquisitions Coordinator:	Carly Stapleton
Copy Editor:	Lisa Theobald
Proofreader:	Paul Tyler
Indexer:	Karen Arrigoni
Production Supervisor:	Jim Kussow
Composition:	TypeWriting
Illustration:	TypeWriting
Art Director, Cover:	Jeff Weeks

RESHAPING YOUR BUSINESS with WEB 2.0

Dedication

To my lifelong inspiration and friend, my all-star who never ceases to amaze me, my superstar with a passion for doing everything perfect, Robbie, Alex, and Veronica, you provide my life with purpose and joy. And to all the voices that stood up to be heard and shaped me: Gloria, Warren, Eda, Clarence, Carole, Ron, Irene, Larry, Mickie, Sam, Ted, Roberta, Joe, Jeannette, and Vera. Special thanks to Manish for your mastery of our subject.

—Vince Casarez

To grande Starbucks dark roast with cream, my Zune playlist, the Web, Jahweh, ubiquitous connectivity, the host of smarter people who were my sounding boards and idea incubators, and, finally, my family who supported me, edited me, and made me better, though they didn't always "get it."

—Billy Cripe

To the countless voices, anonymous or otherwise, and the many crowds that have pioneered and continue to shape the participatory web and inspired me to contribute.

—Jean Sini

About the Authors

Since 1995, **Vince Casarez** has served in many key positions at Oracle Corporation. He is currently Vice President of Product Management for Enterprise 2.0 and Portal products. He also manages the WebCenter development team handling Web 2.0 services. Prior to this, he focused on hosted portal development and operations that included Oracle Portal Online for external customers, Portal Center for building a portal community, and My Oracle for the employee intranet. Previously, he was Vice President of Tools Marketing, in charge of all tools products including development tools and business intelligence tools. Prior to that position, he was Director of Product Management for Oracle's JDeveloper. Before joining Oracle, Vince spent seven years at Borland International, where he was group product manager of Paradox for Windows and dBASE for Windows. He holds a bachelor's degree in biochemistry from the University of California, Los Angeles.

Billy Cripe, director of product management at Oracle Corporation, focuses on Enterprise 2.0 strategy and Enterprise Content Management products. In 1999, he received his master of arts degree from Northern Illinois University. He also received a degree in communications, focusing on Internet-mediated communications, and he studied extensively with Dr. David Gunkel. Billy eventually wound up working at Habitat For Humanity International (HFHI) in Americus, Georgia, as extranet webmaster. It was there that he brought his education in Internet-mediated communications to bear on real-life systems. He and the Habitat team developed and launched PartnerNet, a global extranet linking HFHI affiliates around the world with donation and distribution centers for materials, information, and volunteer coordination. While working at HFHI, Billy first learned and exploited IntraNet Solutions Intra.Doc! content management software. He left HFHI for a consulting position at IntraNet Solutions, which eventually changed its name to Stellent. After six years in the services group as a consultant and manager, and the addition of a new family member (daughter Kessel), Billy moved into product management to help guide and influence the product direction. Soon thereafter, Oracle Corporation acquired Stellent, and he became the Director of Product Management for Oracle Enterprise Content Management.

Jean Sini is currently Chief Technology Officer at BuzzLogic. He joined the company through its acquisition of Activeweave, a Web 2.0 startup he co-founded in 2005. He leads BuzzLogic's core technical vision and architecture, with a primary focus on targeting relevance and influence across social media. His expertise and interests center on the design and development of distributed computing infrastructures and web-scale services. Based in the Silicon Valley since 1996, Jean has honed his leadership and software engineering skills building large-scale, multi-tiered platforms and managing international engineering teams. Jean holds master's degrees in computer science from Telecom Paris and the Computer Science Laboratories at the Paris University.

Philipp Weckerle leads the product management efforts on Oracle Reports and Content Integration at Oracle Corporation, with more than 15 years' experience in the software industry. Philipp joined Oracle originally in 1999 as support analyst for tools in Austria and transferred to Oracle headquarters as product manager for Oracle Reports in 2001, where he took over the team lead role in 2003. His responsibilities expanded to cover Oracle Portal and Content Integration in 2004 and he now leads the product management efforts on Oracle Reports as well as content integration in the Oracle Austria office in Vienna. Before joining Oracle, Philipp worked in software development and project management for more than seven years, dealing with governmental database application projects and implementing solutions based on the complete Oracle technology stack. During his many years working with Oracle products, he has gained significant experience in design, implementation, and support of transactional and decision-support systems based on the Oracle platform.

Contents at a Glance

Contents

Introduction

Traditional business models have focused on a process and interaction approach that hasn't changed for more than 100 years. Traditional models take a hierarchical approach, with an expectation that all good ideas come from the leaders at the top of the organization. Unfortunately, such models create barriers for using the core knowledge and experiences of every individual within the enterprise. However, by injecting some fundamental Web 2.0 technologies such as social networks, these business models can tap into the core knowledge of all their employees, partners, and customers. This notion of *collective intelligence* is critical to help businesses map new Web 2.0 technologies into their organizations and make the Web 2.0 business paradigm a reality.

Enterprise social networks are made up of people who are linked together in some fashion. These linkages can be formal and well-defined, such as an organizational structure, partner network, or a team workspace membership. They can also be informal and fluid in nature, based on shared goals, objectives, expertise, or projects. Information and *metadata* (description of the information) logically link individuals together, thereby providing the social network. Social networks have broad requirements, and the technologies required to deliver the full promise of enterprise knowledge sharing must be comprehensive yet simple to use.

This book started as a collaboration of authors and experiences via a set of wiki pages that leveraged only a small slice of what Web 2.0 has to offer to the enterprise. Throughout this book, each author's voice is heard for his unique point of view, derived from past experiences and brought together in this collected work. We discuss the key Web 2.0 technologies required to build social networks within the enterprise, along with some common infrastructure guidelines for enabling a more fluid and extensible social network.

Social Network Enablers

Enterprises today face ever-increasing pressures to be agile, innovative, and competitive. Traditional methods of addressing business challenges in the current dynamic and global business environment overlook the rich resources of employees, partners, and customers. Building a social network requires technologies that create and share information and discover experts. These technologies range from simple ways for users to collaborate and share information to more complex capabilities that track progress toward specific goals and measure success.

Pages

In the Web 2.0 era, *pages* are arguably the most important way to share information. Composing pages must therefore be intuitive, simple, collaborative, and expressive. *Wikis* are a good start and provide the foundations for collaboration, but they don't go far enough. Additional considerations include the following:

- **Rich, yet extensible, set of available resources**—Call them widgets, gadgets, portlets, or whatever you like—to express knowledge, the right components need to be available for users to compose their pages. Unfortunately, system designers can never anticipate all the users' needs, nor do they have the time or resources to build out every single component. Pages need to include information from throughout the enterprise as well as across the Internet.

- **In-place collaborative text editing**—Users need a collaborative way of sharing information that isn't dependent on passing around the "correct" version of a specific document. Whether the entire page or a section of the page requires editing, creating a wiki page and adding text to an existing page should be an extremely simple process. However, current wiki solutions fall short in their ability to integrate with existing identity management systems. Their permissions aren't granular enough to provide flexibility for the users and still provide enough control for the enterprise. In addition, every person and every team wants their information and ideas to be presented as clearly and professionally as possible. However, not everyone has the eye or skills to make their pages look as if an expert designer created them. Design styles and themes that can be applied quickly and easily to their existing pages will make their ideas stand out.

■ **Ability to share pages or keep them private**—Outside of a well-defined membership space, the Web 2.0 common usage pattern is for all pages to be available to everyone. But when a limited set of users should have access to the information, a user must be able to include some and exclude others.

■ **Ease of interaction and usability**—Users have high expectations regarding the ways they interact with new Web 2.0 applications. They expect all the bells and whistles that are available on the public Internet, including capabilities such as drag-and-drop component arrangement, dynamic layout changes, in-place component editing without leaving the page, and quick page refresh with enterprise data. The Apache Foundation started the Trinidad project to enable AJAX-based controls to help the open source community deliver these types of components.

■ **Ability to mashup components**—To make everything on the page relevant to a particular user or task and enable in-context viewing, users want to be able to mashup components. They also want to combine enterprise information with Internet services. The key standards here are Web Services for Remote Portlets (WSRP 2.0) and the Java Portlet Specification 2.0, JSR-286, along with de facto standards such as Google Gadgets and web services that allow one component to pass context to another. Providing a simple way for business users to pull this information together is the core foundation of Web 2.0 deployments.

Discussions

Obviously, organizations need a place where users can share ideas and refine their thoughts with input from others. Discussions provide a mechanism by which users' thoughts and feedback can be organized. Many users see e-mail as an easy way to carry on discussions, and this is why online discussions need tight integration with e-mail—to help manage these ad hoc conversations in a threaded or related way. In addition to e-mail, a set of web services are required to allow developers to integrate threaded discussions directly into their applications.

Instant Messaging and Presence

Easily locating information and communicating with team members and subject matter experts is essential to making everyone in the organization more productive. Workers need to have the best communication methods available to contact experts when they need to accomplish a task. Information must be available directly at the point of interaction. Users don't want a list of all users or buddies—they want to *know* the presence of and chat with the user who filed the specific report they are viewing.

Tags

Tags are bits of information that each user is able to attach to any object in the social network to help classify the information and make it easy to locate. Tags help users classify all information from a user's point of view. But more important, tags can be integrated with enterprise search to provide a way for every user to influence the results and quickly find items that are used on an infrequent basis. When not limited to a prescribed organizational structure defined by a developer or business users, information workers can create a user-driven categorization, or *folksonomy*. Combining the power of these user-defined tags with some of the other services mentioned here, information and experts can be easily discovered and linked.

Links or Shared Bookmarks

Empowering workers to take control over how new and existing enterprise information is organized is critical for the success of social networks. Connections or links between information, such as links from a document to a discussion forum or from a document to a page, are key enablers. An architecture in which each of these services can easily be added to the system is required, along with a simple user interface that allows business users to link tasks with a specific document or to link a team event with a set of documents. Rather than copying this information from one location to another, it should be easy to link it directly. Tags and links bring all these services together to provide a rich social network of people and information.

Key Enterprise Considerations

Several points are key for an enterprise to consider when establishing a Web 2.0 presence.

Fit with Existing Infrastructures

All enabling technologies must fit within the existing infrastructures that are already in place for each organization. Too often, software as a service (SaaS) offerings rely on their infrastructures to enable all of these technologies, but they don't fit with the rest of the enterprise architecture. The alternative is the need to "upgrade" to the new solution to replace all the backend servers that were already in place.

Before new technologies can provide real business value to the organization, they must provide an adaptive services model to allow any backend system to participate in dynamic social networks. In addition, this adaptive services model must be componentized so that only the services required are plugged into the system. For example, if a company has decided not to include presence and instant messaging within its infrastructure for compliance or regulatory reasons, then the user interface and the rest of the services designed to fit within the infrastructure should still work unchanged. In this way, developers can build their applications once, and then, at deployment or at runtime, the backend connection can be configured to work against existing systems.

Upgrade-proofing

In an enterprise, many stakeholders are involved in a typical application. A balance of application control must be in place for all these stakeholders. Information workers must be able to participate in a simple way that doesn't stifle the growth of the social network. Business users need control over the information that is published and the application evolution. IT needs to roll out new applications and manage upgrades and application patches with relative ease. This places a rigorous demand on the application infrastructure.

Customization patterns are common in the consumer Internet, with sites such as iGoogle and My Yahoo, where a user can create a personal home page and views of information. Although these features have been typically targeted at personal productivity, they enable information workers within the enterprise to share knowledge rapidly and evolve the application. Developers create the initial application and enhance it over time. Business users and lines of business such as human resources can also customize the site. It is important that all changes to these pages be managed effectively.

Avoiding overlapping customizations is impossible, so an effective strategy for choosing which customizations "win" is important. In order for this type of information sharing to enable a social network in a successful way, information workers must be confident that the customizations they implement will remain in place. For example, if information workers customize a component on their shared home page and then IT releases a new version, the new version must not discard or overwrite the information workers' customizations.

Security

Although the enterprise can adopt a whole set of Web 2.0 technologies, it can't adopt the same level of freedom that the Internet enjoys. Not all business knowledge should be shared with the masses; because of this fact, social networks in the enterprise face a difficult challenge. With all the links that exist between people and information, security policies are arguably the most important aspect of social networks. An information worker must never discover information to which he or she doesn't normally have access and must not even be able to discover its existence. Security must be enforced, but the new Web 2.0 capabilities must remain simple; otherwise, users realize no gain in productivity and social networks risk dying a slow death.

As mentioned, information linking is an important aspect of any informal social network. If all this information was in a single place, applying security policies would be straightforward. But this is not practical, and technologies that enable linking information are required to store parts of this data outside the normal security policies, even those as simple as a linked URL. If someone were to link a public page to a top-secret company document about mergers and acquisitions, for example, any knowledge of the existence of that page must not be discoverable by users who do not have appropriate access permissions.

It is important not to underestimate the burden placed on the end users to understand the underlying security models. Consider, for example, a user creating a page and adding a document to it. If the security for the page and document are from the same infrastructure, the model exposed to the user is consistent and simple. If the page and document are separate files, the application must keep the two files in sync, and the user must understand the page security and the document repository security to share the information with others.

Several best practices should be implemented when considering how to secure information in a composite application:

■ Use formal social networks to define information access rights, thereby ensuring that the information itself is secured. To gain access to the information, users must be part of a specific group or granted a specific role and be authenticated as such.

■ For an even greater level of control, information rights management products can be used. These products encrypt the actual information so that only those with appropriate rights can access it. This increases security so that if the information leaves the repository (via an e-mail attachment, for example), the initially defined access rights are still enforced.

Discovery or Search

All information must be exposed with common discovery or search in mind. The primary discovery mechanisms include search, tag clouds, pivoting or lateral searches, and links navigation. Many discovery mechanisms can be blended together. The typical usage pattern for exploring the plethora of information in a Web 2.0 world generally involves combining *search* and *navigation*. A user, for example, could search for a document she remembers as relevant from several months past. After viewing the initial results, she might filter the results based on the author she recalls wrote the document, start pivoting on tag clouds related to the search terms used, or follow links for a document that seems related.

Since many of the discovery connections and end points may be a person, the ability to interact with an author in-context via instant messaging/chat, phone, and e-mail is critical to improving productivity.

Know Your Audience: Employees, Partners, and Customers

Many new devices attempt to move social network experiences directly into real-life experiences. Online gaming across the Internet using a Nintendo Wii, for example, creates a realistic experience, blending reality with computer and user interaction. Online fantasy games allow a teenager to play the game online, text his cousin, and simultaneously plan a trip to his cousin's house to taste his mother's homemade cookies. These "Net natives" send micro-text messages to each other in the Twitter style, as discussed in Chapter 4, even while actively playing an online game.

Every day, every hour, similar interactions shape the experiences and expectations of new workers currently entering the business workforce. They are greeted with simple cell phones and e-mail systems that actually force them back in time. In fact, limiting these Net natives to using such tools would, for some of us, be like going back to the age of character-mode terminals, punch cards, vacuum tubes, and typewriters. If you were to be offered a job at a company that uses only telephones, faxes, and typewriters to communicate, would you join?

Young workers today expect, demand, and require more productive and interactive methods for working in and improving the enterprise. They can multi-task in amazing ways and are able to deal with their personal lives at the same time they are working on the next big project. It's your job to figure out how to tap into all these skills and make employees more productive with tools that have become second nature to them.

Sometimes to Always Connected

Today's workers have moved from a "sometimes connected" style to an "always connected" way of life. Net natives who join companies are constantly updating each other with short bursts of contacts either online or via text messages. These interactions are second nature to them—like breathing.

New and powerful mobile devices have added computing power, and new innovations, applications, and experiences can be used by workers even while they're outside the office or on the road. The mobile sales rep, for example, expects to get the latest sales information en route to a customer visit. He can IM experts directly from his cell phone and receive immediate responses without wasting the customer's time. The platform of systems and services that make such communication possible must be easily accessible to these types of users and interactions.

Shattering the Traditional Business Model

While traditional business models can and do prove successful for some companies, they don't guarantee success over time. If employees want to offer suggestions or ideas, or they disagree with key principles set forth by management, they might have no avenues for expressing their thoughts on improving the company. Many company leaders are fond of statements such as, "Our employees are our most critical resource." However, these same companies have no idea pathways to allow employees to offer refinements of existing ideas; as a result, employees become less passionate about what they do and less motivated to make improvements.

Although a senior visionary might be quite passionate about his or her initial ideas, employees become less and less passionate about the company goals. The new challenge is to find ways to tap into the passions of every individual to increase each employee's stake in the ultimate success of the company and to improve the current business. This is where the intersection of Web 2.0 technologies and the enterprise start to shine.

A second flaw with traditional models is their key dependence on the senior visionary to keep thinking of the next great idea to drive the company forward. Such dependence exposes the company to competitive threats from other companies' visions and ideas. The challenge isn't just to break out of traditional thinking, but also to tap into each and every employee as a source of new ideas and new business strategies.

Old models are also insufficient for accessing and collecting data and business knowledge from every possible resource. Pockets of knowledge or business know-how remain in the minds of key employees instead of in the company arena where it can benefit the organization. When an employee is promoted or leaves the company, everyone else scrambles to recover from the loss of a knowledgeable resource. Even if the key employee were able to document his or her critical understanding of the business, it becomes just one more disconnected source of information that needs to be interpreted for others. The challenge is to enable the collaboration of a team of employees to stimulate the flow of ideas, improve existing processes, and create new and successful processes.

Innovative Examples

Several companies have found ways to address these challenges, and the following examples provide sources of critical new ways of running a business. In the context of solving direct business problems, clearly companies need a way for employees and teams to channel their thoughts, pull in information from other sources, refine the idea based on this new information, and then leverage this knowledge in promoting their idea to stimulate future organizational success. While many companies have difficulty allowing key engineering resources to devote time to innovation, the real question is this: can they afford not to?

Toyota Motor Corporation

Many business stories have been published about the success of Toyota Motor Corporation. Early studies tried to decipher why Toyota consistently showed a growing market share, increasing customer satisfaction levels, and continued customer loyalty. Theories about the company's success ran the gamut from sheer luck, to key management hires, to superior robotic automation. But the speculation ended with the revelation that Toyota's employees were incredibly satisfied with their entire work environment.

At Toyota any employee who believes he or she could improve the production process is allowed to stop the entire multi-billion–dollar production line to fix the problem immediately. No employee is expected to fill out a form and submit a request before a change can be made. They aren't told to educate management on the improvement and build consensus among all the managers. They are instead asked to identify the problem immediately and suggest a solution. Sometimes, even within hours, these new changes are successfully implemented to the overall production process.

Toyota empowers every employee by listening to every suggestion, and each employee knows that his or her ideas might be adopted or at least seriously considered. This provides each employee with an obvious channel for individual passions and expertise and allows the company to improve its relevance within the automobile industry.

Google

The meteoric success of Google continues to astonish onlookers as the company keeps coming up with great new ways of finding, presenting, and delivering information and processes to users. The speed at which users can leverage new capabilities consistently outpaces the speed at which Google can deliver these services.

Key executives at the company consistently credit the fact that luck is on their side. However, they understand that a critical reason exists as to why Google consistently provides new and innovative services that change the way users think about problems and how the service presents information: Google makes sure that every engineer in the organization dedicates a significant portion (some say as much as 20 percent) of their time to creating and developing new ideas. Guidelines regarding their work assignments are loosely defined—in fact, the directions are quite simple: basically, "Work on whatever you want." Needless to say, allowing individuals to work on whatever they choose is a foreign concept in the traditional business model. Many companies find it ridiculous to think that employees actually know what might make the company more successful without direct management guideance.

Whole Foods

Whole Foods Market is the world's largest organic food retailer. Whole Foods' slogan is "Whole Foods, Whole People, Whole Planet," emphasizing its goal of reaching far beyond just being a food retailer. The Whole Foods "Declaration of Interdependence" on the company website (http://www. wholefoodsmarket.com) states the following:

> Our ability to instill a clear sense of interdependence among our various stakeholders (the people who are interested and benefit from the success of our company) is contingent upon our efforts to communicate more often, more openly, and more compassionately. Better communication equals better understanding and more trust.

Whole Foods store managers do not decide on new employee hires. Instead, a group of employees in each area of the store interview each candidate and then take a vote. If the candidate doesn't receive more than two thirds of the team's votes, the person is not extended an offer. Whole Foods believes so strongly in building team dynamics that it makes public to every employee the compensation and financial terms for the entire company. Every employee knows what every other employee earns.

Whole Foods clearly believes passionately in cultivating teamwork and team-based interactions. The company wants to tap into its employees' experiences and visions to improve the products and services it delivers to its customers.

Technologies to Consider

Throughout this book, examples of existing and emerging technologies are provided. We didn't intend to provide an exhaustive list of all technologies; instead, we hope to highlight the possibilities, how you might tie them into existing enterprise systems, and what to consider as you plan for the future. With so many new and emerging services in the Web 2.0 and social computing space that can benefit enterprises, we are experiencing a move up a level from pure coding. We see declarative frameworks such as JavaServer Faces (JSF) and Oracle's Application Development Framework (ADF) as core foundations for delivering these innovations in the quickest and most efficient manner. These products improve productivity for developers to help them provide the solutions that can help users get the most relevant information in the most efficient ways.

In Summary

Before Web 2.0 technologies can be successful within the enterprise, they must be adopted by the enterprise. Ensuring that personal productivity is built into social networking features can be a way to increase adoption in a significant way. Information workers' primary focus is accomplishing their tasks using efficient methods with disparate information. The more Web 2.0 technologies can facilitate an individual's own information organization and access, the more likely these technologies will be used in the enterprise. For example, if a user is effectively able to manage shortcuts to information using tags, he or she can find information more quickly and realize a tangible benefit. The fact that other coworkers can also discover information deemed important by a subject matter expert is another benefit to the company.

Bringing Web 2.0 into the enterprise is more than just providing the latest technology; it's about changing the traditional business model and tapping into the creativity, intellect, and passion of every single employee. Companies must understand the changing trends in business and knowledge so that their workers can do more than simply implement the next hot technology. Web 2.0 within the enterprise helps companies foster the development of new ideas, tap into critical thinking and knowledge, and enable the synergy of teams to revolutionize existing business models and set them on the right path for future success.

At the heart of any successful enterprise social network is the ability to connect information and people based on a set of industry standards. Bringing Web 2.0 features to the enterprise and leveraging existing enterprise information and application infrastructure allows companies to tap into every user's expertise and experience, making everyone more productive. By leveraging an adaptable social networking foundation, organizations can more rapidly achieve their goals in a highly optimized way.

Part I

The Behaviors

Chapter 1

Participation Culture: Opportunities and Pitfalls

By Billy Cripe and Philipp Weckerle

For a long time, Web 2.0 was heralded as the transition to the understanding that "the web is the platform." That insight didn't go nearly far enough. It is becoming increasingly clear that the web, in and of itself, is not the platform driving the Internet economy. Rather it is the community as platform that is transforming business and culture in the wired ecosystem. The empowerment of users working in the community has created opportunities for value creation that have simply never been previously available to businesses. This, more than perhaps any other aspect, is driving the development of the Participatory Marketplace.

Michael Graves, CTO, JanRain, Inc.

Web 1.0 was all about one thing: *presence*. If your company, charity, school, or even you had some identifiable presence out there on the World Wide Web, then you were *da' bomb*. Content was secondary. The information displayed was not as important as *how* it was displayed. Having a web page signified you were on the cutting edge; you (or your organization) were a thought leader. The web page generated revenue, investment, and credibility.

Media theorist Marshall McLuhan's aphorism, "The medium is the message," never held so true. Web 1.0 tilted dangerously toward *medium* on the fulcrum of meaning. It was as if relevancy and meaning sprang out of the web page fiat. With Web 1.0, information posted on the Internet was considered meaningful simply because it was *posted on the Internet*. Much less attention was paid to the message carried by posted information than was paid to the medium that carried it. But with so much information being added, and increasing all the time, was it *all* truly useful and accurate? Had to be. After all, it was *On The Web*. Organizations desperate for a web presence poured out money in a mad scramble to get something, anything, online. The dot-com bubble was birthed.

As Web 1.0 evolved, websites started to add in more and more functionality and became more akin to applications, basic to be sure, but applications nonetheless. Form-based web pages became easy ways of soliciting information from users. Database capability, easily scalable, technologically mature, and relatively cheap, was added behind these basic web applications. The databases stored information collected from the web page forms. Information items such as pictures, book chapters, lists of favorite colors, or HTML-encoded pages were stored anywhere a web server could access them. Businesses, schools, and individuals were driven to get more information, content, and functionality available online. Groups with the money or infrastructure looked for new ways to leverage prior investments and started to use structured data management systems first next to, and then increasingly in place of, file system stores for the raw data that networked web servers and Internet service providers (ISPs) made accessible to web surfers. The complementary technologies of increased capacity, structured organization of data, basic processing capabilities, and web page presentation started an evolutionary process in the web consumer. As web *pages* that were best characterized as standalone, self-contained, hyperlinked information designed to be *read* evolved into *sites* inviting *interaction*, the casual reader of web pages evolved into the casual user of websites. Websites, while still containing static pages, also morphed into collections of related information designed to drive the user from passivity to action. Those actions were often the input of information or placing of a purchase order.

Active participation with and in the creation of information rather than simply the passive consumption of information became a new experience for web users and a new offering from websites. User opinions were solicited, polls were taken, the first items were purchased, the first credit card numbers were intercepted, and users were invited to supply simple data: basic username and passwords and then sophisticated purchase orders and more.

Staying true to the archetype of the public Internet, Web 1.0 technology developed and manifested across internal organizational deployments. It placed an emphasis on the speed and efficiency with which information could be created and published to the World Wide Web. The emphasis on creation and distribution of information came at the general expense of accuracy (specifically) and relevancy (generally). As it became easier to create and distribute information through Web 1.0 channels, the likelihood of proliferating inaccuracies also increased. The relationship was directly proportional. Larger quantities of information produced quickly and made ubiquitously available through the Web meant more inaccuracies. In addition, with the increase in information quantity and availability was a nearly inverse proportional relationship with relevancy. Regardless of the quality of information created, the fact that so much information was so easily available meant that finding the right information became increasingly difficult.

At this point, while the public Web was leading the technological exploration of content creation and web distribution, organizations and enterprises started thinking that maybe this web thing could prove useful for their employees and partners. Years passed, seasons changed, and Web 1.0 evolved and morphed into Web 1.99. During this time, organizations and the clanless rogues out on the public Web were continuously trading places for top spot on the innovation ladder. While the clanless were more adept at leveraging new technology and agile development approaches to produce sometimes cool, sometimes lame Internet stuff, the pure weight of funding and momentum that a business could bring to bear on an issue meant that sometimes they actually did something innovative. Unfortunately, most organizations and enterprises also tend to suffer from Newton's first law. Rephrased for business but keeping the gist, it goes something like this: Organizations not doing anything in a particular area tend to keep not doing things in that area, and if, by chance, they are doing something, they tend to do the same thing the same way for as long as they can. This means that it is rare for them to lead anyone anywhere. When they do, they had better hope they are headed in the right direction, because it is hard for them to stop.

Still, the infrastructure that supported the explosion of public Web content, distribution, and development came from somewhere. While open source projects and those of self-interest tended to focus on software, application programming interfaces (APIs), and standards development, businesses looked to productize and sell software, hardware, and infrastructure. Sometimes they innovated in-house. Sometimes they took and sometimes they bought, and otherwise they blatantly stole from the open source community and the clanless and unaffiliated "developers of passion." Cyclically, the open source community and clanless developers hacked, poked, decompiled, repurposed, integrated, and otherwise innovated against standards that became de facto as they were implemented by a critical mass of big business and infrastructure players. These were enterprises such as the telecommunications companies, ISPs, universities, and early dot-coms that penetrated the business and public spheres and provided the digital backdrop for the emergence and mass adoption of the public Web.

The result was a dual explosion of adoption and content. The mass adoption of web technology and creation of content has been near-exponential. Consider two findings from the web content and technology tracker Technorati (see Figure 1-1): As web content creation and distribution technology become increasingly available and accessible to the public, a near-exponential rise in uptake occurs. Weblogs, or blogs, in this case are taken as archetypes of the most easily accessible form of web content creation and distribution technology.

While the adoption and uptake of technology does not necessitate the continued usage of that technology for its intended purpose, tracking information clearly demonstrates that content is exploding along with and enabled by its technological adoption. Considering the plethora of blog posts—that is, content created by people and distributed on the World Wide Web—as representative of overall web content creation, it is clear that information is exploding. Not only is the quantity of information growing, but also the metadata (such as tags) that are being applied to information is growing (see Figure 1-2). Taken together, the information, and the information about the information (metadata), create a flood of data that constitute the wired tableau in which the current generation of

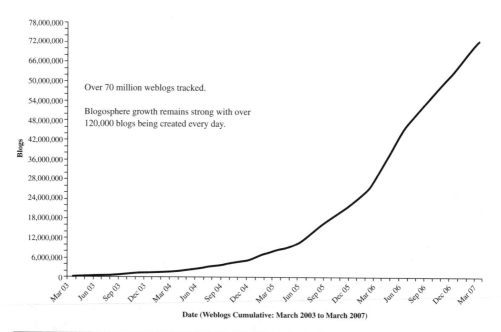

Over 70 million weblogs tracked.

Blogosphere growth remains strong with over 120,000 blogs being created every day.

Date (Weblogs Cumulative: March 2003 to March 2007)

FIGURE 1-1 As evidenced by the dramatic growth in blog creation, creating information, and Internet-enabling, blogging is more popular than ever. (From Technorati's 2007 State of the Blogosphere Report, Sifry, 2007. See References at the end of this book for source information.)

business workers operate. When we consider that these reports do not contemplate other sources of web information creation and distribution, such as automatically generated reports that aggregate information and are distributed programmatically, the implications of this content explosion and the challenges of usability and relevancy are staggering.

It is important to note something that is easily overlooked when considering the intersection of technology and information *as such*: The technological evolution that was (and is still) occurring is *heterogeneous*. No single technology is evolving, and no single species of content is changing in a neatly linear path. Web technologies emerged from the minds of developers, from the mixed-up source code of cobbled-together programs, from an amalgam of languages, methodologies, protocols, and anticipated outcomes. Functional goals for software and the design approaches were (are) often overlapping. But the technology advocates, designers, and developers wedded to their ideas, skill sets, and areas of expertise promote their way of doing *it* (whatever *it* is) over the other guy's way. There is nothing inherently undesirable about this approach, but it is a

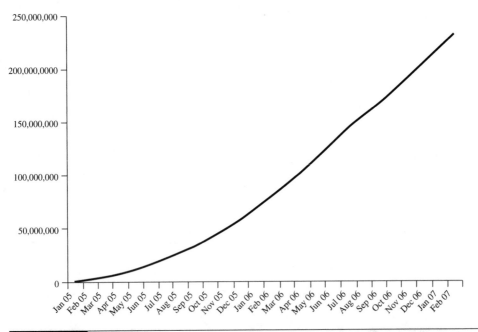

FIGURE 1-2   Information is exploding, and the explosion is fueled by many separate sources—from individuals, to companies, to automatic generation of information. (Technorati's Total Posts Using Tags; Sifry, 2007.)

reality. Technologies and web content that were first to "market" (in the early days, the free market of the Internet where currency is adoption and usage rates, inbound links, credibility, and search ranking rather than dollars or yen) were often followed by numerous overlapping and copycat technologies, many of which incorporated richer features than the original but were competing for the same conceptual space and adopting audience. Those technologies often replaced each other for no other reason than being the latest and greatest. While this pattern of compete, copy, and supersede was acceptable for the public Web landscape, enterprises found it increasingly difficult to focus on and invest in one technology or application stack. The pervading fear was that, by the time their projects were implemented, the technologies and applications used would be passé or, even worse, no longer used at all.

The importance of this trend of creation, re-creation, and adoption should not be underestimated. While it manifested both inside and outside organizations, the ramifications for the enterprise were much more profound from a capital investment perspective. Out on the public Web the proliferation of overlapping technologies was fine. Success was measured in adoption rates, exposure, and individual pride. No web CIO had to answer for all that R&D time and cost spent for…

"…what exactly?"

"Well, the users think it is cool, sir."

"You're fired!"

"You can't fire me, sir. It's The Web."

On the public Web, application developers are accountable only to themselves, and, to a lesser extent, their user base. Meanwhile, back in the enterprise, the large investment in all-in-one applications are showing weakness, especially in comparison to the deeply capable, narrowly tailored, and agilely developed Web 2.0 applications. Think about a customer relationship management (CRM) system that incorporates contact management, business process management, content management, business intelligence, and a busy dashboard-style user interface. Now think about a Web 2.0 application, such as Twitter, iTunes, or Flickr. The immediate contrarian will point out that these two types of systems do not compare—they are apples and oranges. Yet they do compare on an important similarity: Both systems have users. Aside from functional differences, users use the investment-sucking, enterprise-all-in-one applications because they *have to*. Users use the Web 2.0 applications because they *get to*. The patterns of voluntary adoption of Web 2.0 applications hold important and mostly overlooked lessons for business. These lessons are laid out in more detail in the subsequent chapters. But important for our purposes here is that when other applications in the enterprise were purchased to fill in a real (or perceived) gap in the functionality or capability of an old-school large enterprise application, the solutions did not fill—they overfilled. While this is often tactically successful, the ability to leverage these investments strategically on an enterprise scale is severely inhibited, simply because of the extreme glut of interfaces, processes, platforms, APIs, user interfaces, data models, and on and on and on.

Throughout the evolution of web technology and its adoption and implementation, the abilities of websites-cum-web applications continued to increase. Concurrent with the evolving sophistication of applications, the underpinning technologies, development methodologies, APIs, and raw talent were also maturing. By way of just one example, brute-force Java scripting started to give way to object-oriented Java scripting. This increased portability, reusability, and speed of code, and it opened new doors to dynamic presentation and more robust and application-like capability. Web browsers enhanced their domain object models (DOMs), which made it increasingly easier to tap the power of the web browser as a delivery platform for end user–oriented systems.

Communities of interest sprang up around programming languages (such as JavaScript, Perl, Python, PHP, C++, Java, HTML, CSS, and so on) and delivery methodologies (Six Sigma, Rational Unified Process [RUP], Agile, TEAM, and so on). These communities were drawn together by the programming languages, protocols, and methodologies that they were using to create websites, applications, and jobs that often had a community facilitation aspect to them. Such echo-chamber development meant that ideas from communities of developers often informed (which is a nice way of saying infiltrated and subverted) the deliverables and outputs of those developers and were then reflected back to the community. The result: A self-reinforcing wave function, defined as capability, speed, effectiveness, and sexiness, which grew as it was implemented and communicated back to the network.

An endpoint or a final state at which the project was finished was impossible to reach. While applications were certainly released and deliverables under contract were completed, a sense existed that, as the network heard about or got hold of the ideas, something new, different, or better could always be added. The notion of "perpetual beta" emerged, not in an instant but over and through a metamorphic phase. The developer community had (and still has) an inherent "tinkerer" disposition. Programs and applications are interesting puzzles that can always be made to run faster, better, and smarter. As turn-around and completion times for improvements decreased significantly due to technological and methodological improvements and network feedbacks, "new stuff" was released, and whether it was perfect or not didn't matter.

While the public Web was consistently enamored with the latest sexy looking website, meme (dancing hamsters, anyone?), functionality, or other cool bits, the enterprise was still struggling to figure out why the promised benefits and full capabilities of the systems, applications, and software in which they had invested substantial sums (of money, development resources, or both) had evaded them. Where enterprise systems were lacking functionality, hipster employees turned to public Web capabilities to augment their job functions. Corporate blogs were born not on internal sites but on public-facing blogs also used by preteen girls describing their latest boy troubles. Where enterprises lacked hipster employees, they put more money into one system or another that had some feature that, if you could just configure it right, the salesperson promised, could do *<insert sexy functionality here>*.

Concurrently and probably consequently, purchasing at organizational levels lower than the enterprise increased. Departments were more agile and flexible than their parent organizations which often suffered from analysis paralysis. Departments often had control of enough money and development resources to be able to move ahead in designing, developing, purchasing, and integrating line of business solutions to the real problems they were facing. Departments were investing in software that could meet their tactical needs irrespective of what it could (or could not) do for the rest of company.

Today, the result, from a whole-enterprise-IT perspective, is a mess. The mass of systems, file stores, and methodologies has become an organizational barrier composed of overlapping and underused or unused technology and mechanisms that are difficult to manage, authorized differently, platformed differently, and contain only the basest of interoperability. It is a leaky, weeping monstrosity of waggling arms, toes, mouths, sphincters, trunks, horns, and eyeballs. Even worse, the corporate sponsors for each of the parts of this ghastly mechanism are excited to proclaim their piece's criticality to the mess. Caught in the chaos and all too often forgotten are the employees. It is the profound failure of the enterprise that the lessons from the public Web were missed.

What the enterprise learned from the public Web experience is that public Web technologies hold individual promise: There is some really exciting stuff out there. But what the enterprise failed to learn is that the goals of technology on the public Web are different—sometimes radically, sometimes minimally—from the holistic goals and needs of any one organization. Tapping the capabilities offered by public Web technology yielded point solutions that could not be replicated across the organization and that often unintentionally ramified negatively over and against other organizational goals, practices, and personnel. Technological capability and implementation within the enterprise is, in many ways, a microcosm of the public Web. However, the shared context and common purpose of employees within an enterprise drive and focus on the needs for interaction, collaboration, and participation. While the public Web has a similar drive for interaction, collaboration, and participation, it lacks the focus of the enterprise. While web communities may be highly focused on a particular topic, the enterprise as a whole acts as a "community" for the employee. Public Web communities are created out of voluntary association and convenience. However, if a user leaves the community of the enterprise, it is often not voluntary and he probably no longer wants to participate in this community. This community has been a huge benefit and freeing luxury of public Web technology development, but it is a luxury that the enterprise has never been able to master.

The enterprise is not completely insulated from the pressures that current technological, cultural, and regulatory web trends are invoking. With the pace of information creation exploding around the world, the supporting trends manifest within organizations. However, organizations have the added burden of needing to tie all the information to a set of capabilities that allow each employee, partner, or customer to shape it around the task they are trying to accomplish. They have to balance this tactical need with long-term productivity to justify the original investment. This all has to be done while harnessing evolving user expectations about how systems should work, what users should be allowed and empowered to do, and what it means to be an employee. In short, the fact of the existence and power of the emergent participation culture, birthed on the public Web and firmly ensconced in the enterprise, is the formal cause of the challenges as well as the massive potential now facing organizations.

These challenges exist in and around tapping into the power that a disbursed, disunified, and disparate culture of participation can bring to bear on situations within the enterprise in a technologically heterogeneous and functionally overlapping environment while encouraging and enabling behavior that is net beneficial. These challenges are motivated by the nascent Web 2.0 mindset that is cultivated on the public Web but knows no organizational boundaries. As they often do, these challenges also hold an intrinsic promise for the organizations that can successfully manage them and realize their potential.

The Culture of Participation

The *culture of participation* is fueled by three converging trends that span technological, cultural, and regulatory disciplines:

- **Technological** A proliferation of technologies that facilitate participation. Examples include blogs, wikis, discussion threads/forums, trackback pings, social networks/graphs, social multimedia capabilities, mashups, composite applications, intelligent dashboards, and a profound decrease in the barrier to entry that characterizes most of the Web 2.0 technology that exists today.

- **Cultural** The emergent Web 2.0 mindset that promotes, with a force approaching the demands of a human right, hyper-individualized and perspective-based participation.

- **Regulatory** Legal statutes, business regimes, and best practices that increasingly require the persistence of nearly all information created with attribution information stored in an auditable manner. Whether for risk management, for corporate compliance, or from a desire to provide better metrics through richer data sets, information is kept longer than ever before.

The result of more people more easily creating more information that is then stored and archived for more time is *info-glut*, the overabundance of information. When information is created in contextually independent ways by diverse groups of people or programs, the results are disconnected silos of information. Sometimes the enabling and empowering of information creation results in duplication of or, even worse, contradictory data. While the information in those separate silos is possibly thematically connected, and while it is possible at times to find common threads that run throughout differing information stores, these connections are loose and usually exist only informally by association, rather than via intentional implementation.

Connecting Correctly

On the public Web, the loose connection is the only practical mode of existence. Because of the necessary lack of a shared and unifying purpose and context spanning public Web information, it would be a near impossibility to connect and manage correctly the never-ending flood of information created and destroyed every second of every day. Yet even such a statement begs the question of what it means to be *correctly connected*. The reality is that no standard, goal, purpose, law, or reason exists for defining what is a *correct association*. Correct connections are created, and then they exist and persist only in the minds of the consuming audience. Loose-linking and cross-referencing are activities in which information creators (be they semantic inference engines as will be discussed in Chapter 10, web page commentators, or hyperlinking webmasters) engage for the purpose of suggesting or directing the consuming audience to resources the author or originator thinks are important, interesting, or relevant. But hyperlinks can break, information can get stale, and users can be led unknowingly into the Internet wasteland. While this is an implicit risk every Internet user tacitly accepts, this risk is mitigated as relevant connections between information-and-information and information-and-user are constructs held by the individual. The connections manifest through the technology must be mirrored in the mind of the user. Which comes first is a question best left to the philosophers and theorists.

In an enterprise environment, though, this is not enough. Reliability and accuracy of information as well as the associations between unique information sets is vital for the success of a business. While each individual service within an enterprise is responsible for the accuracy of its own data, the challenge is to interconnect those systems and information sets and provide an overall view to the user. Furthermore, the level of reliability and accuracy of the information aggregate must be at least as great as it is for each individual system. But factors that may manifest as minor anomalies at lower singular levels can ramify throughout aggregates and substantially skew results, interpretations, and outputs. The goal is to couple, aggregate, and associate those unique and self-relevant silos of information at different levels of the enterprise so as to leverage synergies, omit overlap, and yield purpose-focused, productive systems in line with corporate strategies and visions.

The biological metaphor is appropriate here: If individual enterprise data systems are cells and organs, then the enterprise is the whole organism. The enterprise organism is becoming self-aware and is curious about itself. No longer is it able to be described as a linear channel of instruction—response messages from autonomous but cooperatively sequential entities. Instead, it is a complex whole, with specialized parts that work together in asynchronous fashion toward a common purpose. At least, that is the vision and promise held by the emerging technology coupled with the emerging mindset.

The culture of participation, cultivated in the petri dish of the public Web and fed on the sugar water of Web 2.0 technologies, has infiltrated the enterprise. Each member of the culture holds small but important data sets, imminently important to the individual but also potentially relevant to the larger culture—the enterprise. With the culture of participation prompting individuals to share their unique perspectives and information with the group and Web 2.0 technology enabling the collection of individual information and aggregation of that information into metasets, the enterprise organism gains access to new contexts, connections, and associations.

Web 2.0 participation or input technologies (such as wikis, discussion threads, tagging infrastructures, blogs, rating systems, and so on) are the new synapses that enable the flow of small, asynchronous, and unique bits of information from throughout the organism. Web 2.0 consumption technologies (such as wikis, discussion threads, RSS, ATOM, and blogs for example) yield the first technologically generated thoughts that spring, from the aggregates. These results are able to be reingested in a feedback loop that brings the participatory capability and desire back to bear on the results in a refining, validating, reconstructive process. While this process is ongoing, at some point decisions are made, sometimes by humans (such as what company to acquire), sometimes by machines (next in line for automatic escalation). The point is that the decisions are made now with greater awareness of the informational context in which those decisions reside. The goal of the technology and the tapping of the participation culture is not intended to create additional information or even to create better context. Rather the goal is to bring a richer understanding of context and relevance to impact, influence, and catalyze the decision-making and actionable processes that make up business.

Managing the Enterprise

Fortunately, and as opposed to the public Web, in an enterprise setting it is often easier to engage the will to participate and implement the relevant technologies. Because the enterprise ecosystem acts as a microcosm of the public Web and because the overall management and ownership of enterprise systems is clearly defined, the barriers to systems' adoption and implementation are not as often systemic—that is, caused by incontrovertible funding, space, resource, or technological systems incompatibilities. Enterprises can make decisions and create technology to implement new systems almost by fiat. The need to sell systems to users conceptually (to spur adoption, for example) within the enterprise, while similar in kind to marketing public technologies on the Web, is nowhere near similar in size or scope. It is vastly smaller. Many do not yet realize it, but when it comes to incubating technologies in real-world business settings, the enterprise has the advantage over the public Web.

Organizations are catching on to the need to manage their burgeoning information with enterprisewide strategies. These strategies must provide a unified foundation or infrastructure that facilitates the management of information, in all its disparate formats (such as documents, images, videos, websites, API-messages, structured database data, and so on). This foundation must also allow for the securing of information even after it exits the information management infrastructure (for example, with enterprise content management systems). Yet better management technology, as good as it is, must manage increasing volumes of data. The challenge businesses face today is not an inability to create information, or even an inability to manage information. It is a four-fold challenge of (1) providing the right information (2) in a meaningful way, scope, and time (3) to the right group of people, or to give those people the ability to access the information they need, (4) when they need it. It is the challenge of relevancy. Info-glut obfuscates relevancy. Rather than challenges from previous eras where creating the right information was difficult, info-glut tantalizes us with the knowledge that relevant information is in there, somewhere.

Rather than applying band-aid solutions to symptoms or adding horsepower to existing infrastructure, the right approach is to go to the source of the challenge—the expectations and outworkings of the culture of participation, where the greatest potential benefits can be found.

Connecting Information, Increasing Productivity

Information has always been connected. The card file and printed phone book connected contact information to an alphabetized schema. As legend goes, the library at Alexandria was organized by subject, connecting like information with like information. Aristotle cataloged the natural world according to a systematic organization, connecting observation with taxonomy.

Nowadays, the World Wide Web connects information with information via hyperlinks, search indexes, and, as discussed in subsequent chapters, emergent strategies enabled by Web 2.0 technologies such as web ontologies. This kind of connection abstracts the *object* of connection from the *mechanism* of connection, allowing the connected information to provide context and meaning apart from the means of connection. In other examples, the means of connection, whether alphabetic, taxonomic, or topical, add to and potentially pollute the meaning and context of the objects of the connection: the information.

When information is connected to other information, it becomes something new and greater. It takes on a potential significance that is bigger, deeper, or more granular than any of the constituent pieces individually. This added context provides a nuance and flavor to the originals that create new meaning from the amalgam of the underlying constituents. It is not simply an additive process. It is a creative process whereby new meaning is created and signals to the consumer that it did not exist before. This new meaning has profound implications and represents the huge potential inherent in Web 2.0 technologies, the Web 2.0 mindset, and the participation culture.

Participation Culture

On the public Web, new and novel ways of connecting information are being unlocked to welcome end user participation. Today, the main source of information connection are the users or consumers themselves. People are inference and deduction engines. We create associations and derive associations between and among bits of information. Then we link those sources, describing the relationships—sometimes formally, sometimes informally, but all the while connecting, connecting, connecting.

While blogs have allowed almost anyone to publish his or her thoughts to the Internet, enhanced commenting and discussion threading capabilities are spawning virtual communities connected by the individual blog post or news story. In some of the most profound cases, the technological enablement of disparate groups of people to connect diverse information sets have brought down institutions.

Remember "Rathergate," aka "Memogate"? During this event in 2004, Web 2.0 blogging, commenting, and research technologies were brought together into a community forged from a shared idea: namely that news anchorman Dan Rather and CBS News producer Mary Mapes were caught passing forged or reproduced documents as authentic originals. The Rathergate event, with the original story broken by the blog Little Green Footballs, was triggered by communities of bloggers posting and commenting and connecting their perspectives, expert analysis, and individual opinions to a common thread. That thread did not exist in any one post or comment or analysis piece, but was the inherent synthesis and construction, deconstruction, and reconstruction of hundreds of relatively small and separate pieces of information. In the end, the mainstream news media (a relative dinosaur in technological terms) got a black eye, Rather got a pink slip, and the blogosphere got some renewed interest (*blogosphere* is generally understood as the collection of all blogs, especially politically-oriented blogs, that post on a similar topic, theme, event, or personality).

It is important to note that, in the case of Rathergate and other less dramatic examples, it was the blogosphere as an entity, not an individual blog or website, that created the story and the information. The story was somewhere "out there" rather than in one specific place. It was the connection of tens and sometimes hundreds of individual pieces of analysis. In a more mundane but no less profound example, end user *tagging* (the attribution of single word or short phrase descriptors) of information such as images, maps, or documents creates new meaning by yielding a collective intelligence over and above the author's or creator's original intent.

Collective Intelligence: Crowdsourcing and Search Engine Technology

Though the examples mentioned so far are only cursory, they demonstrate two key points. First, the information is created and connected by wide and disparate, and potentially unconnected or loosely connected, sources. Second, the connections themselves are important carriers of meaning and information. Consider the first point. Because technology has lowered the bar of participation and because the Web 2.0 mindset esteems credible participation, more information is able to be generated more quickly from a wider audience than ever before. While this contributes to the challenges of info-glut, it also means that more collective intelligence can be brought to bear on virtually any topic. This collective weight of creation, editorial power, and scrutiny means that there is (at least) a presumption that vetting by topically interested but personally noninvested parties will occur.

The technology makes the vetting, filtering, and scrutiny possible. The culture of participation engendered by the technology makes this vetting, filtering, and scrutiny likely.

Studies, theories, and pop and academic works have shown that the greater the numbers of people participating in a similar task, the greater the likelihood that "the crowd" is right. From social movements theory, to SETI@Home-style distributed programs, to the creation of the *Oxford English Dictionary* (see Winchester, 1999), the idea that collective intelligence is something greater than the sum of its individual parts has been around for a long time. But the ability to tap into this power consistently at scale and efficiency is only now emerging—as Web 2.0.

Previous efforts sometimes met with success and other times were failures. Issues arose around early *crowdsourcing* (Surowiecki, 2005) and collective intelligence projects. Problems such as "groupthink" and systemic problems such as the intentional inclusion or exclusion of certain participants or information in the aggregate meant that the latent power of the group was thwarted in some way. But the global scope of the Internet, combined with the vastly increased accessibility of the technology to people from all different stripes, means that truly and radically systemic problems hampering successful collection and use of collective intelligence are no longer a technological risk. This is not to minimize or trivialize the debate surrounding the so-called "digital divide." Rather we emphasize the increased participation yielded by the lowered barriers to participation and the increasing availability and accessibility of the technology in a business context. The most common economic, geographic, and cultural issues cited as intrinsic barriers making up the digital divide are less applicable to enterprises than they are to individuals and communities interacting with (or trying to interact with) the public Web. Instead, where the enterprise has sufficiently intentional promotion and enablement of crowdsourced and collective intelligence projects, the risk is now squarely in the lap of the enterprise, not in the realm of technology. In other words, Web 2.0 technology has evolved to a point at which open participation and accurate aggregation is not merely possible, it is expected and rapidly becoming the norm.

Technological capability, while necessary, is not sufficient for complete avoidance of risk, and that is what this book addresses. Businesses are capitalizing (literally) on the business end of this concept with crowdsourcing— the idea that opening up a task or problem to an undefined or loosely defined heterogeneous group produces better or cheaper results (or both) (Hempel, 2006). But we risk getting ahead of ourselves. It would be pointless to talk about participation if larger and larger amounts of information were not also available for consumption. Because technology has lowered the bar not only to participation but also to consumption, information is amazingly easy to find, and when combined with enabling technology, the invitation to participate is nearly ubiquitous as well as irresistible.

The second key point here is that the linkages and connections between information artifacts and people themselves yield new information, context, and meaning. Both of the key points mentioned in this section need to be well and thoroughly considered by the enterprise because they hold deep promise as well as substantial risk.

Consider the workhorse of the Web, the search engine. Search engine technology discovered early on that simply listing raw "hits," or the matching of search terms with a list of indexed websites and documents, was insufficient to provide meaningfully relevant results to users. As search engine technology evolved, increasingly sophisticated relevancy algorithms were incorporated. These calculated not just tallies of hits, but they also analyzed inbound links to sites alongside more pedestrian hits. Along with other, factors, the search engines sought to provide a more deeply weighted analysis of search hit lists. Simply ordering and ranking results by a tally of keyword or query term occurrence was not enough to meet the needs and expectations of users. Just because something is mentioned often does not mean it is important. However, also including the number of references to a particular piece of information provided an accurate indication of relevance. At the same time, following the loose connections of these references allowed analysis of relationships between pieces of information that otherwise would not have been obvious.

When the analysis of connections is applied to the World Wide Web itself, the semantics around information and the collective interpretation play a big role. Today, concepts for creating loose associations between data and context have entered the popular lexicon. Use of buzzwords such as *tagging*, *clouding*, and *threading* is as common in boardrooms as it is in Internet forums and academia. These terms and concepts appear in virtually all product information management software and hardware. The marketers never miss a turn. The themes and their underpinning technologies are less strictly structured than formal information management principles, but they are also much more widely adopted. As discussed in Chapter 3, anyone can tag content through services such as Flickr, Last.fm, and Google Images, and the more interpretations that are attached to the same piece of information, the greater the presumed accuracy of relevancy determinations.

Those semantics by themselves can carry useful information and provide an alternative mechanism for accessing and interconnecting information. Tag clouds, for example, and services that allow the tagging of disparate sources suddenly create cross-referenced information where no obvious connection existed before. What is obvious, though, is that enterprises are in the process of recognizing that relevancy relies on accurate capture of a user's intent, the context in which she is operating, and the social inputs from the crowd in which she resides as a constituent. These budding recognitions are not the same as successful implementations. However, it does bode well that the pieces of this puzzle are starting to be recognized as an actual image. The culture of participation is collectively helping to piece together the picture, though not in any ordered or organized way. (You will have a much better idea of what that picture actually *is* after you have read this book.)

The Public Web and Enterprise Expectations

Today's enterprise environment involves groups of people who participate in a creative and interactive process. A community of users is involved and connected to the Internet via enabling technologies that let them contribute to the entire community, rather than merely consume information for personal use.

While users of the public Web may be incidentally connected in ad hoc communities of interest, businesses and organizations are built around the core principle of personally and individually vested users who share a common purpose and work together toward that purpose. Enterprises invest in enabling technologies to help accommodate users' needs. However, enterprises also suffer from some limitations that create systemic barriers to innovation. In short, because of the homogenous focus (and often makeup) of the enterprise, their "collective intelligence" is not as good, from a paradigmatic perspective, as the collective intelligence of the public. The principle is easy to understand: Themes and shared perspectives that precipitate from diversity are stronger than similarly shared perspectives that are intrinsic to the makeup and purpose of a particular group. Think of it from a political standpoint, for example: The political process is more effective when liberals and conservatives agree on something than when only one group or the other agrees among its own constituents.

According to author James Surowiecki's thesis, the four core principles that make up a "wise crowd" as opposed to a simple aggregate of people are diversity of opinion, independence, decentralization, and aggregation. Within the enterprise, diversity of opinion can typically be achieved only *after* aggregation of opinions throughout the different organizational nodes and authority chains of the enterprise. This meets the decentralization principle. Finally, opinions must be free not only from groupthink peer pressure from colleagues but also free from vague and unspecified *expectations* of behavior or taboo. Such expectations thwart the principle of independence of opinion. Restrictions on whose opinions are valid (or not) thwart the principle of decentralization of opinion and aggregation. Failure (usually a technological one) to aggregate opinions also thwarts the aggregation principle. These challenges are simple to overcome in theory. In practice, however, corporate culture, power structures, and vague but threatening peer pressure on "what is a good opinion to have or not" stifle and paralyze efforts to bring the wisdom of the crowd to bear on real enterprise business problems and process improvements. These principles are more fully explored in Surowiecki's *The Wisdom of Crowds* (see References at the end of this book for source information).

While businesses and organizations can bring substantial creativity, focus, and resources to bear on a particular problem or issue, the ability to think outside the box is hampered because, after all, they *are* the box. It is no surprise that as technology has matured, the participatory and contribution-as-a-right mindset has grown in the realm of the public Internet over the past years. The growth of this culture was catalyzed by the maturation of technologies that lowered the barrier to participation—technology became easy, quick, and convenient. When convenient technology is combined with attitudes of "if it can be done it will be done," and "it is my right to do it," the result is mass participation—or at least an expectation that we can do almost anything.

It is easy to spot the similarity between the paradigms of participation in the public Web and enterprise spaces. After all, organizations are all about bringing people together to work toward a common goal—selling widgets and services, brokering expertise, and so on. Collaboration and participation are intrinsic to the daily workings of the enterprise. But participation within the enterprise has been governed, bracketed, characterized, and limited by the organizational chart. The CEO collaborates with the head of sales and marketing, not with the hourly quality assurance grunt or road warrior salesman. The boots-on-the-ground sales and service teams collaborate with each other and sometimes inform management of what they are doing. This is why labor unions are in eternal opposition to corporate management and why grassroots political activists in the United States are not often invited to Republican and Democratic National Committee executive committee meetings. The organizational chart governs who should work with whom and how far "up the chain" your suggestions should go. Who you are matters much more than what you say. There is this continual belief that there is a monopoly of good ideas that come from the top.

Corporate politics and the currency of role and title really do affect how information is evaluated in enterprise settings. The assumptions are that people with the "right" titles are supposed to be there (after all, they earned those titles somehow), and therefore their ideas and information must at least be included.

While the market will eventually cull the poor and weak ideas from the enterprise, the timeframe for the process is substantially lengthy.

No organization charts exist on the public Web. The near ubiquity of technological accessibility, from "add a comment" feedback forms on almost all websites, to blogs, to the relatively high and cheap availability of personal computers, means that people are able to participate at will. Combine this factor with the "if it can be done it will be done" mindset, and the result is an expectation of participation that is not limited by who you are or where you come from. The boundaries of role and title that define enterprise interactions are meaningless on the public Web. The currency of the org chart has been completely devalued; instead, the currency of relevance means everything.

In comparison, the differences between the models of participation in enterprise settings and on the public Web could not be more stark. They are both models of participation to be sure, but that is where the similarities end. The public Web's culture of participation respects no boundaries and as such is accessible to virtually everyone (with access to a computer and an Internet connection). Good information is combined with poor information, and the feedback cycle of consumption-participation continually evaluates, builds, edits, filters, and changes into a corpus of information much richer than the original data set. While it is possible for poor information to persist, the likelihood that it will persist unchallenged and unmodified is extremely low, simply because the technology allows and the mindset encourages anyone who can to challenge and modify it, or ignore it into obscurity. (To see how this concept is changing legal precedent, read Glenn Reynolds, "Libel in the Blogosphere," at www. instapundit.com.)

However, the adoption of the public Web's model of participation in the enterprise-located web space is still emerging and is yet to be defined, let alone accepted. This is understandable, however: Those who have the most to lose are the most in power, and those who have the most to gain are only starting to be empowered.

The challenge to this dilemma is twofold: First, and easiest, is a technological challenge. Web 2.0 technology must be brought inside the corporate firewall and then tapped within the enterprise in ways that fundamentally support the corporate goals: making or saving money, time, and quality. Second, and much more difficult, is a paradigmatic challenge. The information, data, ideas, and processes that come from a decentralized, radically distributed, metasourced network of applications, people, and information stores must be leveraged by the enterprise in a way that promotes the goals and purpose of the organization. Inviting the QA engineer or facilities temp to the next board meeting might be polite and might score some points with subordinates or coworkers, but if it is not serving the needs of the business, it is pointless.

This book argues for the integration of Web 2.0 technology, mindsets, and paradigms to enable the enterprise, boost business, increase efficiency, and tap into resources. It does not argue for a popular uprising and revolution of the workers against The Man. In most cases, the abilities and culture of the public Web need to be *mashed-up* (described in Chapter 5) with the needs and culture of the enterprise. The public Web can provide the starting point that then must be evolved to meet the needs and requirements of the organization. Sometimes this may require a rip-and-replace tactic, and most times it will require an amalgamation of ideas and paradigms that leverage the power of the public Web practices and technology within the strictures, structures, and processes of the enterprise.

The Workforce of Today

To ensure that Web 2.0 technology, mindsets, and paradigms are embraced in the enterprise space, several steps need to occur in sequence. First, the independent and participatory-enabled culture of the public Web must be brought in together with technological and organizational changes. Most of today's younger and middle-aged workers either grew up with these new concepts or were introduced to them with the increasing accessibility of the public Internet. Using the inherent capabilities of the public Web in private and business life is second nature that will continue to be a viral driver for enterprise adoption of Web 2.0 technology. The reality is that the paradigms, the expectations, are already here. The enterprises that ignore them, or worse, actively negate them, risk breeding an attitude of frustration and contempt among the employees who will be leading the corporations and controlling pensions a few years down the road.

The problem with viral drivers, however, is precisely that they are viral, with little or no control. While the risk of not meeting employee expectations is real, the lack of an intentional approach to enterprise implementation and adoption of technology risks unintentional but nevertheless harmful exposure of corporate information and practice. An intentional approach does not mean a slow, tight-fisted, or closed approach that would impede efficiency and a shifting of process paradigms. Rather, risk aversion motivates many organizations to do as much as they can to gain the perceptual benefits of a new technology or way of doing business without exposing themselves to unknown risks and entering largely uncharted waters.

Consider an example. Wikis and blogs have become, in some organizations, a vital part of project documentation and communication. The collaborative but disconnected nature of blog and wiki technology caters to the widespread phenomenon of geographically disbursed teams and client, partner, and employee collaborations to accomplish project tasks. Discussion forums and bulletin boards are both public collaborative technologies that were brought into enterprise organizations as a means of collaborative communication. Today, discussion forums are usually a way of persisting threaded discussions. In this way, collaborative communication is kept and stored in an enterprise system.

Industry best practices, legal regulations, and corporate standards demand that corporate information be findable because global legal precedent has determined that corporate communication is discoverable (that is, potentially legally relevant and therefore subject to regulation). As a result, organizations needed a way to store and persist project-based collaborative data before they could embrace a technology that made it easier to communicate.

The Web 2.0 technology is making its way into the enterprise environment, however, mostly in a viral manner but increasingly with official enterprise support. By providing such technologies, employees are invited to participate in broader enterprise initiatives and in projects with greater scope. Sometimes this participation amounts to little more than a corporate "How are we doing?" solicitation. Other times participation is invisible—consider a project team member who posts suggestions in a discussion thread about a project whose comments are included in a yearly audit of project management efficiency.

The challenge is to combine the technology with cultural and generational concerns. Classic IT users (those who came of technological age in the pre-Internet era) largely view technology as a tool required to do their job, not as an environment or ecosystem in which a job takes place. The ecosystem analogy is useful: In a physical office ecosystem, even classic IT users may pick up useful information through informal hallway conversation and corporate scuttlebutt. Seeing two people in a conference room may lead an onlooker to make inferences about what they are discussing. Web 2.0 technology provides a virtual ecosystem that, to many new employees, is just as vibrant and important (if not more) as the physical.

What is clear is that using Web 2.0 technologies and tapping into the growing Web 2.0 mindset in an enterprise environment is different from using and experiencing it on the public Web. Where businesses are beholden to shareholders and boards of directors, technology pioneers on the public Web are beholden to their own senses of creativity and sometimes the requests of their user community. Where private users of the public Web are interested in the experience and can afford to try out the many different technologies available without personal risk, enterprises must invest in a limited set of technologies and implement and secure user adoption over enough time to achieve that almighty benchmark: return on investment (ROI).

Many readers have posted information to (or are at least familiar with) multiple social network profiles on such sites as LinkedIn, Facebook, and MySpace. Such technological extravagance is rarely acceptable within the business environment of today. The goal for business is not personal gain or freedom for the employee, but to help the employee be more efficient, to offer better access to higher quality information, properly contextualized and at the right time. The goal for the enterprise is to improve information relevancy and delivery to users so that they are empowered to make better, smarter, faster business decisions and thereby achieve higher margins, greater revenues, better customer satisfaction ratings, better service, or whatever your enterprise goals may be. This is how Web 2.0 technologies, combined with the emergent Web 2.0 mindset and culture of participation, will lead to the reshaping of your business.

Chapter 2

Many Voices: We're All Publishers

By Jean Sini

Everything would be in its blind volumes. Everything: the detailed history of the future, Aeschylus's The Egyptians, *... the complete catalog of the Library, the proof of the inaccuracy of that catalog.*

Jorge Luis Borges, *The Total Library*

As I arrived home one evening, I was greeted by an irritating dripping sound. One of the faucets in the house had started leaking and was now insistently reminding me of its need for attention. I ignored the drip until the next morning, hoping it would *somehow* just go away. No such luck. On closer inspection, the faucet mechanism—one of those sophisticated, one-handled, pressure-balanced shower-and-tub controls—turned out to be quite intimidating. I could clearly picture serious flooding should anything go wrong while I attempted to fix it myself. So my next move was to reach for the phone: It's an old house, so I had put my favorite plumber on speed-dial. But, inexplicably, at the last second, a sudden sense of pride stopped me: There had to be a way to fix this faucet myself.

I punched the faucet brand and model number into an Internet search engine instead of calling a professional. What's most surprising about the results I got is that, at first, they seemed familiar. Being accustomed to researching all sorts of software-related specifications and APIs, I didn't immediately realize how odd it was that I should find not only detailed schematics from the manufacturer, along with a catalog of replacement parts and an authorized reseller locator, but also step-by-step directions, with pictures and advice from handy folks on which part was likely faulty, on how to take apart this faucet, and last but not least on how to put it all back together.

This is remarkable: Only 10 years ago, it would have been unthinkable for a faucet manufacturer to have anything more than a token online presence. Today, all the specifications are available, indexed, and interactive. Better yet, communities of professionals and do-it-yourselfers have formed, ad hoc, and documented the maintenance procedures for many a home appliance, and they are readily sharing tips and advice. This is a perfect example of knowledge commoditization and open collaboration at play, and the fact that it involves a product as mundane as a tub faucet is telling of the speed and reach of the phenomenon.

This chapter takes an in-depth look at some of the core tenets of the read-write and collaborative nature of Web 2.0: blogs, wikis, and forms of participation derived from these tools. They constitute potent symbols of what the current crop of web innovation is all about: the ease with which anyone can contribute, accelerated dissemination, and innovation fostered in the open. What are the most disruptive paradigm shifts we're noticing, how exactly do blogs and wikis operate, and what opportunities do they represent for the enterprise?

Paradigm Shifts

Beyond the oft-derided rounded corners, improbable names, and daring color schemes that are the hallmarks of many recently launched consumer web startups, one of the most fundamental characteristics of Web 2.0 is its focus on users, not only as individuals but as groups. The Web has become social: it aims at facilitating conversations. This has implications in terms of communication paradigms and ultimately has the potential to affect our culture as it relates to collaboration and information sharing.

Several forces are at the root of the phenomenon. First, the web is becoming an increasingly read-write medium. The wide spread of blogs and wikis, covered in detail in this book, along with a slew of hosting options, has all but eliminated barriers to entry when it comes to publishing online. Technical skills are no longer required to post free-form content to the Web, including rich media elements such as videos and photos. As a result, we're seeing a growing migration of communication from channels such as e-mail or instant messaging (IM)—until now the most readily available systems—to web-moderated platforms with very different semantics.

A few such key differences in semantics flow from the repository-centric model of systems such as blogs and wikis, as opposed to the message-centric nature of e-mail. E-mail systems leave it up to end users to decide whether or not to archive messages, sent or received, for future reference, essentially opening up the risk of the knowledge shared over e-mail to be eventually forgotten. Even when messages are archived, issues arise when it comes to building a cumulative body of knowledge. Participants typically send around only *differential* information (what has changed), assuming each party will adjust his mental model of the knowledge base, or they resend entire documents, either inline or as attachments. Both cases can have drastic consequences, either making it close to impossible for someone coming onboard late in the game to familiarize herself with the knowledge base, or leading to massive amounts of replication in everyone's mailboxes. Instead, the new platforms favor shared rather than replicated repositories and encourage concurrent contributions and naturally support versioning.

Additionally, the asynchronous characteristics of these upcoming platforms enable a looser, potentially less intrusive form of conversation. In this form, subscribers elect to seek out updates from trusted publishers instead of indiscriminately receiving ever-increasing amounts of e-mail, not to mention spam.

The ease with which users can contribute isn't limited to wikis and blogs per se: Many Web 2.0 offerings promote other forms of participation—from bookmarks, to commentary, to votes—further accelerating the ease with which users express their contributions, lowering the barrier to play a role, however small, in the conversation. Progressively, these various forms of expression aggregate and, as they constitute a more permanent trace of a person's thoughts online, they encourage not only participation but the migration to the Web of identity building and personal branding.

The Tools of Participation

Blogs are highly emblematic of the Web turning into a conversational platform. Over the course of their short history, blogs have evolved dramatically, both as a tool and a phenomenon, to the point that early definitions of what constituted a weblog may now appear dogmatic if not altogether obsolete. The nature and reach of the phenomenon is perhaps best understood through a brief overview of the stages it has gone through since users started publishing bloglike sites in the 1990s.

Narrating the Web

Weblogs have actually been around since long before the term was coined by Jorn Barger in 1997. Arguably, they even predate the World Wide Web, as a few Usenet newsgroups started circulating digests of other materials of interest on the Internet as early as 1984. When HTTP and the World Wide Web were introduced by Tim Berners Lee in 1990–91, two related forms of blogging developed concurrently: A handful of diarylike, regularly updated sites were launched, narrating events related to their publishers' general activities. A number of sites also emerged whose focus was the notion of logging web surfing highlights. These were essentially self-published collections of commented links. The name *weblog* originated from this latter strand and was later shortened to *blogs*.

Initially, the technical proficiency required to set up and maintain these sites made them out of reach for most. It wasn't until 1998 that the first online authoring and hosting services were introduced, with some of the more popular platforms launching in 1999, including LiveJournal and Blogger. Six Apart's Movable Type started in 2001, and WordPress was created in 2003. When they were created, these services allowed users to author and publish content via an online service, typically presenting it in reverse chronological order. They offered a choice of software licensing or hosting options, suddenly making it possible for nontechies to establish a blog presence. Software tools quickly made authoring and hosting easier, and they now invariably encompass rich WYSIWYG editors and advanced layout and publishing features that have fueled an explosion in the number of blogs.

Interestingly, the two early facets of blogs—as commented links and as diaries—continue to exist, sometimes simultaneously, with bloggers assuming roles ranging from news commentators, to explorers or guides who are on a mission to dig up and spread noteworthy resources online. Unsurprisingly, given its wide spread, the form has also branched into a multiplicity of variants.

The medium has grown explosively to massive proportions from the handful of sites inventoried in 1997. One of the leading blog search engines, Technorati, tracks more than 112 million active blogs (as of February 2008) and claims it's doing a good job of keeping spam blogs out of its index. Growth rates have been more or less steady, with the blogosphere doubling every 150 days or so between 2004 and 2006, and every 300 days or so since 2007. Technorati indexes more than 1.6 million new posts and adds more than 150,000 new blogs every day. Figure 2-1 shows the cumulative number of blogs tracked by Technorati as of March 2007.

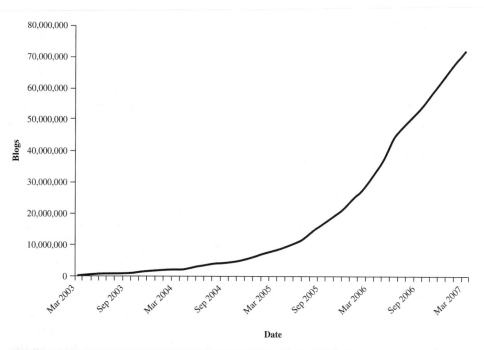

FIGURE 2-1   Number of blogs tracked by Technorati, March 2007. (From Technorati's 2007 State of the Blogosphere Report, Sifry, 2007. See References at the end of this book for source information.)

Characteristics of Today's Medium

What are common traits among blogs today, from a platform standpoint? None of the following characteristics are strictly necessary to earn the blog moniker, but they are among the key invariants we typically associate with the concepts of blogging.

From the reader's standpoint, most salient are the strong assumptions of frequent or at least predictably regular updates and the customary presentation of articles or posts in reverse chronological order. Just as important, and the source of much debate, is the support for comments that invite conversation; they are strongly perceived as critical to the relevance of the read-write medium, even for nonbloggers. Comments, however, can also introduce issues from spam, in which readers or even robots post largely off-topic comments containing links to other sites, to trolling or outright insulting behaviors, where the anonymity of the comments brings out the less civil and constructive sides of some readers. Platforms have equipped individual authors with a range of options regarding comments, and publishers may decide to allow or disable all comments, to moderate them, to require some form of identification before posting comments, or to restrict commenting to newer entries only.

Related to comments, *trackbacks* are a looser form of conversation: After reading a story on a blog, a person posts a response on her own blog instead of leaving a comment on the original article she read. As her response is published, her blogging platform signals the new post to the original blog, which can then publish a link to that response, typically alongside regular comments. This approach encourages a distributed conversation in which each participant simultaneously owns his or her own words and meshes thoughts with those of other bloggers.

Another common trait of blogs is the availability of *XML feeds*, typically in RSS (Really Simple Syndication) or Atom Syndication format. Irrespective of which variant is used, *feeds* are XML documents, available at an advertised URL, that contain a list of links to the most recent entries in the blog as well as timestamps and titles for these entries. They most frequently offer excerpts or the full text of the posts, stripped of the HTML formatting that make up the look of the specific blog. Feeds are suitable for consumption by software components that can harvest them regularly and users who are alert to the presence of new posts, obviating the need for readers to visit and revisit blog sites to find out whether new content is available. In addition to software agents polling feeds on behalf of users to discover updates, most blogging platforms and a number of well-known syndication tools—ranging from search engines to online feed readers to aggregators—participate in a *pinging* scheme, where blogs broadcast their updates to services consuming the posts, to limit the reliance on polling and reduce latency in the transport of stories from publishers to subscribers.

Combined, these characteristics sustain a loose but dynamic conversation model, in which readers, who may engage in commenting or their own blogging, determine which blogs they want to visit occasionally or subscribe to regularly, using tools such as feed readers to fetch updates on their behalf. And unlike e-mail, blog entries are systematically and permanently archived, as are the relationships among stories captured in links.

Finally, a frequent staple of blogs is a sidebar containing relatively permanent links to other blogs the publisher reads or endorses: the *blogroll*. Somewhat reminiscent of the early days of blogging, when the entire set of existing blogs fit onto a short list, the blogroll is now a minuscule fragment of that list, but it's reflective of the author's affinity and establishes a more stable sense of community than the in-post linking pattern.

As far as authors are concerned, the most popular platform choices are Google's Blogger, which is free and exclusively hosted; Six Apart's range of offerings, including hosted solutions such as TypePad or Vox, or the installable Movable Type; and the open source platform WordPress, which also offers hosted or installable versions. In addition, a number of hosting services specialize in running Movable Type or WordPress instances, maintaining them on behalf of their customers to free them from the technical hassles of keeping their blogs up and running. Installing the software requires technical expertise, but it affords maximum control of the blogger's content in case of outages and protects against discontinuation of service. In addition to the hosting versus installing choices, all platforms offer advanced authoring options, blog-management features ranging from look and feel, to comment spam management (Automattic, the company behind WordPress, also makes the Akismet anti-spam package for blog comments), to plug-ins supporting rich content.

Blog Uses, from Amateurs to Professionals

As the medium has matured from a platform standpoint and allowed a broader range of authors to publish, its characteristics from the perspective of content and intent have also widened. With more than 100 million blogs on the Internet, it's clear that a very diverse crowd of individuals is blogging and contributing a mind-numbingly vast array of content types, ranging from link rolls to news commentary, to online journals, to sharing family events and food recipes. Topics covered are numerous and include politics, fashion, technology, lifestyle, and sports, to name a few.

If we focus solely on the growing publisher base without analyzing how much of the content is actually consumed, however, our conclusion would be incomplete and misleading. It is enlightening to study the nature of the most popular blogs (typically ranked in terms of traffic as well as inbound links). Most of the heavily trafficked sites are in fact operated by professional, full-time bloggers who are increasingly organized in networks and focus primarily on news coverage.

Increasingly, popular bloggers are turning into professional pundits, leveraging the more efficient medium to allow for increased specialization, to reach niche audiences (such as technology early adopters, environmentally conscious readers, and so on) while remaining sustainable. A number of options can allow bloggers to monetize their words—from contextual text ads to banners to sponsorships—with questions raised as to the implications on point of view, neutrality, and conflicts of interest. In fact, the smaller the outfit, the more difficult it is to maintain any semblance of the "Chinese Wall" policy that traditionally separates the ad department from the editor-in-chief in traditional publications. Paradoxically, the ethics of blogging are thus called into question on two fronts: Some lament the invasion of the blogosphere by professional, larger outfits, while others complain about the bias introduced by any attempt to tap into ad revenues.

Although only a limited number of bloggers has any significant regular following, the ability to publish with relative ease means that anyone, including lesser known contributors, can circulate a particular story if it contains noteworthy material and reaches significant audiences. Blogs alone cannot deliver on every level, but they are supplemented by tools that focus on aggregating and analyzing content from a vast pool of sources in the blogosphere to uncover clusters of individual stories rather than entire blogs. Additionally, the concentration of most eyeballs on large circulation blogs does not necessarily diminish the relevance of less popular blogs to their small readership: Platforms such as LiveJournal and Vox bridge social networking and blogs and exemplify *social blogging*, or the role of the blog as vector of communication in well-connected communities. Family members, friends, and coworkers use the medium, with its loose conversation dynamics and its long-term archival capabilities, to chronicle and keep one another abreast of events.

To supplement general purpose blogging platforms, a number of services have emerged to encourage various forms of contribution. These have given rise to variations on the blogging theme, including *moblogging*, or the act of blogging from a mobile device, as well as *photo-blogging*, where the primary content is a stream of photos. *Vlogging*, short for video-blogging, offers a spectrum of options ranging from *life-casting* (chronicling activity in video, initially broadcast live and then archived for later retrieval), to video conversations not unlike video voicemail.

A number of emerging services also support microblogging, including Twitter, Jaiku, and Pownce. These services could be described as minimalist, hosted blogs. In the case of Twitter, for instance, users are prompted to answer the straightforward question, *What are you doing?* The service initially had a strong mobile component, and contributions were limited to 140 characters. While some have dismissed the resulting content as inane, others are becoming addicted to the concise, incessant status updates originating from friends. In addition, these services, which typically expose APIs that can be tapped into by third-party developers, are being used to convey all sorts of information to a socially defined group of co-subscribers, possibly coordinating responses to events such as system failures in an IT department. Twitter's limited power of expression, imposed by the 140-character format, encourages contribution, even if it comes in small nuggets rather than full-blown text or multimedia essays.

As millions of individuals take up writing blogs, they dedicate a significant amount of time not only to the content but also to the appearance of their blogs. Thousands of ready-made templates are available as drop-ins for each of the major blogging platforms, allowing authors to craft an online look equivalent to a personal brand. In addition to the visual layout and style, publishers can add a number of plug-ins to the blog to support features such as community-centric avatars, custom feeds for comments, a multitude of sidebar widgets ranging from geolocating readers to embedding a stream of Flickr photos, to showing a tag cloud representing keywords frequently used on the blog.

Along with the creativity brought out in the content, blogging platforms are increasingly facilitating an outpouring of identity building creativity focused on the look and feel of the site, with an array of plug-and-play and customization options for those with minimal technical skills. This contributes not only to a deeper connection of the publishers to the brand they're building for themselves, but also in a blurring of the tool of blogging into a general-purpose content management system.

The pervasiveness of blogs and the wealth of options available for controlling the published content has resulted in an increasing number of corporations using a blog as their content management system (CMS). In a classic case of the innovator dilemma's *low-end disruption*, where the incumbent leader is displaced by a competitor providing lesser value at lower cost, the tool, much less complex to set up, maintain, and learn than more advanced content management systems, has benefited from grassroots support within organizations. Major platform vendors are now introducing basic versioning support and beefing up access controls, while preserving the ease of use that's driven the appeal of the system in the first place.

Blogs' Shifting Roles and Potential Pitfalls

With blogging becoming a ubiquitous platform, and with a lot of mainstream media outlets and former journalists now using the technology to lower their publishing costs, it's easy to overlook the deeper potential to transform and play a disruptive role in the nature of information distribution. It's almost tempting to dismiss the perception, once prevalent amongst enthusiasts, that blogging had the power to revolutionize our access to news, that it had a unique flattening, democratizing ability to turn everyone into a journalist, given the overwhelming proportion of the attention garnered nowadays by major outlets taking advantage of the technology.

Yet the notion of citizen journalism is at the core of the groundswell that has built blogging into the popular phenomenon it has become—news not only told to the people, but by the people. A number of whistle-blowers have used the medium and a number of major news stories were broken by bloggers (such as "Rathergate," discussed in Chapter 1). With the advent of photo and video blogging, the barrier to capturing and contributing raw material has been lowered even more.

Reality lies somewhere between the idealistic view of strictly user-generated news and the pessimistic view that nothing has changed except the delivery technology. Blogs, and the people publishing them, can and do play a number of roles in the information gathering, analyzing, distributing, and filtering chain. First, having the ability to source stories and supporting materials from a broader slice of the population certainly facilitates the intake of potential stories. Similarly, anyone can editorialize, comment on, and analyze any piece of news. By lending their voices to a particular event, bloggers further contribute to its dissemination and filtering. Consequently, users can intervene at any step in the news process to lift, circumvent, and correct any kind of censorship or bias.

Several counterarguments exist to this vision of a perfectly neutral, omniscient, people-powered news organization that gives us unprecedented access to any and all relevant knowledge. The first has to do with quality and noise: Raw materials do not always make a story, and a lot of the content out there is of little significance. Editorializing and making content manageable requires work that few individuals and organizations have the bandwidth to undertake, and most of us look for help. But even in people-powered news sites, such as the popular Digg service that promises to unearth interesting news stories by allowing everyone to vote, an overwhelming majority of the stories are brought into the spotlight by only about 100 power users of the site.

Blogging, or the Remix Culture for News

Another issue, aside from sheer volume of available information, rests on the assumption that most people want to take an active part in the news-gathering process. How valid is that assumption? Stanford University law professor Larry

Lessig has spent a decade working on copyright and hints at signs of what he calls "an awakening" in the younger generation: After decades of their predecessors simply consuming music and movies pushed onto them by the entertainment industry, young people are starting to mashup audio and video tracks in all sorts of creative ways, essentially ending an era of passive watching and listening. This phenomenon signals the start of the *remix culture*.

Whether this applies to the majority of consumers and applications is another story, however. Although we've generally relinquished control over many activities to so-called professionals, we find gratification in producing our own entertainment, even if the audience is limited, and this may be enough to counter the potential drop in quality that results from a lack of training in a particular discipline. But whether that generally applies to news is unlikely.

To appreciate how this applies to the blogosphere, take a look at popular tools such as tech news aggregator and meme tracker Techmeme (or its sibling, Memeorandum, which covers politics) to see how bloggers frequently latch onto a particular story and pile on commentary ad nauseam before moving on to the next hot item. The phenomenon isn't new or specific to the blogosphere, but it shows how many voices do not necessarily translate into many enriching perspectives.

Overall, it's plausible that the medium offers avenues for a broader group to dedicate time and contribute content of general significance, without necessarily turning everyone into a journalist. Meanwhile, many bloggers are able to leverage the medium for other goals, where their content isn't meant as news, per se, but a range of activity from press releases to self-branding.

Truly unique, beyond the lower publishing costs, is the ability of blogs to foster a conversation wherever momentum or enthusiasm gathers behind an item of significance to a group. Also unique is the seemingly improbable mix of two characteristics: that the medium is simultaneously more permanent than e-mail and more fluid than traditional dissemination schemes, such as in its ability to post errata that get the same if not more visibility than the original posting. Without guaranteeing that interesting news will automatically bubble up, by training many to contribute in the open, blogs are contributing to a collapse of the distinction of the public versus private spheres, with possible good and harmful implications for individuals and organizations alike (considering that employees have been fired for inappropriate blogging).

Finally, a review of the risks involved in blogging would be incomplete without a mention of *splogs,* or spam blogs, that most general-purpose and blog-specific search engines work hard to keep out of their indexes. They operate on the premise of syndicating original content and republishing it without attribution or authorization, and they load a lot of advertising on the blog to try and generate revenue. Given the ease of automating the harvesting of content from feeds, their numbers are exploding.

Quick, a Wiki

While blogs have largely drawn on the creativity and personal branding goals of individual authors, wikis have become an entirely different beast. Their influence on the participation culture is just as deep as that of blogs, and it has propagated with impressive velocity, fueled by simplicity and open collaboration from anybody and everybody. The poster child for the disruptive nature of the wiki phenomenon has to be Wikipedia. The site, launched in 2001, has catapulted to become the ninth most popular Web destination, reaching an estimated 217 million monthly unique visitors as of February 2008 (51 million in the United States alone), according to analytics firms Compete and Quantcast.

Wikipedia has grown so fast it blindsided even insiders: In 2002, famous blogger and RSS pioneer Dave Winer challenged Martin Nisenholtz, CEO of *New York Times* Digital, to the following Long Bet (www.longbets.org/2): "In a Google search of five keywords or phrases representing the top five news stories of 2007, weblogs will rank higher than the *New York Times'* website." In February 2008, the Long Now Foundation, ultimate adjudicator in the bet, declared Winer the winner, after carefully pondering, among other conundrums, what constitutes a blog. But what's most notable about the outcome is that for most stories, while neither Winer nor Nisenholtz considered it in 2002, Wikipedia came out ahead of both the mainstream and the blog coverage.

What is a wiki? Let's dig into the Wikipedia example a bit further. Given the traffic it enjoys, most of us are probably familiar by now with the breadth, depth, and relative quality of the site. From a visitor's perspective, the site is chock-full of high-quality content: the English encyclopedia alone counts more than 2 million articles as of December 2007, and studies, notably one covered by Jim Giles in *Nature* in 2005 (see References at the end of this book for source information), have shown that, at least when it comes to scientific matters, accuracy is more or less on par with traditional competitors. Constantly scrutinized by watchdogs and reviewers, the site is also benefiting from its ability to correct errors much faster than any alternative.

What's unique about the Wikipedia site is that it lets anyone be an editor. Other than a few caveats that it has evolved to deal with the consequences of its own success, every page on the site is a click away from being edited by anyone, using a very simple syntax and leveraging a relatively straightforward and possibly rudimentary layout, to make it possible to focus on content creation.

That's the foundation of any wiki. The original wiki, WikiWikiWeb, was designed and developed by Ward Cunningham in 1994, who named it after the Hawaiian term for *quick*, capturing the spirit of the system's reason for being: to enable rapid, unencumbered collaboration among peers creating hypertext content, without requiring familiarity with HTML.

Today's Wikipedia benefits from about 4000 contributors, as of January 2008, who are responsible for more than 28 percent of all edits to the English site. Much larger numbers, approximately 80,000, are regular contributors with more than five monthly edits. In keeping with the general observations made about the asymmetrical nature of the so-called Web 2.0, the underlying ratios of active participants to readers aren't surprising: claiming that the Web is a read-write medium doesn't mean that everyone assumes all roles, and certainly not on a given site. Wikipedia, by far the most successful wiki, exhibits active participation in the 0.01 percent range.

Still, it would be misleading to conclude that all wikis are heavily tilted toward readers. Instead, wikis should be separated as a tool from the large-scale social collaboration experiment that is Wikipedia. Many wikis aren't public and are used instead by corporations to build knowledge bases inside the organizations, and as such they enjoy much higher participation ratios.

Wikipedia installed a number of safeguards that most wikis do not need to cope with and that stemmed from the unique issues surrounding its scale. Some critics have disparaged the organization for being less transparent and less democratic than its claimed ideology suggests. For instance, mailing lists allowing administrators to coordinate actions secretly have been uncovered. In fact, a general debate rages on over whether or not the bottom-up, uncontrolled contributory philosophy underpinning such sites is realistic. In a February 2008 essay on the Technium website, Kevin Kelly, author and cofounder of *Wired* magazine and a strong proponent of the power of smart mobs, highlights the growing number of top-down control mechanisms set up by presumably unfettered contribution services, and how they are necessary to swift success:

> *But it doesn't take very long to discover…that none of these innovations is pure hive mind, and that the supposed paragon of adhocracy—the Wikipedia itself—is itself far from strictly bottom-up. In fact a close inspection of Wikipedia's process reveals that it has an elite at its center…. Turns out there is far more deliberate top-down design management going on than first appears. This is why Wikipedia has worked in such a short time.*

Wiki Semantics

Generally speaking, wikis implement a form of writable web with specific characteristics. Like blogs, the wiki medium is long-lasting and cumulative, as opposed to the transient and differential e-mail, and is shared rather than replicated. Unlike blogs, wikis emphasize an open form of collaboration, where everyone is a potential contributor; the syntax, at least the minimal syntax required to contribute plain text content, is trivial. Even creating links between pages is automated—for instance, by using WikiCamelCase or brackets ([[ ]]). Similarly, to create a new page, a user can simply insert a link to it from an existing page. The link temporarily points to an empty page that the user can then start authoring. The system thus lends itself to constant and simple refactoring, where successive waves of edits can refine not only the content but the structure of articles, for instance, by breaking them into smaller units.

Concurrency and versioning semantics are built into the system to allow easy editing of the site by multiple users, typically with an optimistic, nonlocking approach to conflict resolution on same-article edits. The underlying philosophy is to favor simplicity and remove all barriers to contribute, from technical requirements to access control. Some wiki platform vendors support fine-grained editing, with which multiple users can simultaneously edit different paragraphs of the same article without any conflict. In short, the following is true about wikis:

- Wiki websites are writable by all, requiring little initial learning curve.

- They support formatted, media-rich content with a progressive learning curve.

- Each page is versioned, and all changes are tracked and archived.

- Most support meta-conversation around any page, such as history and talk pages, allowing groups to discuss changes, resolve disagreements, and perform other tasks.

- A number of special pages, such as recent changes and a sandbox, and built-in search, allow users to track new or modified content, to learn how to contribute, and to navigate to content (in addition to following inter-article links).

Of course, wikis can mesh with e-mail to notify interested users of changes for a particular page or category. Assuming a critical mass of contributors is involved, these traits combine for a live medium supporting iterative collaboration toward the building and sharing of a knowledge base. The responsiveness of the medium allows information to be collected and refined very quickly: for instance, it's not uncommon for a skeletal Wikipedia entry to be created minutes after a particular event of interest occurs (sometimes even *as* they occur, such as in the case of sports events), and then be augmented repeatedly by coauthors through successive, rapid-fire edits.

Wiki Dynamics

Overall, wikis in the wild accommodate and foster a more granular form of expression than blogs. Not only do they lower the technical barriers to contribute, they also allow editors to make fragmentary contributions. No edit is too small, and the friction with amending a page is so low that even fixing something as trivial as a typo is meaningful. Paralleling the granularity of the medium is the lack of emphasis on authors. Whereas many blogs are works of personal narration and branding by their publishers, contributing to a wiki is, at least on the surface, a fairly anonymous endeavor.

Perhaps not coincidentally, the distribution of content on wikis is at the opposite end of the spectrum from that of blogs: While 112 million active blogs were tracked as of February 2008, thriving public wikis are a much rarer occurrence. In fact, well-known sites built on the technology, aside from Wikipedia and its massive concentration of content, are hard to come by, and none achieves the scale of the famous encyclopedia. For instance, in the travel vertical, World 66 (www.world66.com) is an established, wiki-based site that attempts to build a worldwide tour book from user contributions. It boasts only 20,000 articles. Wikitravel (http://wikitravel.org) hosts only 18,000 or so articles. Presumably, when it comes to encouraging granular edits, critical mass pays off: A user's typo fix may be small, but its contribution to a heavily trafficked, general purpose site like Wikipedia may make it worthwhile for someone who'd otherwise not feel compelled to commit to that effort.

This helps understand some of the key motivating factors powering contributions to wikis. Some contributors spend inordinate amounts of time sharing their knowledge of a particular field or keeping tabs on articles changing a given area and correcting old or newly introduced errors. They do so without direct reward or recognition and are moved instead by a will to provide others with access to the knowledge they have. They are empowered by the focal point that Wikipedia represents, in terms of reach, as a first stop for many an Internet-based search. (Despite Wikipedia founder Jim Wales's own advice against citing the tool as a primary source in research papers, the people-powered encyclopedia is increasingly being cited in academia.) Not unlike the volunteers fueling the open source software movement driven by the prospect of better code for all emerging from the process, many contributors find the notion of commoditizing information and knowledge appealing, and they see it as a building block toward a more efficient society.

Wiki Uses and Variants

The vast majority of wiki deployments are not intended for public use. Whether physically run behind a corporate firewall or hosted by a provider but access controlled, most wikis are run by small, internal teams collaborating on corporate projects. A number of providers target various segments of the market, from enterprise to consumer customers, from hosted to locally run: Socialtext, Confluence, Wetpaint, XWiki, PBwiki, TWiki, and the MediaWiki software powering Wikipedia are among those, to name a few.

Many of these now offer WYSIWYG editors, making it even simpler for contributors to edit pages without any knowledge of the underlying wiki syntax, and they make it very straightforward to attach images and other media documents to any page. In addition, some vendors have enhanced their platforms to support advanced uses: JotSpot and XWiki, for instance, are categorized as application wikis, where the basic wiki functionality is extended by built-in and user-contributed programmatic plug-ins and templates to support features such as calendaring and spreadsheets. They also support structured, strongly-typed data that is used to automate the embedding of functional mashups in the content and achieve a richer user experience.

The Attention Economy: Taming the Content Flood

Both blogs and wikis are contributing to fostering high-volume, high-velocity conversation. As mentioned, the use of feeds, RSS or Atom syndication–based, as well as pings, allows client software to subscribe and automatically retrieve blog updates on behalf of users. To face the quantity of information published every day, however, better tools are needed. To that effect, two main families of services have emerged: specialized search engines and aggregators.

Specialized search engines, such as Google's Blog Search or Technorati, focus on indexing the blogosphere at a faster clip than the rest of the Web, allowing end users to search over a fresher corpus and get results comprising more up-to-date blog posts. Aggregators, on the other hand, typically operate over a subset of the blogosphere, focusing on a particular domain, from sports to politics, to technology, to gossip. They index the corresponding blogs and possibly include mainstream media sources to discover and extract new developing memes and present these to their visitors in clusters of stories covering the same topic. Gabe

Rivera's Techmeme, for instance, is a site that focuses on tech news, and he runs a collection of similar trackers, each covering a particular area.

In addition, custom meme aggregators have been announced, with which users are able to specify query terms and as a result get the tool to track the blogosphere for memes relevant to the query. Silicon Valley–based Persai is one such service, in private beta as of February 2008. Finally, services such as Digg and Slashdot are people-powered discovery tools that allow end users to keep abreast of the conversation, but these tools lack the clustering ability of aggregating trackers.

These tools, in particular the noncustom varieties, are becoming the de facto gatekeepers of our attention. There is a caveat, however: Attempts are continuously made to game them, and bloggers can derive a lot of traffic by being featured on Digg or Techmeme. Some, therefore, tend to post content echoing the current upcoming stories in the aggregator to be included in the cluster of posts identified as relevant, thus contributing to an artificial inflation of attention and coverage toward a particular event.

The Enterprise Opportunity

So far, this chapter has covered the various shapes assumed by collaborative communication platforms in the Web 2.0 era. It's critical to highlight how the underlying technologies, paradigms, and driving forces represent an opportunity in the enterprise. Authors Don Tapscott and Anthony D. Williams, in their study of mass collaboration and its implications for corporations (see *Wikinomics*, in References at the end of the book), claim that companies must adapt to embrace the new rules of conversation, embodying the next round of evolutionary selection or face extinction.

What's at stake? How can companies tap the power of the tools just reviewed? Opportunities fall within two broad categories: on the one hand, taking part in a conversation, and on the other, building knowledge, both in new, fluid, and efficient ways.

The Conversation Is Everywhere

The blogosphere is, first and foremost, a conversation ecosystem. Better yet, it's a multitude of seemingly independent conversations that can at times intertwine through hubs, people, and topics. As a whole, it's a conversation nobody controls, but we can take part in it, and we'd be foolish not to do so. Why? Blogs are published by individuals and organizations alike at a prodigious pace, and it's likely that there are as many reasons to invest time and write as there are writers.

The infrastructure that all the feeds, feed readers, search engines, and aggregators represent allows the medium to form as the mesh of all posts, intersecting or not. The conversation is simultaneously conducted by a sea of independent authors, yet momentum can build and attention can quickly gather around ad hoc memes. Stories can clump around a piece of news aided by mainstream distribution or a chain of blogroll subscriptions, or they can be carried initially by tighter connections among a group of bloggers reading similar sources and reacting to each other's thoughts. Weak social links are thus established and then strengthened, initially around a given story and later around individual voices. In addition, clusters can develop over time, under the radar, until suddenly reaching a critical mass. Search engines allow patterns to emerge and connections to form among what were first isolated posts. As such, the medium acts as a loosely coupled, distributed system of nodes and has a lot of autonomy and resilience built-in against broadcastlike control. Since no single voice has a monopoly on attention, attempts at owning the entire medium and the message it conveys are bound to fail. This doesn't mean the conversation isn't biased, isn't polluted by a lot of noise, or is necessarily always constructive. But for all their faults, blogs are perceived as personal voices and opinions, not anonymous text, and in the aggregate if not individually, they garner tremendous attention.

From an enterprise standpoint, the opportunities to play a role and have a voice in that conversation are numerous. Incidentally, none of these steps should be considered mutually exclusive, and in fact playing an active role helps with less involved aspects as well, given the focalizing influence that stems from taking active part.

Aside from merely ignoring the blogosphere, a dangerous proposition that's likely to lead to blindsidedness, especially in a time when blogs are far from ignored by search engines, the least involved role consists in passive monitoring. At its most rudimentary level, monitoring is a defensive move. It involves tracking developing stories in posts about a company, its products, its competition, and so on. This is not unlike staying on top of regular press coverage, except the scale and velocity are much larger, and volatility and fragmentation are much higher.

The next step, then, involves leveraging the medium to identify market opportunities and trends. This differs qualitatively from what's usually available in the traditional media: It's likely that members of a target market are blogging about their current experience, not only about their product, but about their various activities, chronicling and narrating their needs and aspirations. All this provides ample raw materials, hints as to unmet expectations, and information about ways to reach a particular audience. What are frequent traveler bloggers complaining about when it comes to commenting on their hotel stays? What would make their stays more enjoyable? When the experience was memorable, what made it unique? A lot of the answers to questions like these can be found on their blogs. Corporations must adjust their hearing aids to sense and leverage that input; this is key to remaining competitive.

Corporate blogs aren't only about listening: Engaging users where they are involved is a transition to a more active participation. This starts with a willingness to comment on posts related to a company's products and technology, and to address customers' issues when they are expressed. It isn't simply about blanketing the blogosphere with PR-speak and rehearsed messages: It's about gaining the trust of authors and readers alike, and it means that some amount of raw, unpolished commentary must be acceptable.

From there, the logical conclusion is to establish a personal voice, a presence in that ecosystem. Obviously, this doesn't exempt business from keeping up with monitoring, scouring, and commenting on stories—quite to the contrary, a blog that's focused only on broadcasting a unidirectional corporate message isn't going to get much mileage in terms of credibility. Increasingly, employees from all groups in the company are blogging, and it pays to have employees outside the marketing and PR departments involved. A variety of bloggers from the product development side and from people at all levels of the organization from top to bottom can offer more credibility, and the galvanizing influence of having an open leadership, as an example, can drive others in the company to start writing. It clearly can't be anything other than voluntary, and it also pays to educate those bloggers about policies that might be needed to protect competitive advantage, intellectual property, and so on.

Bloggers have been fired, some famously, either for inappropriately writing about the inner workings of their professional life or for being too far ahead of the company thinking. Mark Jen, for example, lasted 11 days at Google in 2005, and he claims to have been fired because of his blog reporting on his job there. Ellen Simonetti, flight attendant for Delta Airlines, got in trouble and was fired for her *Queen of the Sky* blog. These and similar stories show that it's imperative for employees to be aware of the company's blogging policy, which assumes one is in place. But this shouldn't deter employees from blogging. Companies should turn employees into evangelists and actors who are not in isolation but in a vibrant conversation. From 2003 to 2006, Robert Scoble was a Microsoft employee who became the company's *spokesblogger* and covered Microsoft and industry news in general with a unique and independent tone. He was not afraid of criticizing teams, products, or decisions with which he disagreed. As such, he pioneered corporate blogging, became a trusted voice in the technology community, and helped give the company a more human face.

Dell is also famous for having turned around public perception of its brand, products, and customer service through the commitment it made to blogging and the support the initiative received from executives. It took a couple of years for the company to find the right tone, after originally being under fire from Jeff Jarvis (renowned journalist, blogger, and City University of New York professor), whose *Dell Hell* posts chronicling his dealings with the company following computer problems starting in 2005 that snowballed to gain massive coverage in the blogosphere and mainstream media alike. *Direct 2 Dell*, the company's official blog, has now become a respected voice in the dialog around company products and customer service. In fact, in 2007, Dell launched IdeaStorm, an innovation community in which users can submit and vote on product ideas. In the process, overall community sentiment about the company has grown from 40 percent favorable to 60 percent (Li, 2007).

Of course, creating and strengthening corporate blog presence is easier said than done. Getting people to participate implies establishing a safe atmosphere of trust and empowerment within the company, so employees are confident that they can safely participate. It also mean adopting a more open approach to conducting business: The company has to be willing to disclose information about what's coming and to listen and react to criticism to build trust in the community.

While influencing the influencers is touted as the ultimate goal, and as good a pursuit as any, beware of shortcuts, which eventually fail under the constant, merciless scrutiny of the blogosphere. Establishing a presence in the community takes time and continued commitment. Instead, *Astroturfing* (PR campaigns masquerading as grassroots behavior, named after the artificial grass product) or other attempts at obtaining or buying the favors of this or that blogger in hopes of getting coverage or even oblique product references usually backfires. Walmart, known for its controlling stance on how business should be conducted, is a great example of how a company is evolving to embrace the form. The company has been attacked numerous times for engaging public relation firms to conduct undercover campaigns using blogs. Recently, buyers at the retail giant, in particular in the consumer electronics division, are starting to find an authentic tone, blogging candid reviews of various appliances—good, bad, and ugly. And while traffic to Walmart employee blogs is still low, they're gaining credibility among readers.

Finally, blogs also represent an internal opportunity as a means to promote informal conversations and facilitate exchanges across traditional organizational boundaries. Blogs are easy-to-use content management systems, and as such they make a good enough platform for departments to post updates and share them with the rest of the team.

Knowledge Building, Crowd-sourced

Like blogs, wikis can be phenomenal information accelerators. Anyone who's had to answer the same question by e-mail more than a couple of times appreciates that a far more efficient way to address recurring issues is to point people at a URL that can be updated to reflect and refine current issues. Such is a frequent occurrence and reason enough to start a wiki.

In their role as an internal knowledge base, wikis are thus fueled at the least by a basic driving force: our selfish need to make our work more efficient. Wikis benefit from a virtuous network effect cycle as well: My contributions enhance the experience of others, who in turn are compelled to participate, improving my experience. In addition, visibility, unlike Wikipedia where identity isn't emphasized and is lost in the scale of the system, is at play in the enterprise. Contributing knowledge for the benefit of everyone in the company is viewed as a constructive endeavor that helps improve efficiency overall. Of course, the ability to participate incrementally, without barrier to entry or friction, makes such low-key implementations possible. One of the key strengths of wikis is the lack of any learning curve, as anyone who has used the Web knows how to use a wiki, at least as a reader. And transitioning from mere reader to contributor doesn't require any technical skill, especially with the rise of WYSIWYG editors. To most, editing a page will seem much like authoring a Word document. And setup itself is simple, with a vast array of hosted options available, some for free.

The biggest hurdle has to do with establishing a culture of participation. There, too, wikis facilitate a progressive approach. The contributor-to-reader ratio doesn't need to be high initially. It takes one champion who's willing to change his own communication habits to start channeling some information sharing away from e-mail, contributing instead a handful of articles to a wiki and then pointing others to it.

Because getting a wiki off the ground is easy, many are deployed from the bottom-up. Yet it pays to foster the trend early and adopt a cohesive policy in the organization by offering a unified wiki infrastructure that helps with performance and multiplies touch-points across groups. The benefits from the network affect the entire company.

In addition to their internal uses, wikis can build communities across company boundaries. Most companies strive to build and nurture relationships in a complex ecosystem of customers, partners, and suppliers. Although all these parties shouldn't be granted the same level of unfettered access to the same wiki, the tool can be leveraged to enable a much higher velocity of information and can help spread knowledge more dynamically. Efficiency, where not at odds with whatever core intellectual property the company needs to protect, yields better results than either secrecy or simply reliance on legacy e-mail for all communication, by leveraging the cumulative and evolving qualities of the wiki system.

Consider Dell's IdeaStorm: It can be viewed as a specialized wiki, where outside parties can submit, edit, and vote on suggestions for products, with employees participating as well. Another straightforward example is with software platforms publishing their APIs and letting developers exchange, build, refine their understanding, and learn from each other together with company employees on a wiki, complementing the traditional mailing lists. Facebook, for instance, uses a wiki to document its F8 developer platform. Wikis thus allow companies to establish a focal point for conversation directly about their products and services.

Pragmatically speaking, such openness initially works best along interfaces and noncompetitive areas. We are not yet in the economy of abundance that would be required for all to be willing to commoditize their information and knowledge completely. Yet when combined, wikis and blogs, in all their possible incarnations, represent a tremendous opportunity to engage with, participate in, and nurture an active community of users and critics of a company's products and services, while simultaneously accelerating efficiency inside the firewall.

They also represent a counterpoint to the prevalent hyperspecialization, currently the de facto path to adding productivity. The shift to participation is turning everyone into active contributors who can play a role and assume responsibilities at more than a single level. It supports the remix culture that Lessig referred to as an "awakening," and it can turn hobbyists and customers into designers.

Chapter 3

The Power of Crowds:
Varieties of Collaboration

By Billy Cripe and Philipp Weckerle

In 1968, J.C.R. Licklider and Robert W. Taylor predicted the advent of
"communities not of common location, but of common interest." Although the
first generation Internet and Web provided some compelling examples and
beta-versions, it is really with the Web 2.0 applications that these "virtual
communities" have become a reality.

David J. Gunkel, Professor of Communication, Northern Illinois University

In today's business environment, most organizations share dramatically similar enterprise information infrastructures. All businesses have some kind of in-house data storage technology, be it a warehousing application, a high availability database system, or a simple homegrown content system. It is rare to hear of a company that does not have some kind of web presence—even if it's only a simple brochure page or splash screen. The similarities exist at a high level, though technology brands, implementation styles, and capacity still differ. However, the high-level similarities mean that any competitive advantage to be gained from technology is less about what brand or application is purchased and more about how the technology is used. It is about the scope of technological adoption within the enterprise.

Winning businesses are no longer required to spend megabucks on technology products. Instead, these businesses are squeezing more efficiency and productivity out of their people and systems. Business is about efficiency, adoption, return on investment (ROI), and getting the most out of the resources available. Consequently, optimization of business processes, and information creation, access, utilization, and sharing, have become the focus. The important questions that smart business leaders are asking is not how can the right information be *created*, but how can the right *efficiencies* be realized and the correct *business intelligence* be applied to business decisions.

Business intelligence—not the old systems of algorithms and queries brought against structured data warehouses, but rather the process of gathering relevant information from disparate structured and unstructured sources to drive business decisions—is not created in a vacuum. It is induced from and precipitated out of the existing corpus of information. Inductive analysis and deductive precipitation of results can be performed by systems (such as legacy business intelligence software) and people (such as the business analyst). But before systems or people can perform these tasks, the information must be available and understandable. Business intelligence systems, while evolving, are still focused primarily on highly or lightly structured information. This is because it is orders of magnitude easier to *programmatically* understand and report on structured information, such as the sum of all fiscal year revenue, than it is to understand the purpose and intention of a series of e-mails and memos circulated through a department during a quarter. The business analyst's job exists because human intuition and intellect are still required to interpret the nuance of meaning in unstructured information as well as the overarching operational context in which those information artifacts reside. While intelligent systems that can start to interpret unstructured data are evolving (see Chapter 10), analysis technology still primarily targets structured information.

Within structured information systems such as databases, data warehouses, and spreadsheets, getting at the information is easy. Columns and rows can be tallied and numbers fed to a dashboard, cube, or pivot table for simple consumption. Unstructured information, however, is incredibly difficult to analyze—at least with the same kinds of tools and strategies used on structured data. From a quantity standpoint, the overwhelming majority of information created in the world, let alone the enterprise, is unstructured. This includes documents, memos, e-mails, marketing images, and videos. Unprecedented amounts of unstructured data are being produced by people, systems, and combinations of systems (pulling data together from various applications). Even the huge amounts of paper-based content are not letting up, especially when the emerging economies from around the world are considered. With this information explosion, it should come as no surprise that more than 80 percent of an organization's information is unstructured, and that number is growing 50 to 200 percent annually by some accounts. The accelerating volume and velocity of information is placing huge strains on organizations simply trying to stay afloat. According to analysts, the amount of digital information "created, captured, and replicated" in 2006 was equal to 161 billion gigabytes (GB), roughly equivalent to the contents of 12 stacks of books extending from the Earth to the sun. In 2010, IDC estimates, the info flow will reach 988 billion GB. It is estimated that each *individual* in an organization will create about 1 GB of unstructured information in a typical year. According to Ferris Research, about 600 nonspam e-mails are sent and received weekly by a typical business user.

Clearly, we are dealing with more than line items in a database. Items such as videos (YouTube), maps, graphics, and scanned images (converting paper invoices to electronic forms) are increasingly generated and incorporated into our daily business lives. A lot of business value is held in the information being generated and not just in the primary purpose of the information. Where a primary purpose for an e-mail might be the *reporting* of supply chain issues to management, the secondary and tertiary purposes might be tracking and aggregation of e-mails, complaints and kudos alike, about a vendor. While aggregation may be considered a kind of ad hoc, unintentional, or invisible collaboration, the presentation of aggregated information back to the user community will help drive additional feedback, participation, and intelligence-driven decision-making. We need help from technology to gain access to information relevant to the task at hand and to help us transform information from a largely static to a dynamic strategic asset. Effective navigation through the swamp of info-glut is what will differentiate successful businesses.

This all means that if business intelligence systems (many of which have enjoyed substantial growth and adoption in the enterprise) are focusing their analysis powers on structured information, they are missing the majority of available information: unstructured information. With the explosion of information creation and our lagging ability to catalog and track, let alone understand, all of what is out there, unstructured information represents the data dark matter of our information universe. Intelligence systems blissfully unaware of the existence of this massive body of information are not getting the whole picture, and the answers these systems provide are inherently incomplete, so data is sometimes fatally flawed. Stopgap solutions, such as bringing in a human business analyst (or, more often, a high-priced team of analysts) to interpret the results of business intelligence systems in light of other contexts, are incontrovertible indicators of the challenges faced. While systems may be unaware of the dark universe of invisible unstructured information, businesses are not quite so ignorant, but they do not have an efficient way to deal with it.

The source of the challenge is twofold: The information needs to be *available*, and the information needs to be *understandable* to people and systems. While getting at the right information at the right time is a relevancy challenge, making information available to people and systems is an aggregation, sharing, and collaboration challenge. Making information understandable to people and systems is a philosophical and a technological challenge. Fortunately, the emancipation of unstructured information from its virtual prison is the purview and goal of Web 2.0 technologies, approaches, and mindsets. Similarly, making the information *understandable* to people and systems not directly or originally connected to its creation or intended consumption is also within the Web 2.0 purview and goals. The creation, exposure, and maintenance of information system–human synergies is what Web 2.0 is all about—knowing who to ask, how to interpret, what to trust, and where to look.

At the time of this writing, we are still in the early days of Web 2.0 uptake in the public Web space and the very early days of Web 2.0 uptake within the enterprise. Important lessons remain to be learned, especially from the public Web, that drive and inform how and where similar technologies and approaches may be leveraged to reshape businesses.

If any theme pervades the majority of Web 2.0 examples on the public Web, it is *sharing*—the sharing of experiences, ideas, and creativity. Sites such as Flickr, MySpace, and YouTube allow individuals to share their stories, thoughts, and impressions with others. Conceptually, these kinds of community websites manifest a key concept of Web 2.0: the power of the crowd. Prior to these community sites information was still consumed on the Web. Websites flourished in the days before YouTube. What is the difference between now and then? The answer provides the foundation for building a strategy around incorporating Web 2.0 concepts and capabilities in a way that makes sense for business.

A key difference between the sharing websites of Web 1.0 and Web 2.0 is that the Web 2.0 sites provide a platform for sharing at a more robust and easy-to-use level. Ease of use is critical for adoption by people. Most of the commonly known public Web 2.0 sites require no training. How can so many business applications claim the same thing? The public Web 2.0 sites not only allow people to distribute their content, but they also provide an interaction layer that offers ease of consumption (for viewing videos, text, and images) and advanced interaction (for participating in discussions asynchronously via threads, rating, and tagging information, pushing information out, and so on). By providing this often anonymous and "crowd-based" interaction platform, Web 2.0 simulates then stimulates the community. Although this community does not need to be well-defined or even long-lived, these people and systems are unintentionally collaborating and being drawn together by chance, opportunity, and theme, coalescing around content they find interesting. Quite simply, the technology enables a widely spaced (geographically, physically, philosophically, and conceptually) and ad hoc network of people to participate with the information as well as with each other. Without them immediately or necessarily noticing, these participants enrich the original content while they raise the value of the aggregated information for others. A feedback spiral emerges, expanding outward from the original intent.

The Power of Crowds

The amount of interactivity on the World Wide Web today has increased dramatically since the early days of static sites (as described in Chapter 2). Blogs have gained in popularity and sites such as Digg.com have redefined the concept of the Web, from a static, one-way interaction to a collaborative environment. But Web 2.0 challenges many of the concepts and predispositions about our ideas of collaboration within organizations.

The business world often thinks of collaboration as involving some *thing*. We work together for a purpose or project goal, creating a presentation or marketing campaign. These are very intentional ways of collaborating after a purpose has been established. While it is easy to understand how this kind of focused collaboration necessarily includes a group or a team, it becomes more difficult to envision the ways in which a crowd—a faceless, anonymous mass—can collaborate. Who is in control? Who sets direction? Who measures completion let alone success? For the business, these are valid questions, but they reflect Web 1.0 thinking. Web 2.0 spirals out the concepts of collaboration to include the unintentional, accidental, and infinite.

Digg.com and StumbleUpon.com are good examples of Web 2.0's new way of collaborating and sharing. Individuals discover interesting, funny, or otherwise mentionable content through research or by chance and they publish those references with a simple button click (no training needed!). These services become a de facto lightweight and intrinsic rating system. The purpose is not to rate a website *on a scale* or to provide an explicit review of the site. Rather these are simple thumbs up or down, binary systems. Although Digg.com and StumbleUpon.com are basically a collection of links, they transcend the banality of a personal browser's bookmarks by allowing the entire population of the Web to interact and collaborate on the unstructured content of the Internet.

Because the "digs" that stories or content receive are aggregated and stored along with the link references, Digg.com serves as a de facto prioritization engine and relevancy index. The prioritization engine becomes possible only through the collaboration of the users—the crowd. The Digg.com user community is not a formally defined group. They have no shared purpose or projects. They are associated only through their common use of the Digg.com service. Such unintentional collaboration is how Web 2.0 is tapping the huge volumes of information from the crowd (by making it overwhelmingly simple for users to participate) and doing the work of collecting all those independent inputs to provide new aggregate information back to the crowd.

Popular services such as Amazon.com and Netflix let their customers rate items and submit reviews. The ability to rate is a kind of structured comment that allows both the users and the system itself to process that information. Explicit ratings are powerful, not only in the obvious way of creating an aggregated opinion, but also in how they are used by other customers who mine data for purchasing recommendations. Community participation is a great source of statistical data for refining search results and providing recommendations based on collected data that a user might not have discovered otherwise.

Similarly, the concept of *social bookmarking* is widely available on the public Web through such sites and services as del.icio.us. Social bookmarking is one of the simplest examples of sharing information across vast user crowds. Social rating and bookmarking services such as Digg.com and del.icio.us percolate up relevance from the aggregation of the crowd inputs. End users take in these references as important weighting criteria when judging whether to look at a story with several diggs or whether to add a highly bookmarked del.icio.us site to their personal bookmarks. In this way, the sharing of pointers to information suddenly morphs into a highly potent decision-making tool that draws its power from the participation of its users. No administrator prepopulates content. No algorithm determines relevancy. Instead, the human element is tapped for "computational" power. It is precisely this potent decision-making capability that holds promise for the business world. But the great potential comes out of vast participation, and the rigid hierarchies of business often run at cross purposes with such social participation.

Web 2.0 could restore the human element to the technological plane of Internet-mediated communications. Both del.icio.us and Digg.com go beyond simple, linear, word-of-mouth transmission (I tell you, you tell your friend, she tells the kid next door, and so on). The inherently digital and asynchronous modes of web operation yield a network effect map of communication. While the information is being disseminated, Web 2.0 services are performing aggregation. Aggregation is a key function that is not available in a linear word-of-mouth model. It brings power to the message. In the Digg.com example, the message is simple: "I like this." If you see that "33 other people like this," your interest may be piqued.

In the anonymous Web, aggregation is a proxy for credibility and trust: The more the crowd trusts a source (or reads it, bookmarks it, uses it) the more *likely* it is that it will be useful to you as well. The success of community sites such as FaceBook, LinkedIn, and other social networking sites hinges on a different kind of crowd-based sharing: the sharing of *connections* between *people*. In personal, professional, and casual contexts, the value of the connections that make up social networks holds immense potential.

Although the social network is discussed at length in Chapter 4, the power of the crowd in a social network context warrants mention here as well. Especially in today's anonymous web-mediated world, connections between people are increasingly important. Even indirect or loose connections between people that have been mediated through stronger and tighter connections between others can raise trust levels. Trust is crucial for the roles it plays in propping up *probable* relevancy and providing the warrant for the Web's most implicit claim. The public Web's most implicit claim, the one that is inherent in every piece of information available on the Web, is this: *You ought to consume this.* The warrant for that claim is the answer to the question *Why?* Crowds provide the answer to this question in many ways. Through aggregation services, the answer is *because lots of us liked/ bookmarked it*. This is positive net peer pressure. Through social networking and social graph services, the answer is a bit different: *because so-and-so is a credible person and she suggested it,* or *because this many other people like you thought it was worthwhile.* While this is not exactly word of mouth, the weight of these words, either because of their quantity (anonymous aggregation services) or quality (social network services) drive our individual decision calculus to consume or not to consume. That, after all, is the point.

Opinion sharing is another example of participatory interaction. Opinions can be shared via blogs or comments on blogs, for example. Web comments represent personal opinions about particular information at a particular time. Web comments often carry additional information that is both unstructured and typically informal. Individually, each comment may not offer much meaning or useful information, but a number of comments about an item can indicate the crowd's interest in or engagement with the topic. Following on the notion that nothing attracts a crowd like a crowd, the indicator of engagement and interest by a crowd is a good clue that the topic(s) being discussed are important and, therefore, relevant. Understanding how to tap these hotspots of blogging *buzz* is part of the core business model for several web businesses, but the revenue potential driving these new businesses has a corollary within the enterprise. If companies can be profitable targeting blogging buzz, then important intelligence can also be gained within the enterprise by understanding what employees, partners, and suppliers are discussing, working on, and talking about—even if they are not talking with each other.

The Power of Teams

Moving one step farther into the realm of sharing, if we break down larger communities into those that share the same interests or work on the same topic, we enter the realm of *virtual teams* of individuals who are connected by topic rather than organization. Yet they still want to share ideas to achieve a common goal. This is where the application of Web 2.0 capabilities, pioneered on the public Web, to business organizations should become most apparent.

Teams and teamwork, familiar concepts in most organizations, also lead to the categorization of individuals. An individual's membership in a particular group offers information about that individual to others. For example, your position on a team will tell others that you are knowledgeable in a particular area. An individual's involvement with several teams can also provide information about that person and possibly trigger actions by others—for example, if someone is looking for an expert in a particular field or a manager who can balance workloads, he or she may seek out a candidate who is involved in groups that focus on particular skills.

Working with virtual teams is familiar to most business people today. In fact, many operational strategies are based on the concept. Whether incorporating partners, offshore resources, or geographically disparate team members, the communicative connectivity provided by the Internet infrastructure allows the decentering of team structures. Ever-shrinking resource and time budgets do not allow for duplication or heavy reorganization; they require flexible pools of experts that can be assembled as needed.

Along with seeking such flexibility on the personnel level, organizations must provide tools so that those virtual teams can do their work as efficiently as possible. Whether teams are virtual because of geographical locations of members or because of their distribution across organizational boundaries, their members must establish and maintain efficient ways of communicating and collaborating, both intentionally as well as unintentionally. The teams need ways to share information in a connected, asynchronous fashion. Sharing in virtual teams is not a luxury, but an absolute necessity. While sharing within a team is less about trust and more about efficiency, the goal of spreading individual knowledge to the group to empower the group is critical. Furthermore, the paradigms that limit virtual teams to the conceptual boxes defined by the team members have already been deconstructed and reconstructed on the public Web. When competitive advantage or speed to a niche market means the difference between being an alpha dog or merely a part of the pack, is an organization able to afford ignoring any *relevant* information source? It is too easy for businesses to become self-congratulatory for their pioneering virtual teams (welcome to 1990!) without realizing that they have swapped a rigid individual hierarchy for an equally rigid virtual team hierarchy, where ideas and information from outside the team are ignored simply because of their point of origin.

The public Web has proved that virtual teams can work together even with the loosest definitions of what constitutes a team and being a team member. Open source software development is a good example of how inclusion in a virtual team is a matter of individual initiative. Sign up for updates, contribute some code or review cycles, and you are "in." While control over code branches, the product these teams are creating, is maintained by the project leaders, access to the information is widely available. Consequently, the power of the participating crowd can be brought to bear on the quality and ease of use of the software product deliverable. Furthermore, the power that is brought is not simply hours of developer time; it is also a variety of perspectives and problem spotting and solving. The powerful virtual team does not succumb to the limited thinking and perspectives that plague so many organizations. Through the power of the crowd, the team transcends the constrictions of "inside-the-box" thinking.

Communication among members of virtual teams is vital in keeping information flowing, and Web 2.0 technologies and paradigms have added significant simplification to the communication process. Technologies such as instant messaging, discussion forums, blogging, and microblogging facilitate communication among geographically disconnected individuals. They can be used synchronously as well as asynchronously, allowing for both real-time communication (the *instant* in instant messaging) and time-delay communication.

For globally based virtual teams separated by dramatic time zone differences, the ability to carry on conversations regarding project goals is important. From an efficiency perspective, it relieves the need for difficult scheduling to consider smaller issues. Within the enterprise, virtual teams can take advantage of communication technologies to discuss, for example, design ideas over the course of a week through a specialized forum or project blog. Decisions can be made collaboratively but without the burden of forcing real-time conversations. While real-time conversations are still a vital part of the decision-making process for any organization, instant communication technologies such as chat, instant messaging, and VoIP (Voice over Internet Protocol) can be used to coordinate and set up important business meetings. These technologies can be configured and deployed to automatically retain the information exchanged. Such retention is vital for maintaining secure, auditable, and compliant business practices.

With any information sharing technology, security must be intrinsic to the concepts of *relevance*—getting the right information to the right people at the right time. That means controlling information so that if someone is unable to access information, the information is not relevant to this person. As well, access is granted to individuals only for information that is appropriate and relevant to their particular task or job. Executives tend to get a bit nervous when considering crowds, collaboration, and sharing. They fear that information anarchists and hackers will exploit proprietary information or try to air company dirty laundry or otherwise cause mischief. Executives should rest assured, however, that this is not the case. Not all information is suitable for all members or people outside the group. Access policies and privileges need to be attached to information that is stored within a common area to ensure that only those entitled to this information can take advantage of it.

In an ideal world, everything published on the Web would be trustworthy, and information would not need to be protected against misuse. But this is not an ideal world. That said, can nothing be trusted? Fortunately, the answer is that most information can be cautiously trusted, but its source, context, and intended purpose must be understood. Web 2.0 brings to the technological world the same kinds of common-sense capabilities that we humans use in everyday life. We determine trust by considering the source of information. Personal connections to a source, direct or via known proxies, significantly increase the level of trust. Ratings, tags, and collective opinions of information are all sources of trust.

Consider how many of us buy a new television. Before we commit to purchasing a unit, we search the Internet for ratings, and if we see that a lot of people rate a particular TV highly on an opinion site or the vendor's own rating page, we figure that the TV is probably a good one. And if we know one or more of the people who have rated the television, even better. Nothing trumps the word of a trusted friend. This phenomenon applies equally to the business world. Information is as good as its source. The more the sources agree, the better the information. However, with exponentially more sources, it is exponentially more important that we are able to trust these sources as well as audit their credibility.

Opinions are sometimes more valuable than facts when determining relevancy, and Web 2.0's participatory nature is an important driving force behind the technology. Participation is one significant difference between the public Internet and the enterprise web; although the number of contributors out there is huge and contributors are usually anonymous, enterprises are and must be controlled ecosystems with a clearly defined and easily identifiable number of contributors and sources. Due to the lack of relative anonymity in business settings, information posted on the corporate web will typically be viewed with less skepticism than posts on the public Web. In this trusting enterprise environment, the quality of information could be directly inferred from the credibility of the source.

While the concepts of *trust* and *credibility* are closely related, they are rarely connected technologically. While an opinion might matter to you, because you might know the source, the source might not be credible in a professional sense, even though he is trustworthy in a personal sense. Similarly, an acclaimed subject matter expert's opinion on a topic might simply be ignored because the person has not "entered the inner circles" of your network. Web 2.0 is about creating a controlled environment in which trust and credibility can be established and fostered. At the end of the day, both concepts should be the result of the contributions and decided by the community. The power of the community brings corrective power to claims made by people seeking credibility. The recognition of credibility by the community can ease the earning of trust. The reflective feedback loop empowered by the community establishes and then tunes relevancy. While credibility could be defined by a third party, trust needs to be earned.

Crafting Meaning: Tagging

Another common mode of participatory interaction is *tagging*, the categorization of content along various axes that describe the scope of the information, its aggregation, and its topics. Tagging allows users to label items used infrequently to find them more quickly when required. Tagging speeds user discovery and increases user productivity directly. Tags greatly enhance information in a number of ways. They can enhance the discoverability of content by creating cross-references that were not known by the authors. Tags enhance the ability for users to consume information quickly by combining into topical "maps" the concepts contained in a document, web page, or collection of artifacts. When exposed to social networks, tags self-organize into community-based and theme-driven thesauri by tapping the power of the crowd to draw out ideas contained in an artifact or collection of artifacts. Such conceptual topographies did not exist when a particular piece of information was created. By interconnecting information based on user behavior, tags make locating relevant content easier. Similarly, since the items returned are correlated with user interest, the relevancy is significantly enhanced.

As mentioned earlier in this book, the information explosion is fueled by three converging trends that span technological, cultural, and regulatory disciplines:

- **Technological**   The proliferation of technologies that facilitate content creation. Examples include blogs; wikis; social network sites such as LinkedIn, MySpace, social video; and image sites such as YouTube and Flickr.

- **Cultural**   The emergent Web 2.0 mindset that promotes, with a force approaching the demands of a human right, hyper-individualized and perspective-based content creation.

- **Regulatory**   Legal statutes, business regimes, and best practices that increasingly require the persistence of nearly all information created. Whether for risk management, for corporate compliance, or from a desire to provide better metrics through richer data sets, information is kept longer than ever before.

The result of more people more easily creating more content, which is then stored for more time, is *info-glut*, an overabundance of information. Businesses are catching on to the need to manage and leverage this information. Successful strategies provide a unified foundation or infrastructure that facilitates information management, interaction, and contextualization. But the challenge of understanding information at the right time and in the right context has never been greater than it is now. Exacerbated by the vast quantities of information being produced and stored, this is the challenge of relevancy.

Reshaping Relevancy

At its core, the problem of relevancy is a search result problem that presupposes a *relevant to what?* question. A search result is relevant based only on what the searcher wants. The possibility of relevancy is a function of either or both how well a search term or phrase actually reflects the searcher's desire or how well the search engine anticipates the *actual* desire of the searcher. The ability of the searcher to translate his or her desire into an accurate and appropriate middle language (query string, form value, criteria, and so on) is an implicit limitation to the degree of relevancy that is possible in the search results. For example, if a user seeks information on Australian shepherd dogs and searches the Web for *animal*, the relevancy of the results is substantially diluted.

Many of the early attempts to deal with relevancy sprang from a structured content mindset: database thinking. Interactive search forms provided more user-friendly ways of writing database queries than developer-based solutions such as SQL. But these forms dealt with relevancy only indirectly. Any and all results were assumed to be relevant simply because they matched the query criteria. In today's info-glutted system, simplistic criteria-matching is no longer sufficient to assure relevancy. Relevancy cannot be driven simply by the searcher's ability to phrase a search accurately. When a search yields hundreds, thousands, or millions of results, the relevant item is effectively buried and therefore lost.

Fortunately, new approaches have organically arisen from the emergent Web 2.0 world to deal with the challenges posed by the needs of relevancy. These approaches share two key themes: First, the strategies incorporate a participatory social or democratic approach to the solution. Second, since Web 2.0 is intrinsically participatory, the more users participate, the more relevant the information.

Relevancy is determined by the seeking individual. When that individual is aggregated into a "seeking audience," the collective responses can help to define relevancy. Better relevancy scores and rankings result. The idea is that the more information that the seeking audience affiliates with the content that describes "what it is" and "how it is used," greater accuracy will be produced by the relevancy algorithms the next time they are applied. But relevancy is also expressed in the collective agreement of groups. This is the power of social and democratic approaches to relevancy solutions: They foster a hyper-personal interaction ability for information inputs while facilitating amalgamations that precipitate out (or percolate up) from the interactions of the individual contributions. Social and democratic relevancy disciplines make it easy for individuals to contribute while understanding how to interpret, weight, aggregate, and publish the results. This is the power of the social and democratic approaches to relevancy.

Four advantages to tapping the power of the crowd to determine or increase the relevancy of information are immediately evident:

- *It decreases the central burden.* The social approach is decentralized, relieving the burden on and responsibility of a top-down approach. Centralized approaches such as corporate taxonomies, predefined option lists, normalized database schemas, and myopic most-recent-therefore-most-relevant approaches place an enormous burden on human staff such as central administrators, corporate librarians, and records managers as well as on technologies such as search indices and query engines. The cycle of tuning and tweaking the systems to serve the end users can become never-ending.

- *It increases the accuracy and granularity of relevancy.* Relevance is directly proportional to specificity. A social approach to a relevancy solution tends toward greater accuracy and granularity since it takes a bottom-up approach to relevancy determination. Rather than relying on a central authority to establish relevance across all the permutations of ranking and ordering of results to all the permutations of queries that the end user community might use, the social approach allows the user community to establish relevance on the go, as they use the content they find. This process also relieves the burden of random categorization as individuals stuck with strict schemas are required to select "the closest," which is not always "the most accurate" choice.

- *It provides self-correcting and self-tuning results.* A social approach to relevancy is inherently self-correcting and self-tuning. As social and democratic input is included over time, anomalies are statistically marginalized to the point of immateriality, and gaps are filled in. In this manner, a system learns and corrects and then provides increasing levels of accuracy and granularity that determine relevance.

- *It is hip to Web 2.0 culture.* A democratically based solution to the relevance problem is inherently Web 2.0 and invites and requires participation by end users. It is radically decentralized and fosters reuse and repurposing of content, yielding efficiency gains. It reveals a potential for content that often transcends original intent and represents a nascent semantic web.

But what exactly is the social or democratic approach to a relevancy solution? The following concrete examples from the World Wide Web should help describe the various socially based solutions to relevancy.

Google

The Google search engine measures *inbound* links (other sites that link to it), among other factors, to the websites it indexes to determine relevancy. The more inbound links associated with a site, the higher its ranking. The implicit presumption is that links to a site are a currency of relevance; they are an arbiter of one of the few items of value in the online world: credibility. The "richer" the site, the better the chances it will provide relevant content—ergo, it gets listed higher up in the search results. To be sure, this is an oversimplification, and other factors, such as purchased keywords, query matching against result candidates, sophisticated algorithms, and so on, affect ranking display (Elworthy, 2006; see References at the end of this book for source information). Nevertheless, the point stands. After all, other website owners would not link to sites without "cred," would they? But the answer is not straightforward. Consider, for example, that some mischievous individuals seek to manipulate the perception of credibility through popularity analysis. They create "front" websites, blogs, or comments in response engines containing only links to the target site—the website whose result ranking they desire to increase. These attempts are real, though they prove the inherent point: Popularity is a presumptive indicator of credibility.

For determining hipness or popularity, the inbound link model is fine. But this approach does not determine relevance as much as it leverages a potential side effect of relevance. The potential of relevance stems from the expectation that a popular site will offer something important about the topic. For determining relevance, especially in relation to the relevance of information contained in lesser ranked sites, this approach provides little to no relevancy benefit. In other words, a site appearing on page 9 of a Google results list might actually be the best site out there, despite the fact that it has few inbound links. Search engines are also limited by how fast they can keep up with finding, logging, and indexing new content.

Despite these possible shortcomings of the Google model, it does serve to exemplify the social and democratic approach to relevancy, and, at the end of the day, it does a pretty good job of pointing us toward the information we want.

Flickr

The photo sharing site Flickr is an example of a site that popularized the *tagging* concept. Tagging on Flickr is a web form-input field whereby the photo owner may apply one or more keywords, or tags, to a photo that she has uploaded. Images are notoriously difficult to index in meaningful ways due to the lack of machine-readable, human-understandable, textual, associated data. The quickest way around this snag is to associate human-input textual data with the image and then leverage that data, in aggregate, as a ready-made index against which searches may execute. Flickr implemented this notion with its photo tagging capability, and it took this one step further and aggregated the most popular tags into a *tag cloud*—a visual representation of the tag aggregate in which more common tags are differentiated from less common tags by appearance.

The tags in a tag cloud represent subsets of content that precipitate out of the aggregate or totality of data. Users with no connection to each other may tag their content using the same words and thereby, independently and democratically, add it to the set of content that then becomes available for the community to view. Such an organic and subversive approach is immediately and intuitively appealing to a Web 2.0 mindset.

Tag clouds are also incredibly powerful mechanisms and alternatives for form-based query builder search tools. By presenting the user with a visually represented search interface, the cloud taps into the power of the human brain to understand what it wants better than a query language can translate that desire into a machine-understandable request. Visual relationships are clearly understandable without the end user needing any training or instruction. As long as the user understands what the visual differences of the tags in a cloud signify, the user is engaged and invited to participate with the information to find what is most relevant to him. By aggregating and presenting keyword tags, the user is invited to drill down into the subset that most likely contains the content in which he is interested. In the Flickr example, larger tags indicate larger quantities of likely data in that subset while smaller tags indicate smaller subsets of data (see Figure 3-1). The different styles of tag clouding are discussed a bit later in this chapter.

While tagging is an individualistic activity, relevancy can still remain an elusive goal. No suggestion engine or central application engine enforces tags on images. Subsets are defined democratically insofar as individuals make their own decisions on what tags to apply to their content. Yet, if one user tags a photo of his Australian shepherd with *dog* and another user tags a photo of her car with *dog*, both photos will display in the set of photos using the *dog* tag. The results are only

07 africa amsterdam animals architecture art asia australia baby band barcelona beach berlin birthday black blackandwhite blue boston bw california cameraphone camping canada canon car cat chicago china christmas church city clouds color concert cute dance day de dog england europe fall family festival film florida flower flowers food france friends fun garden geotagged germany girl girls graffiti green halloween hawaii hiking holiday home honeymoon house india ireland island italy japan july kids la lake landscape light live london macro march me mexico mountain mountains museum music nature new newyork newyorkcity newzealand night nikon nyc ocean paris park party people photo photos portrait red river rock rome san sanfrancisco scotland sea seattle show sky snow spain spring street summer sun sunset sydney taiwan texas thailand tokoyo toronto travel tree trees trip uk urban usa vacation vancouver washington water wedding white winter yellow york zoo

FIGURE 3-1	Flickr uses font size and weight to indicate data popularity.

as good as the fidelity of the tag to the image to the end user's expectation. Maybe the woman's car is a "dog of a car," or maybe she calls it her "dog." Nobody knows except the tagger herself and possibly her friends. These colloquial or microsocial contexts are neither known by the end user community nor communicated by the tag *dog*. Therein also lies a challenge that owner-defined tags pose to relevancy. Social tagging relying only on content owners for input is beholden to the whims of the owner and whatever taxonomic baggage she carries with her.

Despite the shortcomings of the Flickr owner-tagging model, it does serve to exemplify a democratic approach to relevancy and actually does a pretty good job of pointing us toward a set of information that probably contains what we seek.

Last.fm

Another kind of social tagging is presented in clouds similar to the Flickr model but takes a different approach to how tags are created. Instead of content owners being solely responsible for applying tags to their content, the entire end user community is invited to tag content. In this manner, the audience defines the content. As participation by the audience increases (as measured by the number of tags applied over time), certain terms emerge as more common while others remain outliers. In this way, the end users vote on the term or terms that best describe or fit the content. Over time, the fit gets better as more votes are tallied.

The sense of fit, though, is flexible. Because fit responds to the community, it also reflects community trends, preconceptions, and understanding. Of course, all this presupposes continuing interaction with the artifact by the community. But if that is granted, then democratic tagging and clouding becomes an incredibly useful and dually faceted tool.

One facet is the democratic tag cloud as a snapshot of perceptions at the time. The way the cloud looks at any given moment is a good reflection of how the using community perceives and interacts with the content item. This provides very useful real-time intelligence and feedback on the nature of the consuming community as well as the desirability of the artifact. The other facet emerges when considering snapshots of the democratic tag cloud arranged in time. As successive snapshots of the cloud are arranged historically, the changing perceptions, and the layers of interaction, interest, and even demographics of the consuming community, can be mapped. These changes are valuable to organizations interested in using historical trends to predict future behavior. Trend mapping and spotting is facilitated with the preaggregated and continuously correcting nature of democratic tagging user interfaces and cloud-based presentations.

The music site Last.fm uses this style of democratic tagging to label the genres of the artists it hosts. The cloud formed from this audience-based tagging approach typically indicates a single leading tag. But rather than declare an artist's genre as the one "winning" tag, the entire cloud is left such that the relation of the "winning" tag to the other tags is apparent. This has the effect of flavoring or moderating the genre. Consider this cloud for the band Arctic Monkeys that appears on the Last.fm site and is shown in Figure 3-2.

While the presentation is identical to other tag clouds, what is interesting here is what the cloud as a whole communicates to the end user and the implications on relevancy. This artist is clearly tagged *indie* and *indie rock*—arguably two synonymous or nearly synonymous genres. But *alternative, british,* and *britpop* also appear in the cloud. From this information, the audience can generate a much richer inference about this band, its likely sound, and its influences than simply

00s **alternative** alternative rock arctic monkeys artic monkeys awesome boisterous brit brit pop brit rock british britis indie british rock **britpop** britrock classic rock confident cool dance emo england english favorite favorites favour favourites fun garage garage rock great lyrics i like **indie** indie pop indie punk **indie rock** indie-rock indiepop love male vocalists modern rock pop pop rock post punk post-punk post-punk revival pukkelpop punk punk rock **rock** rock werchter 2006 rousing seen live seen live twice sheffiel< very british the best uk want to see live whatever people say I am yeah

FIGURE 3-2   Tag cloud for the band Arctic Monkeys

indie rock. The cloud is a living metadata asset to the content—in this case, the band's listing on Last.fm (Figure 3-3).

The cloud serves another purpose as well. It is a collection of hyperlinks. Clicking *indie rock* allows a user to drill down into a collection of other artists who have been similarly tagged by the audience of Last.fm users and listeners. From a search relevancy perspective, this provides a list of results relevant to indie rock and related or similar to the Arctic Monkeys. For the user, such a related relevancy engine exposes him to other content (artists) with whom he may not be familiar or have considered and provides a visual indicator of how accurate the tag (*indie rock*) is as a metadata indicator (in this case, genre).

1	▶ Arctic Monkeys	3,718
2	▶ Bloc Party	3,242
3	▶ Death Cab for Cutie	3,103
4	▶ The Killers	3,078
5	▶ Interpol	2,940
6	▶ Franz Ferdinand	2,931
7	▶ The Arcade Fire	2,844
8	▶ Modest Mouse	2,586
9	▶ The Strokes	2,473
10	▶ The Shins	2,041
11	▶ Radiohead	1,922
12	▶ Yeah Yeah Yeahs	1,858
13	▶ Kaiser Chiefs	1,793
14	▶ The White Stripes	1,763
15	▶ The Decemberists	1,544
16	▶ Broken Social Scene	1,514
17	▶ Pixies	1,440
18	▶ Muse	1,405
19	▶ Snow Patrol	1,348
20	▶ The Libertines	1,331

See more top artists...

FIGURE 3-3   Artists tagged "indie rock"

Gaps, Deficiencies, and Missing Features

The preceding three case studies illustrate the general state of democratic approaches to the relevancy issue. To be sure, some sites and developers have implemented relevancy strategies, some of them socially or democratically oriented, that surpass the strategies of Google, Flickr, or Last.fm. Other site developers have not started to consider a relevancy strategy. Before businesses begin to consider a relevancy solution, be they technologies, development approaches, or off-the-shelf applications, they should consider what is missing in, but needed from, the current approaches.

Missing from popularity analysis of inbound hyperlinks is an evaluation of *inherent* as opposed to *probable* relevancy. Missing from author-originator keyword labeling is an ability to overcome the baggage and preconceptions about the content that are imported by the author. Missing from the democratic or voter-style of tagging is any kind of data seeding as well as any ability to attribute tags that capture the meaning and originally intended purpose of the content. Finally, missing from both tagging approaches is an understanding and appreciation of the differences between and power of owner-originator keyword aggregation and social tagging.

Democratizing and socializing technologies are both accessible to the users. They have little or no barrier to entry and participation. However, socializing technology is understood in this context to be accessible to the users as well as fostering a synthesis of concepts. It is a process in which *n*-inputs (such as tags or keywords) are aggregated to impact each other and form a new whole (such as a cloud). This whole is a new kind of object that contains traces of the constituent parts, where no constituent part goes unflavored or unnuanced by the others. Dissimilarly, democratizing technology, while accessible to the people, is understood in this context as fostering a tallying of inputs. Inputs remain distinct. If aggregated, the aggregate is a report or a display rather than a uniquely new whole. The aggregate provides a presentation of multiple tallies for purposes of visually determining ranking preference or popularity.

Tags and keywords are also differentiated along a similar polar opposition. In this context, tags are understood to be connotative or suggestive and social, while keywords are understood to be denotative or clear labels but rarely social. Keywords are supplied by author-originators and are denotative. Tags, on the other hand, are supplied by consumers. Tags are provided with the intent of signifying or suggesting concepts that are potentially accompanying or associated with possible meaning and purpose of the information. In this sense, individual keywords represent a "what the content might be or mean to whom" while tags represent a "how or for what the content might mean."

From implementation and application perspectives, the ways in which keywords and tags are used is also best differentiated. Keywords, as author-originator selected, are ideally situated for one-time application and then tallied and presented according to democratic principles. This best taps both original intent and purpose. This snapshot can then be tallied and algorithmically evaluated to perform more in-depth democratic-perspective-over-time evaluations and presented to display current meaning. Alternatively, tags are ideally suited for ongoing and unstructured application to content. This best taps the organic and ongoing meaning and purpose of the user community. When presented back to the consuming community, and end users can consider that information when making final relevancy-based selections. If an item is insufficient, the consumer is invited to participate in the ongoing social tagging in a kind of pay-it-forward relevancy model.

Popularity

While popularity of information objects is important to capture, popularity itself is not a guarantor of credibility. Nevertheless, popularity tracking of, on a macro level, websites remains an important strategic goal. Neither are analyses of inbound links guarantors of credibility. The phenomenon of Google bombing illustrates this point. *Google bombing* is the manipulation of the Google algorithms to make certain pages appear closer to the top of search results, thereby giving the impression that they are the most relevant (Moulton and Carattini, 2007). Such tactics and others like them, though, serve to illustrate the central supposition that popularity, as indicated by incoming links, is presumed to be an inherent indicator of relevancy. Were it not so, Google bombing would not be a problem that demands a public response from Google.

Consequently, and at best, popularity analyses are indicators of the likelihood that something important may be found. A relevancy solution should take these metrics into consideration but not stop there. The good news is that these kinds of metrics are relatively simple to track and capture. Website traffic meters typically track hits, popularity, and incoming links. Most business intelligence tools and search appliances incorporate more sophisticated algorithms to track, capture, and report or serve up this information. But a relevancy solution that stops at this point is missing some of the most powerful processors available: the end users.

Author-originator Tags and Keywords as Data Seeds

Data seeding is a springboard set of tags, keywords, or both that attempt to prevent initial obscurity. If socially or democratically applied tags are the only data points that can be indexed or that can appear in an end user–facing tag cloud, then the barriers to inclusion in initial search results are quite high. Consider, for example, a new artist added to the Last.fm queue. Without either an end user community "in the know" about the new addition or an alternative way of listing the addition, the new artist will remain in obscurity until someone stumbles upon her listing and decides to be the first to tag her. For any content, obscurity in the info-glut storm is already a significant risk. A tagging solution should not also exact an "obscurity toll" as the price for possible eventual relevancy.

The lack of a communicated original intent is also a problem with purely democratic tagging mechanisms. While it is nearly a guarantee that, in the mashup-loving, socially-empowered–Web 2.0 world, content can be repurposed, the force and thrust of content will still be greatest in its original intent. Content will typically be strongest when consumed according to its original purpose, which should be captured as metadata. While Flickr keywords provide a sense of meaning, the lack of a tagged intent that is able to be aggregated and machine interpreted or presented is a deficiency of both the Flickr and Last.fm models. An ability to capture the initial purpose as part of an overarching relevancy approach is still required. Promotion and enabling of author-originator tags and keywords as a denotative content purpose is one strategy that ought to be integrated into a larger relevancy discipline. Data seeding tags and keywords alone are not enough to guarantee relevancy or even encourage users to participate. Alone they are lacking the structure of keywords, the organic nature of social tags, and the power of popularity rankings. They must be integrated into a larger relevancy discipline to realize the potential they hold.

Risks in Folksonomy: Implementations and Solutions

Democratic and social practices for adding information to or about content is known as *folksonomy* (or folk taxonomy, an organization of the content that emerges from all the users labeling information). A dash of consideration of the risks and problems with folksonomies is warranted.

First, as with the communication of all content, the medium selects what it allows to pass. So as a tempering influence on anything that smacks of universal, tagging must be recognized as an inherently *textual* process. No mechanism is available for aggregating and rendering image-as tags, video tags, or audio tags that is as immediately accessible to the user as textual tags are currently.

Second, social and democratic tagging and keyword labeling strategies presuppose user involvement. While democratic keyword application strategies may be configured to compel author-originators to provide textual inputs in a keywords field, neither the quality nor the propriety of the content can be compelled. Furthermore, social tagging strategies, by their nature, cannot be compelled—they can be encouraged, users may be enabled, and strategies may be made convenient. However, all social input strategies rely on the good graces of well-intentioned users habituated to provide input over time to succeed.

Third, even when users are actively participating in democratic and social strategies, the information they provide may not be relevant or appropriate. Social strategies will self-correct for this problem over time under the presumption that more users than not will provide "good" information. Democratic strategies that take new end-user inputs under consideration but rely on a core set of administered keyword artifact sets may be effectively protected from such problems, but at a sacrifice of flexibility and responsiveness to trends in time. Under social tag structures, the risk of "tag bombing" or flooding a tag input mechanism with distasteful or irrelevant data can severely undermine the goals of enhanced relevancy and user experience.

These three potential risks, among others, are shared by all democratic and social relevancy strategies. As such, they are not uniquely disadvantageous to democratic and social relevancy strategies as implemented in an enterprise content management system. Instead, these problems are indicative of the need for a solution used consistently rather than a fix-all elixir. In a nutshell, beware of quick-fix shills that promise comprehensive relevancy solutions if only you buy the newest product.

Key Business Requirements

So far, the information presented in this chapter has demonstrated the following:

- The overabundance of content precipitated by advances in information and communication technology is masking the content we want when we want it. This is the problem of relevancy.

- Various solutions to the problem of relevancy implement Web 2.0–style tactics. Many of these tactics are democratic, social, or both in nature.

- Democratic approaches focus on tallying and reporting while social approaches focus on aggregating and swapping nuance.

- The multiplicity of approaches, be they democratic, top-down, social, bottom-up, taxonomic, folksonomic, consumer, or contributor-based, may be necessary but are not sufficient to solve the relevancy problem.

What is required is a solution that is a discipline that incorporates best-of-breed enterprise information management technology with enabling democratic, social, and legacy approaches to provide the right users with the right content at the right time.

Democratic Author-originator Keywords

Because it is easiest to start with the tactics that have most of their constituent parts already in place, we'll first tap into the flexibility of a metadata framework for a democratically oriented keyword solution. As discussed earlier, keywords are ideally situated as author-originator–provided artifacts. This section describes an easy way to implement a simple author-originator keyword system with a keyword cloud for display and prompting for input.

A metadata framework should allow for the easy creation of new metadata and taxonomy or schema fields. Author-originator keywords should be set during contribution. The input field should be large enough to display author-originator inputs, and keyword delimiters (commas, in the example shown in Figure 3-4) should be automatic or at least commonplace.

Additionally, keyword sets should be loosely administered artifacts that are predefined and presented in preset user interfaces, such as a multi-select list, that also facilitate suggestions from the contributor community. Suggestions should be regularly gathered and considered by an enterprise taxonomy working group and then incorporated back into the user interface. Enterprises should be cautioned, however, against maintaining too tight a grip on taxonomies that are part of democratic relevancy strategies. Even the best-intentioned reviews and regular update processes can miss important input from the user community the taxonomy is designed to serve.

Finally, other author-originator keyword generation tactics may be implemented, including: preset user or contribution defaults, automated keyword extraction, and human validation workflows, or even rule-based keyword derivation.

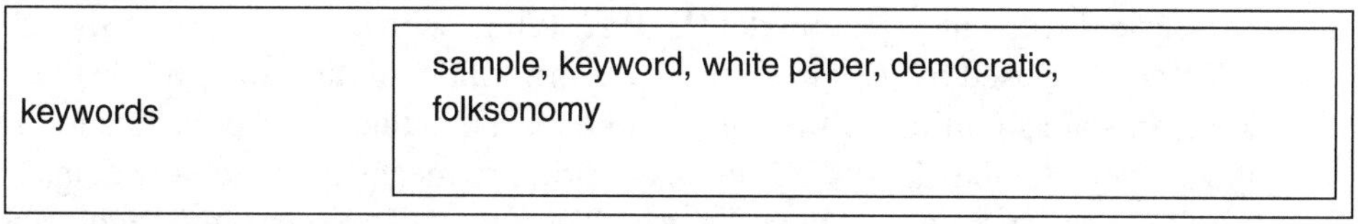

keywords	sample, keyword, white paper, democratic, folksonomy

FIGURE 3-4   The input field for author-originator keywords

These steps, however, are not all that is required. Once keywords are entered, whether manually or automatically, they are stored and then able to be exposed through the framework application programming interface (API) and service-oriented architecture (SOA). With a simple user interface mechanism, the keywords may be aggregated, tallied, and displayed as a cloud (as depicted in Figure 3-5) in any web-enabled context and user interface the enterprise desires. If display is not the primary objective, the keyword aggregates and tallies may be queried through web services, or other API calls and leveraged for additional relevancy enhancements and systems integrations.

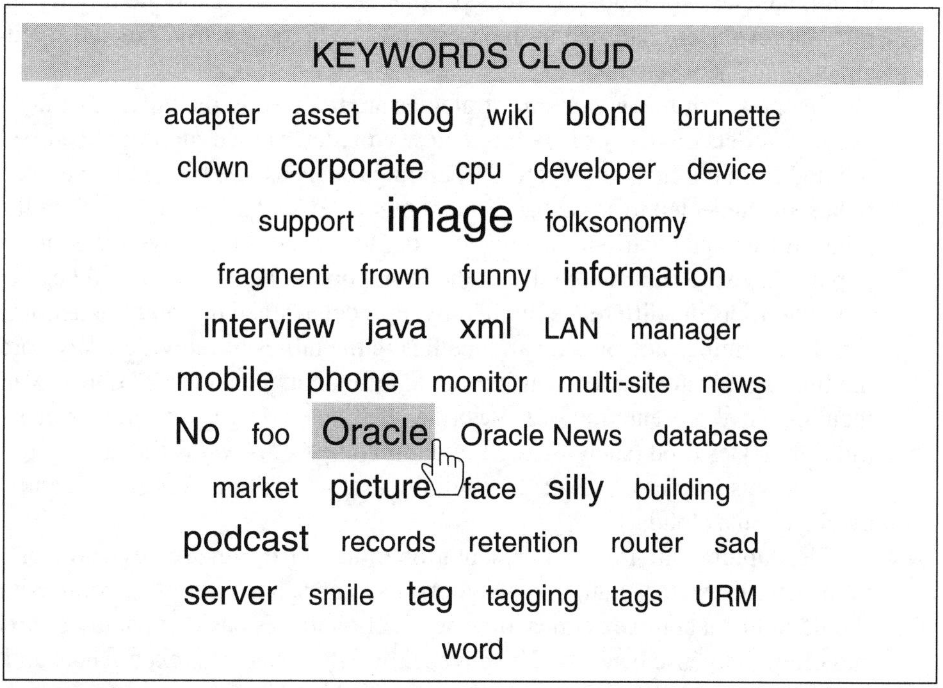

KEYWORDS CLOUD

adapter   asset   blog   wiki   blond   brunette
clown   corporate   cpu   developer   device
support   image   folksonomy
fragment   frown   funny   information
interview   java   xml   LAN   manager
mobile   phone   monitor   multi-site   news
No   foo   Oracle   Oracle News   database
market   picture   face   silly   building
podcast   records   retention   router   sad
server   smile   tag   tagging   tags   URM
word

FIGURE 3-5   Keywords displayed in a cloud

Basic document object model (DOM) styling with cascading style sheets (CSS) can be used by the tag cloud to govern font color and size. While the keywords are signifiers of the content in the system that the user is able to "see" if she wants to, the cloud's styling is the primary means by which the democratic signifiers are communicated to the user. The keywords represent thoughts about individual content items. The size, color, and position of any single keyword indicates its democratic weight within the aggregate of all content. To indicate relative popularity, size and weight are used so that bigger and heavier fonts signify a larger tally. To indicate the most popular keyword used, the styling offsets the color—light gray in Figure 3-5. Finally, a styling "hover effect" is implemented to indicate to the user that a drill-down click-through capability has been incorporated into the cloud. Clicking a term immediately executes a search for items containing that particular keyword.

In this way, items sharing keywords are dynamically associated without additional author-contributor input. As a further enhancement to a basic keyword cloud, a keyword *constellation* can be included, in which all keywords from items having at least *n* keywords in common are highlighted. When clicked, all highlighted keywords are passed as parameters to a search and the refined and relevant results are returned to the user who had no necessarily preconceived ideas about what she wanted.

The power of the democratic strategies are realized in the tallying of the keywords. Sets of keywords falling below a predetermined minimum can be omitted from the final aggregate. Depending on needs, the remaining keyword tallies are subjected to some basic mathematical calculations to determine the items' difference, distribution, and spread. *Difference* is the tally of the most popular keyword minus the tally of the least popular but still included keyword. *Distribution* is the difference divided by a predetermined distribution denominator, which determines how much variance lies in the tallies of individual keywords in the final aggregate: Larger distribution denominators mean less variance. Variance then, in visual presentation of keyword aggregates, governs the number of different styles used (such as small, medium, large). *Spread* is the tally of unique variance sets (such as 3 small, 12 medium, 2 large) within an aggregate and displayed in a cloud.

The capture, tallying, and presentation of author-originator keywords in information systems, content management systems, and enterprise composites should not be a complex endeavor. The functionality is basic, typically preexists, and offers immense benefits. The payback in efficiency, user experience, and user adoption is high when this strategy is combined with social tagging and an enterprise system's infrastructure that can fuse the functionality with other applications and systems. Tagging capabilities are not systems as such. Instead, they are functional enhancements to existing systems. Furthermore, this step is necessary in the journey to realizing a highly relevant system as well as a dynamically semantic system.

Social Tagging

The ways of implementing social tagging strategies are nearly limitless. The only requirement is to be able to capture the tags and the unique identifier of the data or content item to which they apply. Additional features that social tagging solutions should contemplate if not provide outright include the following:

■ **Automatic tag creation timestamping**   Timestamping of tag creation enables tracking of the progression and evolution of tags and the nuance of meaning and purpose over time.

■ **Automatic tag modification timestamping**   Timestamping of tag modification enables microtracking and capture of first impression, gut reactions, and overall usage.

■ **Capture of response information**   The capture and inclusion of any header and result-set data that is present are important criteria. Useful data such as username, the page or site or item on which the tagging took place, the search query run by the user to get to the page or application screen, the number of results returned, the complete result information, and other information should be made available through the API. Furthermore, the header and result-set data can be leveraged to perform even more complex operations before or during the tagging event. This means that, for example, if the username is present, you could query for him most-used tags for similar content items and return them to him while he is tagging suggestions.

■ **Extensibility**   Any information may be captured and "mashed up," or combined with or into the tags. This provides an exceptionally rich interface and potential. To be sure, intentional forethought and clear goals are required when designing a tagging schema. However, this is not bad. Too many tagging strategies available today lack a purpose or goal and wind up being little more than added form fields with which users are burdened.

For tagging to be social, the tagging user interface must be accessible to the user where he consumes the content. Different contexts will place different demands on the implementation of the tagging solution. Public-facing websites have an anonymous user context where content is typically accessed by browsing or drilling down through a predefined navigational structure. Public-facing sites run the risk of ingesting irrelevant tags from passersby. Intranets and extranets have a context where users are known, identity is default, and content is searched for as much as, if not more than, it is browsed or navigated to.

Consider an example in which a tagging user interface is placed on a search results page for each result. This allows content-specific *micro clouds* (tag clouds that pertain to a single item) to help guide the user to the most relevant result. This works because the micro clouds nuance each result, providing a glimpse into a bite-sized collective opinion. More helpful than raw metadata, micro clouds give users a much better clue as to the pertinence of the result. Examples abound of how best to present a tagging user interface. Usability studies and the particular user cultures intrinsic to each organization should be weighed when considering an appropriate approach.

To provide a seamless user experience, a resulting solution architecture should leverage SOA capabilities. For example, a Simple Object Access Protocol (SOAP)–based service request could be made that executes both the tagging and the retrieval of new tags via AJAX (Asynchronous JavaScript and XML). This is important, especially in a results and efficiency–oriented environment such as the enterprise. A poor Web 2.0 tactic would allow users to tag items but require that they either navigate away from their working context or rerun the entire search in order to execute the tagging function.

In keeping with the Web 2.0 mindset of "show it if you need it," a simple visibility toggle wrapping the Tag This function is often a good idea. Web 2.0 expectations abhor clutter; clean lines and simplicity are the order of the day. It is always a good idea to take advantage of browser DOMs and dynamic HTML or other scripting to create an on-demand user experience. Clicking a Tag This label, as shown in Figure 3-6, dynamically displays the tagging form, thereby enabling the consumer to supply her own tags.

The input field should take as many tags as the user wants to provide, within reason. Tags should be delimited (commas or spaces are common) so that they can be machine-parsed. Bearing this in mind, the ability to add phrases, URIs, or other objects should also be considered. Along with the actual tags, the tagging form might also submit other useful information, such as the user's ID or name, the unique ID of the item being tagged, and the time and date when the tagging occurred. While the social data is not necessarily displayed, its capture provides

| FIGURE 3-6 | Tag This function |

a rich set of data for later analysis. These data sets are then submitted to the tagging function and any callback functions for full AJAX-capable responses. After the submission is completed, any AJAX callback functions return data that may then be parsed and rendered for display. All these actions should take place asynchronously—the end user does not see a page redraw, and the server does not rerun the query. The tags are supplied and the new cloud appears.

Information Ratings

Incorporated into this example is an information rating capability that combines democratic-style voting with the social aspects of ubiquitous tagging and presentation of the tag cloud. In Figure 3-7, users vote on whether or not the item is helpful with a simple checkbox selection. Other rating schemes include the familiar four or five stars ratings (Figure 3-8) or simple tallies of users who have interacted with the data.

Such democratic tactics are not uncommon: Amazon.com, for example, uses similar democratic tallies in conjunction with customer reviews. Netflix uses star ratings for movies rated by viewers. Content-rating mechanisms may be sophisticated or simple, but some basic considerations are useful. For example, if the Helpful checkbox appears only for users who are not the author of the content

Tag This

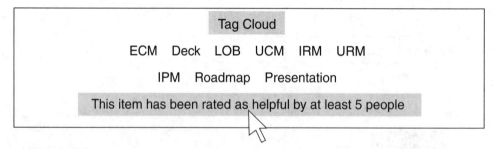

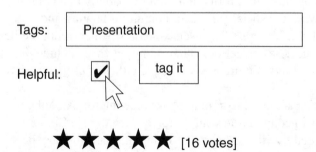

FIGURE 3-7   Users vote by clicking a checkbox.

Tag This

Tags: Presentation

Helpful: ✔   tag it

★ ★ ★ ★ ★ [16 votes]

FIGURE 3-8   Star ratings

item, this prevents an author from skewing socially held notions of usefulness by inflating his own work. Only non-author users can indicate whether an item was helpful. After some minimum number of non-author users have indicated that the content items were helpful to them, the cloud displays a small symbol that indicates that the user community has found the listing to be helpful.

More sophisticated strategies can incorporate the idea of power users or experts and add the concept of "weighting" to tags and content ratings. This mashes up the user's identity and social network with the way that relevancy is determined. To accomplish this, the user management system needs to allow rating on users to identify them as subject matter experts, or this could be determined by the system itself. Tags and ratings from expert users or power users would be weighted more heavily than tags and ratings from anonymous or non-expert users. Alternatively, a different cloud could be presented, showing all tags or filtering out the anonymous ones on request.

The strategies of user ratings and weighting hail back to the notions that credibility is the currency of the Web. With signifiers of content credibility, we can infer that the likelihood of relevancy is high or at least greater than the surrounding data points. Content ratings are one kind of indicator of content credibility. Incorporating weighted responses from in-network, expert, or power users leverages the credibility those users gained in achieving membership in those communities. Rating algorithms that weight ratings from expert and power users infer that such users are better or uniquely suited to discriminate relevancy among all the results in a set. We, the consumers, infer that, due to their earned credibility, these experts are well situated to help us find that most relevant piece of information buried within all the results with which we are presented.

Clouding

Although clouds are a convenient and intuitive way to present information, these keywords, tags, popularity rankings, usage metrics, and rating scores can be more data that contributes to the problem of info-glut if they are not made useful to humans, applications, or both. Consequently, the benefits of folksonomic inputs are realized only insofar as they are exposed. Exposure may mean that the data is included in a search index and/or human-oriented user interface. However, with the focus of folksonomy in general, human-centered display most often is part of the exposure.

Because clouds are beneficial for information presentation, democratic clouding can be implemented for any metadata container. Democratic clouding, as opposed to social clouding, is mentioned intentionally here because metadata fields are typically not open to all consumers for modification. Consequently, the clouds, while still providing nuance over an aggregate of data, are still tallies. The power of clouds lies in the presentation of the aggregate of ideas. A single cloud may signify an aggregate of ideas over an aggregate of content as in the keywords cloud example presented earlier. Alternately, it may present an aggregate of ideas over a single piece of content.

At their core, clouds of democratic or socially input tags are aggregators of information. Aggregators make it a lot easier for employees to find new business information sources. That is good for business systems with lots of information. Aggregators enlarge the potential audience for the information and expose lots of otherwise hidden but relevant information. That means tagging, as an aggregation engine, can drive better business decisions, better business intelligence, and better business.

Search Results and Micro Clouds

Micro clouds contain tags for each individual item. Presented in a search result set, they provide flavored or nuanced meta-information over and above what is presented by default. This facilitates human inferences of relevancy. Because the search engine has already run and provided its set of results to the user, to determine which is the "right" content, the user has little recourse but to open and scan each item or make inferences based on metadata such as a title. Providing micro clouds related to unique content items facilitates the human sorting effort.

Nano Clouds

Dialing down even further, nano clouds provide aggregated tags and keywords that spring from sections of unique content items. If the task of enabling and prompting users to provide keyword and tag feedback for content items were not daunting enough, the presumptive level of effort in tagging discrete sections of content is nearly overwhelming. As a result, while users may be enabled to provide social feedback, nano clouds may be automatically generated as keyword aggregates from full-text indices.

It may be possible to leverage the capabilities already present in automatic XML renderers and XSLT converters, though the technologies are not limited to those two. For example, an item might be automatically converted to an interim XML format and have an XSLT transformation applied. The XSLT can render or feed different sections of the original for consideration by people or analysis engines or, conversely, preclude sections of the item from consideration. Each chunk can then be fed iteratively to an analysis engine (human or machine) for rules-based suggestion and precipitation of keywords and concepts that can be stored as metadata, tag attributes, or both. The net result is that the system can precipitate keywords to be stored and aggregated into section-relevant *nano clouds*—clouds of tags or concepts that pertain not to a document, web page, or photograph as such, but to parts of a document, web page, or photograph.

Nano clouds can be useful for application-based processing and generation of inferences. The implications for the automated creation of compound, complex, and conceptually related but heterogeneous content through this kind of a content mashup is profound. Imagine a system that can autonomously assemble a real estate contract from a boilerplate document, a spreadsheet of addresses, another spreadsheet of property valuations, an agent directory, and a report pulled from a banking system with loan rates and amounts and payment schedules, and then route that content through a workflow for final editorial reviews and then signatures by all transacting parties.

Real-life nano tagging has been implemented in a number of sites on the Web, including the popular Facebook social networking site. Using Facebook's photo-tagging API, users can create separate tags for regions within the same photograph. The technology is not earth-shattering. Image-mapping has been available as part of the HTML specifications for years. However, the realization of Facebook's photo-tagging API and other similar implementations takes simple coordinates within the photo and ascribes a tag to that set of coordinates. The information artifact (a photo in Facebook's case) then contains a collection of localized tags. The aggregate of tags for a specific location, such as a friend's face in a photo, becomes the nano cloud.

Cloud Constellations

Cloud *constellations* are presentations of cloud aggregates that may appear as "clouds of clouds" in 3-D modeling and interactive arrays or oriented spatially in 2-D. Their purposes are variable, and different benefits are promoted through different presentation modes.

Clouds of clouds let the user drill down to locate content. For example, clicking a tag at the top level yields a second cloud of more specific tags that either also include the first one selected or come from content. So, for example, clicking the top-level tag *Bread* yields a cloud constellation with terms aggregated from three distinct items. Remember, the constellation is the combination of tag clouds from three items. One tag cloud comes from tags about a bakery. One tag cloud comes from colloquial terms for currency. One tag cloud pertains to the 1970s' band from Los Angeles. All three clouds combine into the constellation. The user can click

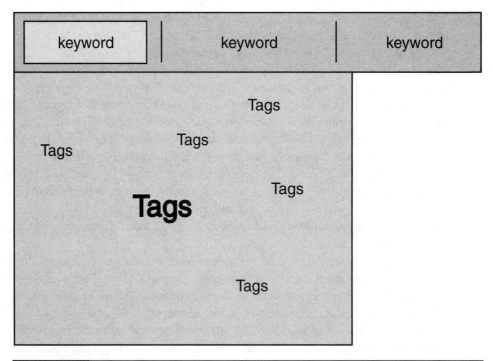

| FIGURE 3-9 | Stacked tag clouds combine as cloud constellations through which the user may drill down into increasingly narrow and specific results. |

one of the tags in the constellation, say a tag reading *Pastry*, and drills down into a cloud with terms pertaining only to the workings of a local small bakery.

Other, nonhierarchical cloud constellations may be useful as well. For example, a 2-D cloud of clouds, if not too cluttered, may be useful for providing a detailed comparison of democratic and social attributes of several content items. The search results page may be considered a 2-D cloud of clouds, where the individual micro clouds are oriented linearly in a page that acts as a cloud.

An Alternative Navigation Paradigm

As an alternative to browsing or querying navigation paradigms, the 3-D–oriented tag or keyword aggregates provide some unique opportunities. Because tag and keyword aggregates can function as containers of containers, navigation schemas may be built around keyword ontologies and tagged folksonomies. Consider a navigation bar organically generated from the web page context containing the democratically most popular keywords.

Clicking a keyword might drop down, instead of a list of additional options, a *tag cloud*. This would visually represent the folksonomy of the content in that page pertaining to the selected keyword. In this way, usage patterns and what is relevant at the time drives site navigation. Websites, in this way, respond to trends before marketers even know that a trend is developing. Matched up with legacy business intelligence applications and usage analytics, end users of a site or application can navigate to the most relevant content within a selected context. To be sure, this cannot be the only kind of navigation on a site, but as part of a comprehensive relevancy discipline, the benefits are at least interesting and, sometimes, profound.

Tag and Keyword Constellations

Tag constellations are fascinating ways of associating tags and/or keywords within a container, commonly a cloud. Tags or keywords from disparate sources are visually associated when they meet a certain minimum criteria. The criteria may be that at least two tags or keywords from different content items match, for example.

The visual highlighting effectively denotes a subcloud within the container. A nice visual example of this is found at the Google News Cloud site depicted in Figure 3-10. The constellation creates an ad hoc content association that requires no human input. Such associations are useful tools to act as content promotion and suggestion engines. They can help to expose users to content that they may not otherwise have decided to investigate. Furthermore, tag and keyword constellations help expedite and alleviate the outlier risks associated with social tagging. While over time, social tagging will address errantly or oddly selected tags, tag constellations will associate outlier tags with more common tags, thereby lending the outliers some context and nuance that may otherwise be missing.

Suggestion Engine

Suggestion engines such as those found on Amazon.com were implemented after careful studies indicated that they work. The principles that govern these kinds of retail "soft pitches" also have benefits to offer users of enterprise Web 2.0 systems. Typically, suggestion engines are one of two styles: either they offer suggestions based on what the user has done in the past or they offer suggestions based on what other users who have accessed that same content items have done in the past. For named users, tags they have provided for content in the system can be aggregated to form a personalized baseline *interest set*. That set represents the user's interest

FIGURE 3-10   Google news cloud (from http://fserb.com.br/newscloud/)

within the context of the enterprise application(s). Against that baseline set, *interest spikes* can be found by analyzing the baseline set for tag patterns that precipitate out over short time periods (such as one or two weeks). Additionally, by comparing the interest set of one user to that of other users who have tagged a certain amount of the same content or have significantly overlapping interest sets, suggested item or page links may be recommended up to the user.

This can be done for baseline interest sets as well as for the smaller interest spikes. Because a relevancy discipline must implement multiple and diverse strategies to get the right content to the right people at the right time, any advantage that may be gained by proactively getting the content to the user before she asks for it is substantial. Combined with autogenerated nano clouds, content items containing only pieces and parts that might be relevant to the user may be suggested, opening the possibility of introducing the user to entirely new areas of content previously beyond her view.

Role-based Relevancy

Hyper-personalization is a hallmark of Web 2.0. To get the most personally relevant information to the individual based on information known about that person, *term-term* or *word-word* relevancy should not be the only factor. *User role-term* relevancy should also be considered. User attributes such as role, role description, access levels, security clearance, manager, organizational structure, and interests can be evaluated against keyword and tag aggregates. Automated role-based relevancy calculations are performed that may leverage thesaurus-style comparisons of user metadata information against tag and keyword aggregates. Thesauri themselves may be social tag artifacts and be built up democratically—they get better with time and use, presuming good intentions and adoption of the paradigm.

Final Considerations

Capture, storage, evaluation, aggregation, and presentation of democratic and socially produced relevancy information is only the tip of the participatory web iceberg. Once this information is captured, it can be used for other user experiences and intelligent calculations.

If users are wedded to their hierarchies (such as within visual nested folder metaphors for information placement like thos displayed in Windows Explorer), the ability to create and present dynamic hyper-personalized hierarchies emerges by displaying the folder order based on conditionally calculated democratic user tallies. The most used (that is, most popular) folders and folder chains would be displayed at the top of the folder hierarchy. Popularity would be determined by a democratic tally evaluation of keywords and tags and usage statistics captured for each user.

The information explosion has had dire consequences for the goals of relevancy. Getting the right information to the right people or systems at the right time continues to be a challenge. What the emergent Web 2.0 mindset has generated are a number of tactics that share an inherently social aspect. Democratic practices foster user involvement for the purposes of tallying or voting on something. Social practices foster user involvement for the purpose of enhancing popular understanding of what content *is about* and what information *is for*.

Folksonomic implementation strategies within enterprise Web 2.0–enabled systems combine into and become part of an overarching relevancy discipline. This discipline has a number of real benefits across not only relevancy goals, but also business intelligence, analytics, user experience, and semantic web goals.

Chapter 4

Social Networking:
Discriminating Connectedness

By Jean Sini

All people appear motivated by an inbred striving for self-esteem that is in large part fostered by the approval of others.

Alan Greenspan, *The Age of Turbulence*

It's well past noon and you're getting ready for lunch. You haven't yet read your e-mail or talked to anyone else in the office today. Yet you know that Bob, two cubes down, stopped for a cappuccino on his way to the office. You know which costume Alice's kid is wearing to the Halloween party tonight. Mary from marketing is eating sushi she bought from the new bar you checked out last week. Scott from accounting is out shopping for a new laptop; you feel a sudden case of Mac envy. You'd like to ask your boss to join you for a burger, but he's 6000 miles away, done for the day, and probably about to sit down for dinner. You feel rather smug, knowing your coworkers' every move. Sure, keeping up with all their whereabouts and coming up with incessant quips might eat into your lunch hour, but that sense of connectedness is priceless, right? Or is it?

If you're not convinced that exposing people you know to the minutiae of your life is the way to go, you likely haven't succumbed to the fast-rising appeal of social networking services. They form a crucial component in Web 2.0, and some claim they have the potential to disrupt the established mechanisms on which people rely to communicate and interact. Are they merely a fad, a dangerous time-sink, or are they the way of the future?

The Software-augmented Social Life

Social networking, perhaps thanks to its many existing, tangible incarnations, from Friendster, to MySpace, to Facebook, to name only a few, is free of the endless controversy surrounding what the more general Web 2.0 is or isn't: There is little debate over the definition of the concept of social networking. This apparent simplicity is, however, not really the case. Understanding the ramifications and implications of social networking begins with deconstructing it into its constituent parts.

First things first: People are at the heart of social networks, online or otherwise. Social networking services, whether sharply focused on real-life relationships or facilitating new bonds directly online, revolve around the central notion of *member profiles*. These repositories of personal information range from rudimentary demographic details, to professional background, political inclinations, photos, and other media. They are aimed primarily at expressing and shaping each user's identity. These profiles anchor what is one of the most important aspects of today's social networking sites: They are all about carefully carving, almost manufacturing, an online presence, identity, and persona.

Next, and just as important as individual members, are the relationships that connect them. Lately, with various social networking services gaining in popularity, the terminology describing their underlying components is being formalized to sustain finer-grained scrutiny and comparisons. In particular, the set of intermember relationships captured and maintained by such services is increasingly designated as the *social graph*: The people in the network are at the vertices, and their connections are at the edges.

Social networks offer ways for users to navigate the graph, following edges from member to member to explore existing connections and establish new ones. But sites vary when it comes to *qualifying* the graph. Certain services (such as Facebook) make it undirected: Relationships are symmetrical. Others (such as Twitter) maintain a directed graph: I could be a follower of yours, without you following me. Requiring mutual friendships or allowing one-sided connections flavors the services significantly by influencing the sense of control users have over who can be witness to their online activities. In addition, and irrespective of directedness, edges in the graph can carry quite a bit of information: They can go well beyond a binary arc between two members, because they can capture the *type* of relationship these users have—friends, coworkers, roommates, spouses, and so on. They can also point to dates, places, and other members meaningful to the relationship: Bob and Alice are friends, and they met through Charlie in 1996 in Michigan. Regardless of these subtleties, the graph is what makes the service social. Without it, we're almost back to the days of GeoCities. As such, the social graph is without doubt the most coveted component among competing services, acting to lock members in: Stick to your network or face the ordeal of re-creating all those relationships.

What comes last is perhaps the most potent element of social networking, due to its addictive, mesmerizing quality: information flow. You can think of a social network as a two-way electricity grid, where (appropriate in these times of global warming) every building both consumes *and* produces power. People are the buildings, and the graph is the all-important wiring infrastructure connecting them. But the reason for being of the whole grid is the electricity flowing along these wires. In social networking services, that's information, disseminated via activity streams and notifications.

The graph lives both as an abstract representation of relationships and as a set of communication channels able to transport information of all kinds among connected members. Without that information, the network grows stale. The brilliance of the successful social networks is in making it compelling for its users both to produce and consume information about themselves and their friends. That information flow dictates the pulse of the system for its participants.

When looking at the meaning, benefits, and pitfalls of social networking applied to the enterprise, the overarching factors determining success are going to be the quality and the quantity of information that members are prepared to inject into the system and consume from it.

Fickle Users: Fleeting and Localized Success Stories

From 2004 to 2006 or so, the most devoted members of the larger social networking sites were primarily teens and young adults. Unsurprisingly, their affections have tended, at least initially, to shift heavily and abruptly, with one network enjoying a lot of attention and hype one year, only to fall out of favor the next. While hundreds of networks are around, only a handful have achieved and sustained massive scale.

Today's global social networking market is somewhat complex and fragmented. Aside from inhabiting the dominant networks we hear about daily, such as MySpace and Facebook, communities segmented by background, interest, age group, geographic location, and other factors are also flocking to a multiplicity of targeted sites. For instance, Google's Orkut, albeit little used in the United States, is hugely popular in Brazil and India. Bebo sees 62 percent of its growth happen in Europe and has grown 300 percent from 2006, according to comScore. CyWorld, similarly, is a virtual world with social networking features serving a massive user base in South Korea and Asia. More traffic statistics are presented in Figure 4-1.

The first service to implement the complete mix of the required ingredients was Six Degrees, launched in 1997 and shut down in 2000. Instant messaging (IM) services allowed users to post rudimentary profiles and maintain a list of friends, and they were perhaps the closest ancestors to formal social networks, but they lacked a number of distinguishing elements. In particular, they didn't expose the underlying social graph to their users.

Social networking's early days were tumultuous, with a number of community-centric services appearing from 1997 to 2001. These included AsianVenue, BlackPlanet, MiGente, and CyWorld. LiveJournal, a blogging platform, also added support for one-sided connections in 1999. In 2001, Ryze, LinkedIn, and Tribe.net launched, with the first two focused on professional networking. LinkedIn continues to thrive as a business networking site.

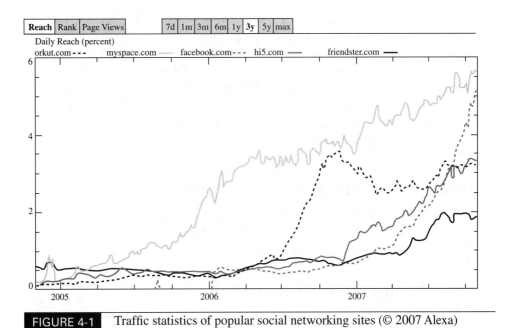

| Reach | Rank | Page Views | | 7d | 1m | 3m | 6m | 1y | 3y | 5y | max |

Daily Reach (percent)
orkut.com - - -   myspace.com ——   facebook.com - - -   hi5.com ——   friendster.com ——

FIGURE 4-1   Traffic statistics of popular social networking sites (© 2007 Alexa)

The launch of Friendster in 2002 marked a shift. The site attracted a significant following, growing by word of mouth to more than 300,000 members in about a year, before massive press coverage began introducing social networks to the mainstream. A series of technical glitches ensued: The site had difficulty scaling to accommodate the rapid user growth, a number of policy missteps led to a deterioration of the trust users had in the service, and the site lost a lot of its momentum with US audiences (but kept growing abroad).

MySpace, which launched in 2003, benefited from the dissatisfaction of Friendster users. It made a point of allowing the infamous Fakesters (profiles of nonpersons, such as colleges or bands) that Friendster had been trying to ban. In particular, it started nurturing the presence of bands on the site, thus enlisting the support of music fans. It also reacted promptly to implement features based on user requests and adopted a permissive attitude toward the copying and pasting of code, allowing users to customize their profiles much beyond what had been possible. The service grew quickly among both young adults and teenagers, and it eclipsed Friendster in popularity. It now counts well above 100 million users.

Facebook began as a Harvard-only social network in 2004. It expanded over time to accept members from all universities, then high schools, then corporate networks, and then everyone. This policy of growing from a niche to a wide-open network, coinciding with social networking becoming mainstream among consumers, has contributed to make Facebook one of the most talked about networks. Facebook counts more than 70 million active users worldwide (as of May 2008), still lagging behind MySpace but rapidly catching up to it in terms of traffic. Of the major networks, it has grown the fastest from 2006 to 2007, adding 270 percent new users, compared to 75 percent at MySpace and 78 percent at Orkut (according to comScore).

Strategic Underlying Constructs

Socials networks have been around for only a few years, and their architecture is still very much in flux. Let's take a closer look at some of the elements making up most services, from a strategic perspective.

The Omnipotent Social Graph

The social graph that maps the connections among members of the network is the object of much envy among competing services. At stake, ultimately, is the tension between market domination and network interoperability. This is nothing new, however, as battles to "own users" have been raging whenever a new type of service with built-in network effects emerges. From telephone networks to IM platforms, operators have been reluctant to open their networks, aiming initially to keep their users locked in instead.

Despite a lot of talk about getting the social graph to open and about its portability, the dominant social network operators have so far guarded their graph carefully. In the case of Facebook, for instance, the service's terms of use are clear when it comes to accessing and storing a user's connections: It places strong limits on the duration for which third-party applications are allowed to store that fragment of the graph. In addition, the API doesn't expose any unique interoperable identifier, such as an e-mail address, that other systems could use to map out someone's connections. This effectively quells much of the portability potential.

How many of Facebook's 70 million users care about being locked in? Today, admittedly, very few are concerned. While Facebook is occupying an increasingly central role in the life of its users, moderating a lot of their online life, it is still perceived by most as having mainly entertainment value. Few people worry about the cost of packing up and joining the next, better service when it comes around. Yet, as the use of social networking services extend and they permeate more of our lives over time, the freedom to move around is going to become critical, all the more so that both incumbent and upcoming players are gearing up to vie for more and more of our attention. This is bound to lead either to fragmentation (some have called this the "balkanization of social networks") over a multiplicity of coexisting networks or to a push for portability.

But there's more to interoperability than mere portability. E-mail is an interoperable system: It doesn't matter which client or server I use, or which server or client you use. We can exchange e-mail. Your company's decision to switch servers or your own decision to switch clients involves only your company or you. Nobody else needs to know, and the messages keep flowing. Similarly, you can switch from one mobile carrier to another, and phone number portability ensures that your choice is transparent to anyone trying to reach you. This isn't yet the case with social networking services, by any measure. Even if you were able to export your contacts out of the confines of a particular service, you would still need to convince all your friends to switch as well before you could resume your conversation elsewhere. That's anything but an independent decision!

This brings up several key characteristics of various networks' handling of the graph. First, is it open, and is it portable? Asked another way: Who, of the users or the provider, owns the graph? Not every service is following Facebook's approach in that regard. An interesting example is Plaxo. Primarily an advanced synchronization service to keep multiple address books and calendars up to date, Plaxo manages the contacts of more than 40 million users (according to the Plaxo site as of May 2008). Its Pulse is a social networking overlay that pulls the members of the network closer by weaving activity streams from multiple sources together. The company has taken a clear stance on its relationship to the social graph: It claims solely to be the *guardian* of your data, not its *owner*.

Similarly, you can examine whether the graph repository is centralized or distributed, possibly with some amount of replication to keep various fragments and copies synchronized. Again, Plaxo exhibits distribution and replication traits, allowing copies of your contacts to exist and be imported and exported in multiple applications and by using its visibility into the whole graph to establish social communication channels.

Beyond understanding where the graph lives and how much of it is exposed, it is interesting to consider the mechanisms by which the graph is formed. While we've mostly covered examples of networks where the edges in the graph are volunteered by users explicitly (as they claim or accept friendships and business contacts), there is tremendous potential in implicitly deriving connections from actual interactions. Several software add-ons are available to scan address books and inboxes on the fly and suggest as friends the senders and recipients we exchange mail with frequently. Xobni, for instance, is a San Francisco–based company whose main service was announced in August 2007. It embeds itself in such popular e-mail clients as Microsoft Outlook and performs an implicit analysis of traffic.

By extrapolating to IP-telephony and IM exchanges, we can envision the ease with which the social graph can be not only collected but also qualified. (Is this a professional or personal connection? How frequently do we interact?) Initially, grouping contacts further allows users to control how they expose and develop various facets of their persona; ultimately, it allows them to rely more heavily on social networks as an information dissemination channel for critical exchanges.

Endless Activity Streams

In Facebook, activity streams are embodied by the mini-feed, where members can, at a glance, view a summary of most of the activity occurring in their neighborhood of the graph: who's establishing or breaking connections; who's sharing photos, video, or thoughts; who's writing to whom. Initially, Facebook users could write private messages to each other or write instead on their friends' *walls*, public whiteboards of sorts to which friends could contribute. They could also perform a handful of predefined actions, such as *poking*. (Twitter, a micro-publishing platform, lets users *nudge* others.) All these interactions involving friends were reported in the mini-feed. With the introduction of the F8 platform in mid-2007, which lets third-party developers write applications that Facebook members can install and use, the mini-feed also started carrying notifications about countless new types of interactions generated by those new applications.

As such, the mini-feeds, or activity streams in general, provide the glue that keeps friends together on Facebook. Any moderately active network, as small as 50 or 100 friends, will generate an endless stream of information. The constant stimulus is intense and drives many to visit the site dozens of times *every day*. F8 restricts how many of the generated notifications from all of these available applications actually make it to members' mini-feeds in hopes of curtailing spamlike tendencies. Users also get to set hints or interest levels per type of mini-feed event, but the granularity of those controls remains coarse.

When is this incessant flow of information too much or simply distracting? One could argue that the signal-to-noise ratio of these activity streams is low, or that with so much going on, it's becoming difficult to avoid missing some if not most of it. In fact, with massive growth both in terms of individual participation and interconnectedness, the sheer quantity of events pushed onto activity streams is growing tremendously. Ultimately, managing the growing amount and frequency of information requires matching improvements in the users' ability to filter and sift through that information efficiently to control what types of updates they want highlighted and which ones they don't really care about.

Applications Galore

Facebook's F8 launched in May 2007 and approximately 7500 applications had been developed for the platform by November of that year. As of this writing, some of the most popular apps count more than 20 million users in total and are used by more than 2.5 million daily. So it's no wonder application developers see the opening of social networking platforms as a golden opportunity.

In November 2007, Google, along with a series of partners, announced OpenSocial, with a set of APIs enabling third-party developers to write applications for one social network host and have them be reusable on any of the other participating networks. Household names—MySpace, Friendster, Bebo—as well as white-label networking infrastructures such as Marc Andreessen's Ning announced their support for the APIs. At the time of writing, only a rudimentary version of the APIs had been made public; it was also unclear whether Facebook would join the coalition. OpenSocial primarily sets out to make social networks interoperable for applications, and it is yet unknown whether it will enable graph portability.

What is the significance of third-party applications inside social networks? Interestingly, fewer than 50 of the 7500 applications written for F8 have more than 100,000 daily users. It is also unclear, for lack of data, how much money—if any—is being made (typically from advertising) by independent applications developers, given the fact that click-through rates by users on the network are little understood. A number of the early entrants that achieved critical mass, partially by inviting and notifying users aggressively before Facebook tightened the mini-feed rules, are now acting as embedded advertising exchanges, effectively selling users to new applications.

Of the applications achieving critical mass, an overwhelming majority are extremely simple, entertainment-centric gadgets, aimed at embellishing existing features of the network (Top Friends, SuperPoke, Super Wall) or providing ways to interact with friends in predefined ways (Zombies, Vampires, Moods). By and large, we're witnessing the infancy of social networks as communication and productivity platforms. Dismissing the potential of applications as fun but mostly useless glitter solely based on the early evidence may be premature. As social networks become more tightly woven in our daily lives, we may well end up congregating around the de facto aggregator that they represent to conduct increasingly complex tasks facilitated by third-party applications. Opening their platform to such applications effectively affords networks an opportunity to position themselves at the core of their users' online experience, not unlike the "walled gardens" of ISPs in earlier days.

Ambient Social Networks

The rise of these applications makes it clear that social networks want users to spend most of their time on network sites. But isn't this inside-out? Isn't the Internet, as a whole, the platform we should aim to make social, as opposed to any particular destination, that's bound to remain a "walled garden"?

Nothing about the coalescence of profiles, graphs, stream aggregation and consumption, and applications is technically mandatory. Plaxo's Pulse service, for instance, feeds off the existing activity streams that users' friends produce elsewhere (mostly by auto-discovering and tapping RSS feeds from Flickr, Twitter, blog posts, shared bookmarks, and so on) and simply aggregates them into a mini-feedlike format. As such, it is separating the place where activities are captured from the place where users come to get updates on their friends' whereabouts.

This example hints at a distinctly different approach to engineering socially enabled applications: Instead of the centralized approach currently advocated by popular networks, where applications have to write widgets for specific containers, we can envision reversing the model so that social awareness is distributed to applications where they live (that is, browser- or desktop-based apps). In the long run, we can imagine a thorough decoupling of all the functions currently collapsed in social networks: The graph is portable and can be tapped by any application a user trusts. That application emits feeds of activity (such as Flickr photo streams), while other services can aggregate those streams and present them to users according to their interests and formatting preferences. All this achieves the same independence of choice enjoyed, for instance, with e-mail today.

As mentioned, Plaxo's Pulse is an example of an aggregation service. Another example is Flock, a Firefox-based *social browser* that has all the familiar trappings of its popular ancestor but adds a twist: It is socially aware. Once users indicate their credentials to networks and applications such as Facebook, Twitter, Flickr, or YouTube, the browser maintains a sidebar, the aptly-named *people bar*, that summarizes the activity streams of friends, from status to media updates. Interestingly, the browser goes to great lengths to detect consumable blog, media, or activity feeds on any web page the users visit, and it does a great job of both masking the underlying technology and automating the task of subscribing to favorite streams.

In January 2008, Google announced its Social Graph API, a project led by Brad Fitzpatrick, who founded LiveJournal and sold it to Six Apart. The API allows application developers to query information about relationships possibly embedded into any web property—such as XHTML Friends Network (XFN) or Friend of a Friend (FOAF) format—and extracted by Google. Such capabilities further the opportunity for an ambient social network to emerge from the aggregation of partial graphs, where no single entity owns the graph, the applications, or the streams making up the network. Instead, such a network will be diffuse, ambient, and available everywhere users browse.

Who's Doing What?

Today, the vast majority of social networking services' users are consumers. Before we delve into the significance social networks can take in the enterprise, it is worth briefly investigating the current makeup of members and uses of those consumer-centric sites.

The Audience Is Listening

One of the most interesting characteristics of observed usage patterns involves deciphering the expectations of privacy; in fact, there is almost a complete lack of any such expectation. Where communications were once envisioned as a mostly private, one-to-one affair, the overarching behavior on social networks, especially among younger members, is to perform most exchanges in public. Researchers who study social networking behaviors from a sociological standpoint have learned that social networks are all about managing relationships, and users tend to engage in these relationships at least partially *for* the audience. It is well understood that everyone is watching, and social networks are the perfect stage for life's dramas to be played out. These dramas might not hold any interest to the general public, but they are at least somewhat titillating for spectators who happen to belong to one's circle of friends.

All participants understand that networking services that persist and archive our actions, exchanges, and photos act as a public memory of sorts, indexed by search engines for all to discover. When asked, young users acknowledge that the risk of a recruiter (job, college, or otherwise) eventually stumbling upon potentially embarrassing pictures and text is real and known, but this is an acceptable price to pay for the benefit of sharing those "special moments" with friends. Those artifacts are perceived overall as a component of their identity worth remembering, not hiding.

Exhibitionist and stalker behaviors are widespread, with both tendencies far more acceptable on networks than they would be offline. Overall, the relative safety of having interactions brokered online fosters confidence and bolder behaviors. For example, when MySpace was heavily covered in the press following its acquisition by News Corp., concerns were raised about the safety of children and teenagers using the service and unsuspectingly befriending participants they had never actually met.

Overall, reputation management is evolving, and it seems that social networks are facilitating and accelerating our migration to a global village, in which the small-town dynamic of yore is reintroduced, even amplified. Anonymity is no longer available to provide cover; instead, everyone is aware of their friends' and acquaintances' every move. It seems that the growing demand for the convenience and entertainment value brought by massive information flows (with users volunteering data on a proportionally large scale) trumps the need for privacy.

A related phenomenon is the accumulation of contacts beyond the realm of real-world acquaintances, in an attempt to be perceived as "most popular." With social networks' platforms in transition, other justifications could be made for using the graph to track more than just our closest friends: Using the network to mediate a lot of our interactions, perhaps business-related or looser contacts, might become a common use. As of this writing, Facebook imposes a 5000-friend limit that has a few hyperconnected members grumbling.

Some networking services have gone as far as internalizing the underlying behavior of seeking validation from others. Yahoo!'s Mash network, launched in September 2007 to replace its previous social network, 360, exposes a tidy Ego Boost widget on each member's profile, allowing users to send predefined compliments to others. The gift of gratification is a click away, and if anyone reciprocates, the widget should ensure that nobody suffers from deflated self-confidence!

This exchange of predefined messages is a particularly fascinating trait of networking behavior and etiquette. Most networks feature, in various forms of sophistication, the ability to express yourself and interact with friends in codified ways. For instance, a palette of *canned* behaviors is made available for users: Why not poke someone today? Why not throw a hot potato, have a food or pillow fight? Buy someone the virtual gift of the day (which could be a burger, a cocktail, or, if you installed one of the popular third-party applications on Facebook, a *naughty* gift). Similarly, users on Mash get to customize their profiles by selecting text fonts, colors, and sizes; background images; and other graphical elements to extend their creativity, though in fairly constrained ways.

This *constrained expressiveness*, the perception of many choices that are in reality well canvassed, could superficially seem at odds with the raison d'être of the network as an unfettered communication platform. Paradoxically, these preset actions actually fill two roles that contribute to the production of information in the platform. First, they help drop the barrier to contribute: Picking a verb (poke, bite, or tickle) isn't nearly as intimidating as starting from scratch. Second, and related, they implicitly limit the amount of personal responsibility involved: "Sure, I sent you a bouquet of roses today, but I am not entirely accountable, and I don't necessarily fully acknowledge the gesture's meaning. This is merely the gift of the day."

It is also important to note that some of the behaviors enjoyed by teens on social networks relate to identity building and, more specifically, identity play. This involves experimentation with various personae and personal styles, and similar activities have been the norm for teenagers well before social networks were available. Many assumptions were originally made about the transient nature of these behaviors, but as the long-term memory characteristics of the system become better known, users quickly adjust their privacy settings and public behaviors. For instance, while the vast majority of MySpace profiles were originally public, more than half are now restricted.

Time Sinks

This acceleration of information flow leads to another observation about social networking habits: They occupy an increasingly central role in their users' daily activity and take up an increasing portion of their time. Of the 70 million or so Facebook users, about half visit the site every other day or more frequently, and many check for updates several times a day. Networks also act as a de facto e-mail replacement: Conversations are increasingly occurring inside the network, either publicly or privately, rather than outside of it in e-mail form, with students reporting 20 percent of their e-mail traffic occurring inside Facebook, for instance. Students polled (Patel, 2008; see References at the end of this book for source information) also indicated that they were wary of the potential for distraction, stemming from the constant stimulation and need to participate.

Opportunities for the Enterprise

When it comes to assessing the applicability of social networking services to the realm of the enterprise, questions from skeptics fall into two broad categories: Why would we even want to promote this kind of activity within the company? If we deemed it a worthy goal, how could we create incentives for our employees to participate?

On the one hand, some corporate firewalls ban workday access to MySpace and Facebook, which are viewed as a major waste of time and threat to productivity. On the other hand, some corporations are attempting to launch their own internal social networks, asking employees to establish and nurture relationships within the company's intranet, on a more informal basis than that afforded by static organizational charts. These seemingly extreme and opposite reactions likely stem from the relative immaturity of social networking as a medium, leading to poor understanding of its levers, its users' motivations, and ultimately its potential for the enterprise.

Net Natives

As this book goes to press, the first truly net-native generation is joining the workforce. Students who have spent the last 12 years on the Web, and the last 6 years chronicling online the bonds they formed, nurturing MySpace and Facebook relationships and communicating as much as possible over those networks, are getting their first jobs and bringing along their instinctive mastery of the medium. Embracing and leveraging the real-life networking opportunities that overlap their online experience is likely to be a differentiating factor for companies striving not only to recruit but also to help those most-connected new hires develop and thrive on the job.

This brings up two issues about social graph ownership and architecture. Net natives manage their entire contact list through their network of choice. In addition, networks are working to implement grouping features, or categorization of one's contacts, and to offer fine-grained controls over what information is shared with which group. This empowers users to continue leveraging the graph component of the network while compartmentalizing their communication and exposure. Similarly, professionally focused networks such as LinkedIn and Yahoo! KickStart are used by members to capture and keep business connections up to date, irrespective of members' current employers. As long as relationships rely on explicit user actions for creation, maintenance, and even approval, an incentive is required for members to keep their connections up to date in the system. Ownership appears to be an obvious incentive: If the data representing your subset of the graph is trapped behind a company firewall with no hope to follow you should you ever change jobs, it is unlikely that you will spend much time managing it.

This doesn't preclude a form of dual ownership. In fact, many networks set the stage for a role-based ownership by tracking not only the existence of a connection but by qualifying it as a friendship or business contact, and further specifying, for instance, which position was held when forming the connection. Identity-based ownership is also in play. If Alice met Bob while she worked as a senior marketing director at XYZ Corporation, Alice would unconditionally maintain that relationship upon leaving the company, because Bob currently is a personal acquaintance. Charlie, Alice's replacement, could as well be put in touch with Bob, based on his inheriting her active role-based connections.

What does this hint at, in terms of architecture? The social graph will likely be heterogeneous, mapping relationships both internal and external to the company. As such, its storage and management is best suited for logically centralized hosting (even if it is physically distributed) as opposed to being replicated by each corporation. This indicates companies should not attempt to replicate the social graph–bearing infrastructure, but be given means to tap into a brokering service, such as Plaxo, operating independently from any particular organization. As far as activity streams are concerned, choices are more fine-grained: Some streams may need to be made secure and kept behind a firewall, while others could intertwine events from multiple corporations and travel through firewalls.

Social Norms

A few social networking participants will certainly get caught off guard, with embarrassing pictures that remain archived and accessible longer than anyone involved anticipated. But just because conversations and interactions are happening increasingly online doesn't mean all hell has to break loose. The corporate edifice will not collapse if employees are allowed to participate. Given the tools they need to cordon off certain areas of their private life, users are no more likely to misbehave online than they are to misbehave after having one too many drinks at the company holiday party.

Assuming goals are clearly defined at work, a responsible employee is going to strive to get her job done, poke and Super Wall notwithstanding, much the same way she would without the network's presence. And the network isn't the only distraction, after all—and few workers spends their days talking on the phone with friends just because telephones are sitting on their desks.

Social networks, and their underlying components, are about capturing and making apparent the connection graphs and activity streams underpinning groups and organizations. The focus on entertainment or flirting-oriented activities prevalent in large, general consumer networks today isn't a necessity in the enterprise. Numerous business-centric services already exist whose value isn't predicated on poking or winking among members. At the same time, enticing team members to participate implies that communications needn't be strictly limited to business topics. Water-cooler conversations don't necessarily start from work-related situations, but they offer an informal stage where local networks develop nonetheless, to the benefit of the enterprise.

Reaping the Social Networking Benefits

Where do employer and employee goals align when it comes to social networking? And how can productive, socially aware applications be implemented and deployed?

First, it is not necessary to conceive of social networks as monolithic, isolated services concentrating all our social intelligence somewhere in a cloud. Instead, the various components powering these networks can be envisioned as decoupled and embedded within existing applications to make them social. In the short term, intermediary steps can entail the implementation of groups and applications or widgets specific to the enterprise within larger public networks, meshing enterprise or industry concerns into the social fabric of the network.

For instance, expertise location is one application that naturally fits the social networking dynamic. Empowered employees can clearly see value in contributing, for instance, their collection of bookmarks, because that helps establishing their expertise. This helps identify them as the go-to people when questions arise about their area of interest and responsibility. Some public networks, either for entertainment or business value, already offer mechanisms for users to ask questions of their social connections. This could be specialized through custom applications within the enterprise.

Consumer social networks are captured in the mix of the social graph and the chronicling of and notification about activities, such as uploading pictures and videos, an activity in which users engage for their own and their friends' benefit. Similarly, the key to a successful enterprise social network resides in its ability to capture and broadcast selectively the *implicit, preexisting* behaviors of its members: Deriving social graphs from inbox or VoIP activity, or turning bookmarking into events chronicled by the system, helps ease any uptake burden and brings the network to life. While the alternative of building enterprise-specific components for existing networks, such as Facebook and OpenSocial, by leveraging their APIs is available today, the benefits of tapping into the existing connections and activity streams to make them implicitly social are much larger.

Precisely because companies are controlled environments where policies are set with regard to which e-mail, voice, or chat applications can be set, where extensions to those applications can be deployed to the entire user base, and how existing services can be converted into socially aware ones, businesses stand to take great advantage of bringing social networking to computing. Additionally, social networking helps foster what some researchers have called *weak links*. We are strongly linked to people we interact with most frequently, such as our bosses, direct reports, and immediate peers. But because we are so tightly connected, it is likely our networks overlap strongly. And if we are facing a particular challenge and are stumped, it could be that those in our immediate network are stumped as well. Through the periphery of our network, the weak links, we extend the realm of our connections to wider circles and can thus tap the expertise of a vastly greater network. Because of the leverage effect brought on by the efficacies of online social networks, individuals can maintain a broader network of connections to provide more resources in times of challenge. This should not be equated with the wisdom of crowds, however: This is about locating expertise of individuals away from the core of our network, not merely averaging random contributions from a large and unqualified group.

Distributed teams (across geographic regions or across companies) and telecommuting arrangements are obvious situations for which ties, weak or not, can also be strengthened through the use of social networks. Knowledge or information workers, in particular, are seeing their world flatten at a fast clip. Teams charged with delivering a particular project end-to-end often pull together contributors based thousands of miles apart. Social networks and socially aware applications offer those team members a unique chance to stay in touch casually and develop stronger working relationships.

So far, we have examined the services' applicability for the enterprise solely as internal communication and collaboration tools, perhaps involving cross-company links. But a business can also view the medium as an opportunity to engage its customer base in community-related activities, to build its brand through sponsorship or targeted ads.

In November 2007, Facebook announced and rolled out a number of advertising-related features that were aimed at monetizing its massive and passionate user base, by offering means for companies to advertise easily and effectively on its network. Two features particularly stand out: *Beacon* is a system that allows partner companies to tap into the viral effects of the network, by turning users into free evangelists. Users get to spread to friends, via their activity streams, endorsements for third-party products or services they like. The system is rather aggressive in three regards. First, it allows such endorsements to occur even when users are not visiting Facebook and are instead using a partner site (such as buying movie tickets on Fandango). Second, and somewhat controversially, it is opt-out, because notifications can be automatically triggered by partner sites unless users choose not to do so. Third, Facebook receives information about the browsing habits of even those users who opt-out. *Facebook Ads*, on the other hand, promises a highly targeted ad platform to businesses. The service opens up its demographic and stated-interest data to advertisers, allowing them to display banners only to those users who match specific criteria. Both *Beacon* and *Ads* are still very rudimentary in terms of targeting mechanisms and are unproven in most regards, ranging from user acceptance to size of the target audiences, to accuracy of the stated data, to overall relevance in the absence of defined intent on the part of users.

Beyond those direct uses of social networks as ad platforms, the ability for a company to maintain a presence, to establish a voice and communicate with its audience over the social medium can become, just like blogs done right, a potent ingredient in a successful branding mix.

Part II

Technologies

Chapter 5

Mashups: A Behavior and a Technology

By Vince Casarez

In technology, a mashup is a web application that combines data from more than one source into a single integrated tool; an example is the use of cartographic data from Google Maps to add location information to real-estate data from Craigslist, thereby creating a new and distinct web service that was not originally provided by either source.

Mashup originally referred to the practice in pop music (notably hip-hop) of producing a new song by mixing two or more existing pieces.

Wikipedia, circa June 2008

Although this Wikipedia entry provides a reasonably good overview of what a mashup can do, it doesn't really explain why a business user would be interested in mashups—other than perhaps how a mashup might be used to help the IT department deliver a solution more quickly. But mashups can also enable business users to manage their products, services, employees, customers, and partners more efficiently. And mashups can provide much more since they are tied into the existing IT infrastructure. A slightly more abstract definition of a mashup, provided next, may help clarify how it applies to business.

Enterprise Mashups

The term *mashup* originated in the music industry: one artist would work with a song created by another artist to create something new, or both artists would work together to produce a brand new sound as a combined work. In the enterprise context, a mashup is a web application that combines data from one or more sources into a single integrated web page; it's a way for a user or developer to alter or shape a web application to direct its content to solve a specific business problem. Similar to the music mashup, software industry mashups keep the core components the same. The synergy of the joined components makes a mashup extremely valuable to business users.

Given the origin of mashups on the public Web, a core set of capabilities typically characterize them:

■ The resulting page is a simple page (HTML) that includes URL-based resources or components.

■ The components being mashed up handle the storage of their core data, business rules, and often their default presentation.

■ These components can be snapped together by a developer using any development language (Java, PHP, PERL, and so on) and often allow business users to assemble these pages using a browser-based tool.

■ The resulting mashed-up page does not change the original components; it simply blends together each of their unique data elements to provide a tailored "composite application," sometimes referred to as a *situational application*, since it was created for the user's specific situation.

Within the enterprise, users are often asked to accomplish specific tasks. They spend much of their time visiting different applications that provide isolated pieces of information to compose a mental picture of what they really want to know or do. For example, when a manager reviews a simple expense report, the act of approving the expense for reimbursement can be quite simple: Click a button and the employee, partner, or contractor gets paid. But the manager needs to understand the entire picture and the impact of this specific request on the rest of the business before she can approve the individual expense. To help her understand where the group stands in terms of budgeted expenses and actual expenses, additional information is often found in a business analytics or reporting system. The manager also needs to understand other budget commitments for other projects before this specific project can be approved. Project tracking information is also likely to influence whether the invoice should be paid directly or held for verification of delivery. The manager needs to understand any pending expenses where overall priorities might influence the timing of when this specific expense is paid. The manager often discusses the budget allocations with peers and partners to make sure all efforts are covered in the project or proposal. As a result, this additional information is likely stored in spreadsheets, tables, or documents. Managers also use e-mail, instant messaging (IM) systems, discussion forums, and wikis to collaborate with others in determining which projects to fund. These unstructured sources of information also need to be available at the point at which the manager is about to approve the expense.

To get the full picture of the project's progress and determine whether the expense should be approved, the manager needs to integrate all this information. Bringing together all these sources—enterprise application data, business analytic data, freeform spreadsheets and documents, web pages, wikis, and collaboration interactions such as IM—requires an *enterprise mashup*.

Businesses can improve the productivity of their employees, partners, and customers by combining all the data gathered from sources regarding the task they are trying to accomplish and delivering it in one single page. Figure 5-1 illustrates

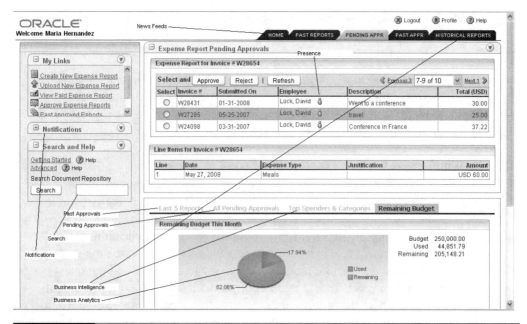

FIGURE 5-1   An enterprise mashup brings together different sources of data into a single page for business users.

a view of an enterprise mashup with many different sources of information pulled together in one screen and placed in the context of approving a marketing expense.

All Mashups Are Not Created Equal

One of the reasons why mashups are so popular today is that they don't require sophisticated programmers to bring together all the data. The components are often easy to understand, the providers document their services quite well, and developers/ users needn't use any single language to build or integrate these components. This is why mashups provide so much promise to many companies both big and small.

Business users must often schedule time with company IT departments to build out the new services (such as a project expense status report) before they can deliver a solution. Using this Web 2.0 mashup concept, IT can produce or consume the components that are required to deliver a quick solution. Since mashups are so simple to produce, business users can devise a solution to a problem without involving IT. This makes the mashup a powerful enabler to help businesses meet the demands of many users while reducing the specific demands and costs on IT.

Mashups can be created with development tools used by professional developers as well as browser-based tools used by end users. With every passing day, new and innovative products and services become available to compose these new solutions.

Another consideration is the type of mashup that is required to assemble the appropriate information. For example, can you pull together a couple of different feeds or services to provide an aggregated source of information—using a list of existing orders from an enterprise resource planning (ERP) application and connecting it with a feed from the order fulfillment centers to understand the quickest inventory turns? Or can you connect information on the page using a list of potential customers from a customer relationship management (CRM) application and the contact information for each customer stored on a service such as LinkedIn?

Many providers of services and products bring their company heritage with their proposed solution. For example, enterprise platform providers such as Oracle, IBM, and Microsoft can provide a set of mashup capabilities that let you quickly plug into a corporate infrastructure and provide large-scale reliability over the duration of a project's lifetime. Internet providers often focus on the best way to present information to the user and make it easy for any type of user to bring these components together. However, Internet-assembled mashups might not be as robust or provide the rich integration required for enterprise applications to solve critical business problems. This is not to imply that one viewpoint is better than the other, but it does highlight the options available when deciding on the best approach to any specific mashup.

Consider, for example, a manufacturing clerk who is required to track shipments from various warehouse locations to a specific storefront. A mashup using order shipment information from the company's enterprise order entry system and a Google mapping service would work perfectly. On the other hand, suppose a senior executive of the same shipping company needed to determine where the company could optimize its package shipments. The mashup components required for such a decision would come from all the back office systems currently running within the company. This type of information would need to be tracked often at different points in time; therefore, a service level agreement would need to be established with all the application owners so that the executive would be able to get this information anytime it was required.

Mashup Types and Suppliers

Many vendors and industry analysts talk about mashups in various ways. Four major categories of mashups are often used in the enterprise. Although more nuanced divisions of these types of capabilities exist, this discussion provides a quick method for cataloging mashup efforts.

- **Data source mashups**   Mashups produce, aggregate, and assemble data feeds from web services, XML streams, Really Simple Syndication (RSS), and other sources to form a combined result.

- **Process mashups**   Often called SOA orchestration, mashup assemblers (developers or technical business users) leverage a set of existing Business Process Execution Language (BPEL) processes and connect them together in the context of their required task.

- **Developer assembly**   Mashups are built using different programming languages (Java, Perl, PHP, .Net, and so on) to call URL-based or web-based Representational State Transfer/Plain Old XML (REST/POX) services and link them together.

- **Visual assembly**   End users shape all these components into a form that more directly allows them to complete a specific task.

Because of the rapid pace of changes in this technology, rather than provide a detailed explanation of each vendor that offers mashup and enterprise mashup capabilities, this discussion focuses on the types of mashups that are available today and describes a representative vendor for each type. The following sections describe each of these types with a specific vendor example for each.

Data Source Mashups: Kapow Technologies

Kapow Technologies (www.kapowtech.com) delivers a set of products that help users and developers create mashups. The core of its product set enables users and developers to connect information from any data source to another data source to provide a coordinate set of information. Kapow can integrate and combine information from the following sources: REST/POX, RSS/Atom, content management systems (CMS), databases, spreadsheets, text and PDF files, and web pages.

Figure 5-2 shows Kapow's architecture for integrating different data sources into a consumable mashup component. Information can be included from any source in which it currently resides and can be delivered as an aggregate. This means that the business user doesn't have to wait for IT to deliver an aggregated report. IT can simply provide a feed of the product sales system behind a secured access point, and the business user can derive the necessary information

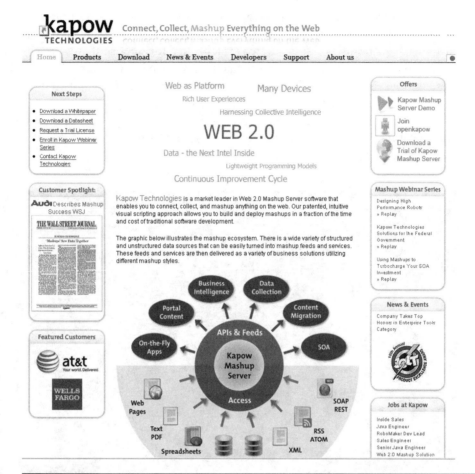

FIGURE 5-2   Kapow Technologies data aggregation/mashup architecture

to determine whether sales should continue for a specific product or whether something new should be offered to the company's customers.

Process Mashups: Serena Software

Serena Software (www.serena.com) focuses its products on delivering mashups that solve business problems that are typically process-driven. In service-oriented architectures (SOAs), technologists like to refer to this type of mashup as *process orchestration*. Process orchestration often involves no user interface (UI) components and provides integration of the backend system processes. For example, suppose a business has Siebel CRM installed for tracking leads and orders but will use Oracle eBusiness Suite (EBS) for tracking shipped orders to the customer. This business wants the two systems tied together so that when an order is entered in Siebel, it shows up immediately in Oracle EBS. The method by which these two systems are linked is referred to as *process integration*, which doesn't involve any user interaction or user intervention.

Serena's process mashups can help coordinate different process orchestration events that might or might not require some user intervention. Figure 5-3 shows some of the process mashups available by Serena.

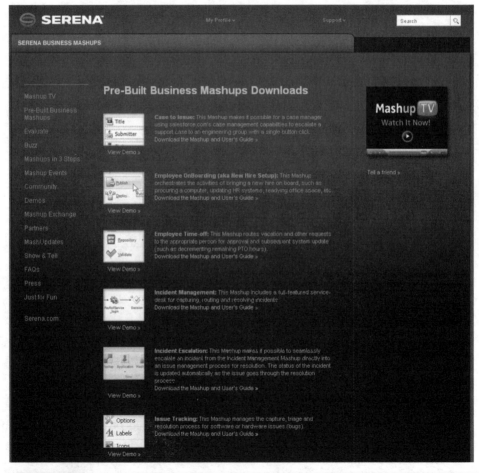

FIGURE 5-3   Serena includes a listing of prebuilt process mashups, or what the company calls "business mashups."

Developer Assembly: BEA Systems

Developers often need an easy way to include different components, portlets, or gadgets onto their pages without having to jump to full-blown frameworks for consuming these components. They simply want to add a URL to their application that pulls in the components from other systems. This can involve supplying security information or application context to shape the results. For example, if an existing Perl application lists all the customer issues reported to people within an organization, and developers from IT have supplied a portlet to show off all the new fixes from the product development team, the Perl application would benefit from using these components directly. But Perl doesn't have a model for using standard portlets. BEA Software (www.bea.com) lets the developer use these standards-based portlets so that existing applications such as Perl, PHP, .Net, and others can use them directly, just by calling them through a URL. This is also known as REST/POX–based usage of these components.

In addition, parameters sometimes need to be passed to these components so that only the desired information is shown. In the preceding example, the developer would set up a couple of variables to pass in the name of the product being shown, and then the portlet/component would show only the fixes for that specific product. The following code listing shows an example of what a developer would add to a Perl application to produce a listing of all the customers and phone numbers managed by a particular sales representative:

```
// create our simple function to return the data to be mashed up

function getMyCustomers() { }
getMyCustomers.getCustomers = function () {

// set the URL to a JSON service,
url = "http://siebelcrm.mycompany.com/getMyCustomers.html";

// get the list of customers from the mashup source
var resultCustURL = environment.getText(url);
var responseCustomers = eval("(" + resultCustURL + ")");

...

// Define the Customer result layout to match the XML description
function getMyCustomerList (name, city, address, contactNumber,
date)
{
```

```
        this.name = name;
        this.city = city;
        this.address = address;
        this.contactNumber = contactNumber;
        this.date = date;
}
getMyCustomerList.toString = function(){
        return this.name+": "+this.contactNumber;
};
```

Visual Assembly: Oracle USA, Inc.

Although Oracle provides a Java development environment called JDeveloper
that lets developers build mashups, the most exciting offering by the company
lets business users drag-and-drop items into a browser to assemble their mashups.
With Oracle WebCenter Composer, users can consume the available components
without any help from IT, thus avoiding being slowed down by IT's applications
backlog. Users who need a tailored view of their existing applications are
directly able to deal with dynamic business changes that might not justify a new
application being built.

Oracle WebCenter (http://webcenter.oracle.com) provides a browser-based
tool called WebCenter Composer that makes it easy for users to move and connect
items on the page. So, for example, a product name can be easily passed from
one component to the next. Oracle also provides a business user view of all of the
components that can be added to a page in a resource catalog. The resource catalog
is critical, because users need a role-specific view of what can be added to their
pages. For example, a developer would like to see lower level components, such
as SQL connections or web services along with portlets, to add to a page. But a
business user would get confused with this view and would rather see items such
as Customer Accounts, Quarterly Sales, or a Customer Profile. Figure 5-4 shows
the Oracle WebCenter Composer and business user view of the resource catalog.

Mashup Styles vs. Enterprise Portals

Many might interpret this conversation about mashups as the same conversation
the software industry has been having about enterprise portals for years. Enterprise
portals provide a starting point for all employees, partners, and customers for
understanding a company's key goals and initiatives. These portals are accessed by
a URL such as *http://myCompany.com*. Although some of the examples discussed
so far could easily be fulfilled with a good implementation of an enterprise portal,

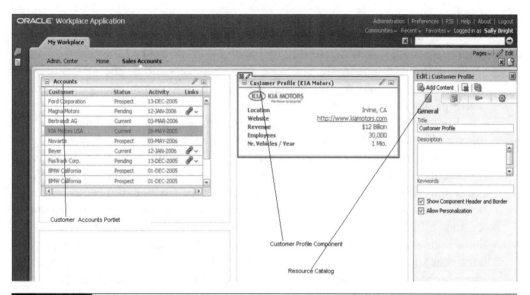

FIGURE 5-4   An example of mashing up a set of customer accounts connected to customer profile details using WebCenter Composer with a business user view of the resource catalog

the challenge is to provide the user with an easy way to alter the enterprise portal consistently until it fits the exact task that the user is trying to perform.

Many enterprise portals provide features called *customizations* and/or *personalizations*. Although these features can easily serve as the foundation for producing a mashed-up web page, they are only part of the experience for the business user. As mentioned, the mashup often needs to occur in the context of the enterprise application with which the user is interacting. Enterprise portals provide a launch point into these enterprise applications, but they fall behind when the user needs to do his work within the application. Enterprise portals are a fine place to provide and enable enterprise mashups, but they can't be considered the end solution for all the different user requirements. Therefore, when looking for technology that will provide a solution to both enterprise portal users and enterprise application users, you should consider technologies that can be easily added both to an enterprise portal and enterprise applications.

Another type of tool related to but slightly different from the enterprise portal is a *dashboard* style of mashup—a combination of components that allows executives to get a read on the key performance indicators (KPIs) that show how their business is running. It could be a listing of all the open orders, the number of orders that were filled on the previous day, the number of incoming issues with product deliveries, and the amount of product returns. The key distinction here is that the information is pushed to the user from the different systems providing the metrics on intervals determined by the applications used by the organization. These dashboard-style mashups enable many managers and business users to analyze information that is required regularly to help them understand the overall performance of the business.

The third type of enterprise mashup is sometimes called a *situational application*. These applications are mashed-up pages that shape enterprise applications and include capabilities that weren't originally intended to be included in the application but have proven to be useful to the business user. For example, a sales representative often prepares information in anticipation of meeting with an existing customer by reviewing all the current orders that have been shipped to the customer. In addition, the salesperson will verify that any customer-reported issues have been resolved to the customer's satisfaction by checking with the company customer support organization. Finally, the sales rep will evaluate the requirements the customer has provided to determine whether additional products can be offered to the customer. The IT organization often provides this information, but it is contained in distinct applications that the sales rep would have to visit one at a time. These "situational applications" are assembled by the user, in this case the sales rep, to include components from several different applications, and information is passed from one component to the other to place all the related information in the context of the customer selected. In this example, *in context* means that all the other systems are filtered to show only the relevant information for the selected customer. The key element of this type of mashup is that the user gathers relevant information to accomplish a specific task or goal—in other words, the user is pulling required information from the different systems.

The last type of enterprise mashup is a *geographically determined* mashup, which is the type of mashup most popular on the Internet today. Business information is placed over a context map to provide a richer way to inspect it and derive conclusions. Suppose an air conditioning service repair technician is going to inspect a particular building. He knows that a few items are necessary for performing the service call: schematics of the building, location of exact equipment in relationship to the building, and the location of one customer call relative to the other service calls for the day. The service tech can start with a broad view of the map, charting each call. Then, as the tech clicks each customer service ticket on the map, he is able to drill into the specific floor plans for each building. Finally, the tech is able to inspect each floor to determine the type of equipment that will need repairs. All of this critical information is often stored in different applications that the customer or service repair company maintains for its customers. A mashup can be designed by an IT developer and then enhanced or altered by the service repair tech to reflect what is needed to do his job. In this case, the tech could add more information to the mashup, such as the names of local parts companies that could provide components necessary to fix the identified problems.

Mashups and Self-Propagation

All of this might seem a little too complicated for the average business user to be able to create a mashup and be productive on her own. But the various types of mashups discussed so far apply to different types of users and the ease with which they can assemble these new pages/applications. The interesting part about mashups is that by definition they are a *self-propagating experience*. This means that when a user has completed a specific mashup, she immediately provides a new component that can be mashed up by others. Such components can be stored in libraries, which are fundamental to the creation of mashups.

Consider our air conditioning service tech example. Once the technician has provided his changes to the mashup to show the parts suppliers along with his customer service calls, another service tech can reuse the mashup. Rather than having to re-create the entire mashup, she can use the other tech's existing mashup and overlay the best spots for lunch when she's out on her route.

Users and developers don't have to start from scratch when producing mashups, nor are they limited to mashups created by their coworkers. Several Internet sites are dedicated to showing off the best and most popular mashups; these sites also provide a great source of ideas and components to mash up. Figure 5-5 shows the most popular mashups available at the time of writing on a website called Programmable Web (www.programmableweb.com). Once users and developers have created their mashups, they can publish them for others to use on the Programmable Web site. This allows a whole community of mashup builders and consumers to work collaboratively to make these components more relevant and more interesting.

Within a company, lots of sensitive information cannot legally be published outside the work context or on a public Internet site like Programmable Web. Like Oracle, these companies can instead provide a resource catalog that offers both business users and developers a way to publish all of these company-specific mashups so that other users and developers can use company-relevant components. In addition, the people who produce these mashups can use the catalog to provide a description of the mashup's use and tag it or provide a label so others can search for and find it. In this way, other business users will find mashable items that are relevant and described in their terms.

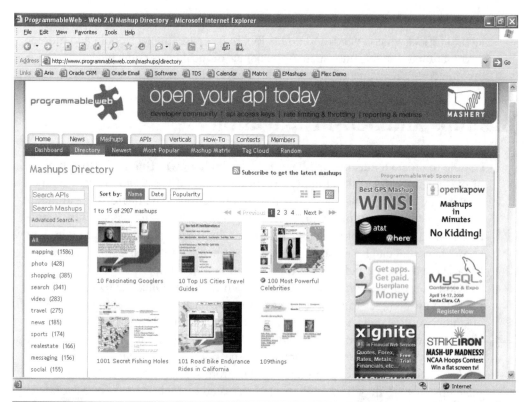

FIGURE 5-5   The Programmable Web site lists popular and useful mashups available for others to use.

Creating Mashups

Now that you know the backgrounds of several mashup types, some companies that provide products to produce mashups, and other basic considerations, you're ready to produce a simple mashup. To help you get started, the Programmable Web site offers several basic options for you to consider (from www.programmableweb. com/howto). In this example, we'll mash up a current stock price with an RSS feed of all the recent company news.

1. Choose a simple example of what to mash up so that the list of sites and services you use can be filtered to a reasonable subset.

2. Decide where to acquire the necessary data. If you're creating a mashup for company use, you might need to discuss with IT the information that is

already available via existing reports, or you may request that IT produce a secure feed from existing systems. In this example, we'll use two different free services: QuoteRSS.com to determine the RSS feed with a delayed stock quote from Yahoo!; and Yahoo! to select all the recent stories for a particular company. (QuoteRSS.com and Yahoo! allow anyone to access these services for their own personal use. However, if these services are required to help solve a business problem, a licensing agreement may be required. Not all services or APIs require an agreement, but many times the creation of the mashup can be done in parallel with the signing of an agreement. Keep this in mind as you select data feeds.)

3. Assess the coding skills of the people creating the mashups. Developers and business users can participate in creating mashups in many ways. Consider the languages being used by developers or the browser-based tool for business users, consider the amount of time available to create the mashup, and determine the server infrastructure from which this mashup will run. In this example, we'll keep with a simple example with a no-coding approach, but it will require a little bit of technical expertise to understand URLs and link items together through drag-and-drop. Many services on the public Internet can help you build these mashups, such as Yahoo! Pipes, Microsoft Popfly, Dapper, and Pageflakes. For this example, we'll use Yahoo! Pipes.

4. Sign up for the required services or APIs that will be used in the mashup. As mentioned in step 2, some services or APIs require that an agreement with the provider be created to allow a specific Internet domain to make repetitive requests to a service. As more and more users depend on their ability to access a mashup service daily, the service must be available whenever they need it; this is critical to the success of the mashup. For this example, we'll use the services from QuoteRSS.com and Yahoo!. We also need to sign up for a free ISP account, such as Yahoo! Pipes, or install a mashup server for companywide use. Many ISPs offer free accounts that anyone can sign up to use to get started.

5. Finally, begin creating the mashup with the correct building tools. For example, if a developer were building in Java, he could use something like Oracle JDeveloper or Eclipse to build, test, and deploy the mashups. For this example, we'll use the services as described and, more specifically, Yahoo! Pipes.

Creating a Stock and News Feed Mashup

To get started, go to http://pipes.yahoo.com and click the Create A Pipe button at the top of the screen. You'll be prompted to log in with a Yahoo! account or asked to create a new account.

1. Once logged in, the Yahoo! Pipes editing environment is displayed. The following illustration shows the starting point for building all new mashups in Yahoo! Pipes.

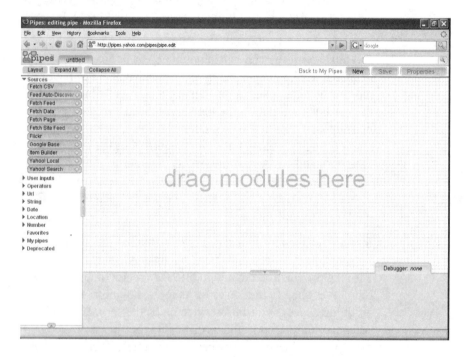

2. The user needs to get the stock symbol of interest and feed this into the system. On the panel on the left side of the user interface, User Inputs allows you to prompt the user for some basic information. Click User Inputs to see a list of choices to add to the mashup.

3. Drag-and-drop Text Input to the area on the right, as shown next. The Pipe Output component appears at the bottom of the interface. This will be used when the mashup is complete to provide one ending page to view all the information.

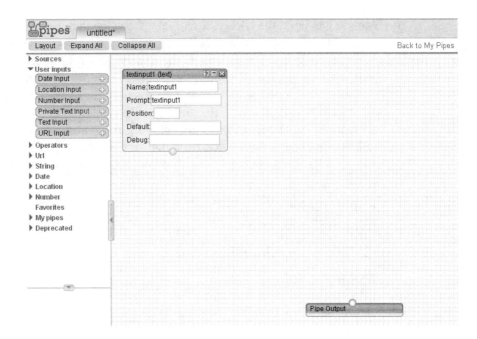

You can fill in the prompts and labels to help other users understand what is required.

4. Now provide a name for what you want to track: In the Name field, type **companysymbol**. Next, add a prompt so that the user will understand what should be entered: In the Prompt field, type **Stock Symbol**. A default value is required so that the page isn't blank when it first shows up: Type **GE** (the stock symbol for General Electric) in the Default field. The next illustration shows the new entries.

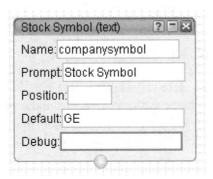

5. Now we can build the URL that will take the value that the user has supplied for the company symbol and gather all the news stories for this particular company. You can get all the news stories for a specific company from Yahoo! using the URL http://finance.yahoo.com/rss/headline?s=GE.

However, we don't want to return results only for General Electric. We need to provide a way to pass in the stock symbol to this URL before the financial service returns this information. To do this, we use the URL Builder component. Click URL from the panel on the left and drag-and-drop the URL Builder component onto the page, as shown next:

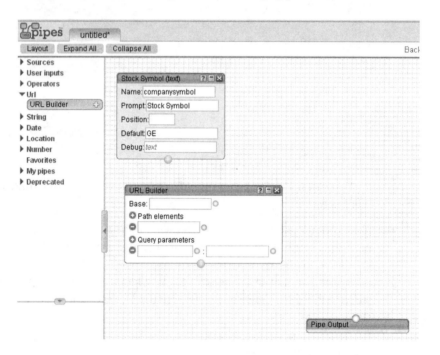

6. Construct the URL by including everything up to the question mark (?) in the example in step 5 into the Base field. The question mark signals to sites on the Internet the changeable values that will be supplied next. In our example URL, the parameter name is *s* (for *symbol*) and the value will be *GE* (which we entered in step 4) for our default example. So enter the letter **s** into the first entry under Query Parameters, as shown here:

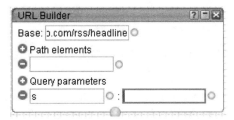

7. Now we need to get the company symbol from the User Inputs component to be supplied as the value for the URL Builder component. Click the circle at the bottom of the User Input component (the Stock Symbol) and drag-and-drop a pipe to the circle to the right of the value entry for the Query Parameters area of the URL Builder. As you click and drag, the pipe follows the mouse to draw a line from one area to the next, as shown next:

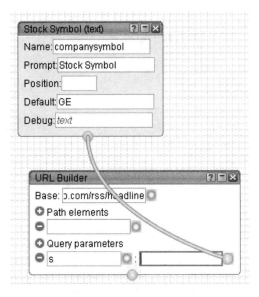

Note: Once the pipe has been created, it sometimes goes behind some of the other components on the screen. At any time, you can rearrange the components on the page to provide a better view.

8. Click the title of any of the components, and the Debugger area at the bottom part of the interface will report what will be run when the component is ready for others. In this case, click the URL Builder and the Debugger area will report the following:

```
Time taken: 0.000745s Refresh
   http://finance.yahoo.com/rss/headline?s=GE
```

This is the exact URL that we will use later to provide a listing of all the news stories for GE.

9. To get a delayed stock quote, we'll now use the QuoteRSS.com site. The URL created to retrieve stock quotes looks like this: *http://www.quoterss.com/quote.php?symbol=GE&frmt=0&Freq=0*. It's a little more complex than the first URL, but it follows the same principle. It includes a base URL (http://www.quoterss.com/quote.php) with three parameters this time (*symbol*, *frmt*, and *Freq*). Drag another URL Builder component onto the page, and in the Query Parameters field, enter **symbol**. Create a new pipe from the User Inputs (Stock Symbol) to this symbol parameter, as shown next:

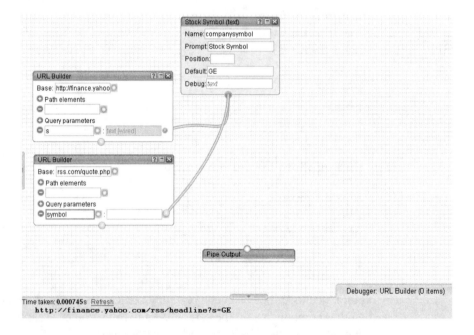

10. To add the other parameters, click the plus sign (+) to the left of the Query Parameters label and a new set of entry fields will appear. Do this twice and enter the **frmt** and **Freq** labels along with a value of **0** (zero) for both:

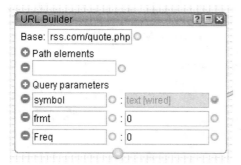

11. Now that we have two URL sources of information, they need to be brought together in one component to display to the user. Open the Sources panel on the left and drag-and-drop the Fetch Feed component on the page. The next illustration shows the new component added to the page to retrieve all the content from the two different sources of information:

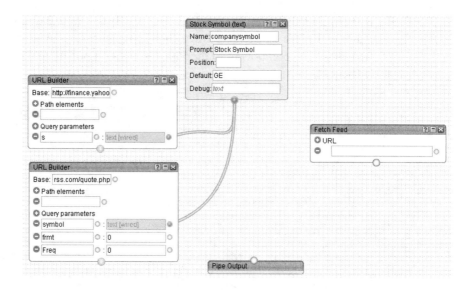

12. To connect the two URL sources that we've produced into one list, we create pipes to supply the URLs as inputs to the Fetch Feed component. Click the plus sign to the left of the URL label to add a second item to connect into this component. In the next illustration, the two URL Builder components are connected to the Fetch Feed component:

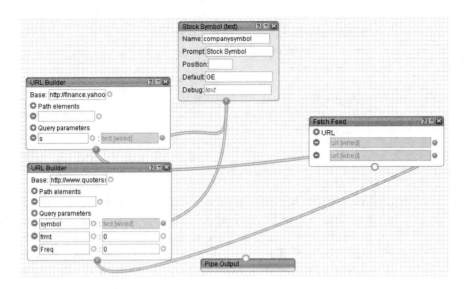

13. You can do more with Yahoo! Pipes, but we'll stick to this quick mashup example. Before we can run the example, we'll create one last pipe from the Fetch Feed component to the Pipe Output component at the bottom of the page.

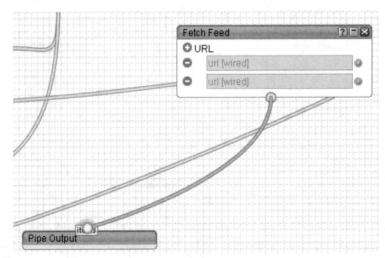

14. To see the results of this example, click the Save button at the top-right corner of the UI and type in a name. Once saved, a prompt at the top of the screen will allow the mashup to be run so that it can be tested and refined. Click the Run Pipe link at the top of the page.

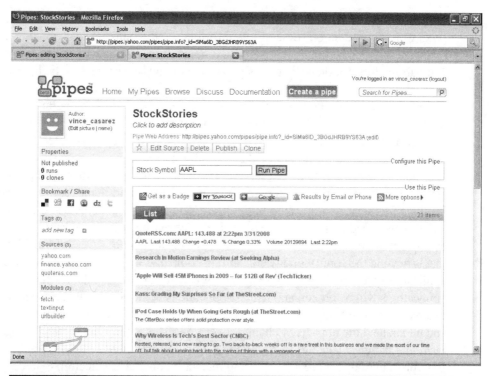

FIGURE 5-6   The mashup is run using Apple Computer's stock symbol.

The resulting listing of all recent stories and the current stock quote for GE are returned. In Figure 5-6, the user has entered a different symbol (AAPL) to see stories and stock quotes for another company, Apple Computer.

Managing Flexibility to Minimize Complexity and Costs

Now that you've taken a concrete look at building a mashup, you might understand more clearly that some key considerations are necessary to leverage this across an enterprise. First of all, our stock quote example isn't really an enterprise mashup—it's a mashup that would be helpful in some enterprises, but it doesn't give users a better view of their business or shape the information around the task they are trying to accomplish. It does demonstrate how easy it can be to shape the information once it becomes available. But if one of the base services used in the example changes, users will be left with a blank screen. This isn't a big issue with a set of public Internet services, but, clearly, if business processes or user tasks were dependent on some of this information, it would cause a slowdown or stoppage of work within the consuming organization. This is why the agreements and partnerships for delivering these services reliably are critical to the long-term success.

In addition, ensuring that the services will be maintained and upgraded over time is just as critical as getting the feeds or information right in the first place. In our trivial example, imagine if the news feeds failed to be updated after a particular date. Quickly, users would notice that the information was no longer "recent" and they'd move away to a new service. If we move this scenario to an enterprise setting and the sales figures stop getting updated, users and managers would not leverage this service or mashup in the future and it would become useless.

You also need to understand where enterprise mashups are being stored. Our example is stored on Yahoo!'s servers and, as a result, Yahoo! saves information that is beyond the control of any consuming company. While helpful, if the base applications were to change, there's no easy way for IT to understand which applications will be broken and which applications work. Storing this information in a more open and common system is critical to being able to track changes and understand the impacts of changes over time. This key concept, often called *metadata management*, has to do with managing information about the application. Enterprise mashups are really just using metadata about an application to understand how to pull it all together for the user. Managing this information is critical to insulate users from changes over time but more importantly to understand what the users want to change and influence how the application can be improved over time.

Based on our example, you can see how easy it is to add components, which could quickly overwhelm users trying to find a useful mashup or inundate the infrastructure trying to organize the mashup components. You learned that Oracle provides a resource catalog library that is organized by the type of user and then by the types of components. In whatever solution you select, a library or catalog is a critical element that needs to be considered.

Obviously, the tool you choose to build mashups must be appropriate for the users who need it. One tool doesn't usually fit all users' needs. Therefore, your choice of system for enterprise use should focus on appealing both to developers and end users. A different tool might be required for each user population, but the mashup components that are created should be accessible or consumable by both toolsets and both user populations.

Products and services will continue to mature in this area, and eventually a much wider set of users will be able to participate in creating and consuming these enterprise mashups. As a result, many companies will need to consider how they want to embrace these new models for their companies and users. Simply allowing them to leverage public Internet tools is a good starting point, but it will always leave users wanting more from their IT groups.

Everyone involved wants a more productive set of workers that leverage secure and managed services to get their jobs done. To achieve this, these enterprise mashups need to be quick to create a set of supported feeds and services, easy to maintain for both the users/developers and IT, and fast to find when they are needed to solve a business problem. The ease with which they can be created is just as important as the ease with which they are managed. Consider these aspects when looking for a solution.

Chapter 6

AJAX and Beyond: Merging the Desktop with the Web

By Philipp Weckerle

More and more applications these days are being webified—*meaning "made to operate on the Web using a browser or made to function in a similar manner." This is because the Internet is capable of significantly augmenting human interaction, with its decentralized system of ubiquitous data accessibility.*

Ebrahim Ezzy, ReadWriteWeb

Much of Web 2.0 is about social networking and collaborative services, but it is more than this. Users these days expect highly interactive user interfaces (UIs) along with rich services. Not long ago, web users worked with character mode applications that provided base functionality through a simplistic and minimal interaction model. This concept spread across multiple platforms, from mainframe applications all the way to early desktop PC implementations. These applications were usually transaction-based, requiring that the user fill out and submit a form, and wait for a response from a server.

With the introduction of graphical user interfaces (GUIs) on those machines, the era of desktop applications began, mainly for the PC. Users required a richer experience in using their applications. After a couple of years, management and maintenance issues made it necessary to split the presentation layer from the actual business logic and data management. The best thing since sliced bread was introduced with a bang: client-server computing. Under this model, the UI remained on the client, while the business logic and data management were centrally controlled on the server, where they could be easily modified and backed up.

Then the Internet came along, and with it the idea of eliminating local installations altogether, replacing them with applications that are served from a server and rendered in a client framework. The web browser did not require any application-specific installation and hence minimized the total cost of ownership (TCO) of these applications. Due to the limited capabilities of those web browsers, users bit the bullet and said goodbye to their rich, highly interactive applications and learned to live with simple application UIs, mainly text or simple form-based applications in a submit-response model; they stepped back a decade to a model they thought they had left behind.

As the potential of form-based, submit-response frameworks increased over the years, those applications evolved, and eventually browser applications provided something that closely resembled the rich interactions users had left behind. A new era of rich Internet applications (RIAs) had begun.

The biggest concern with client-server applications was the distribution and maintenance of the clients. Even though system administrators employed concepts and technologies to distribute software updates to the clients automatically, the process still imposed additional cost with every update released. RIAs, on the other hand, do not require any client-side install; or, if installs are required, the applications distribute these during execution—while downloading Java applets, for example. RIAs combine the ease of use and interactive characteristics of client-server applications with the simplicity in management of web applications.

If we look at the way Web 2.0 applications have evolved, we can see the clear tendency: After features and functionality have solidified, the user experience becomes the focus of improvement. In some cases, the enhancements are subtle and revolve around minimizing page reloads; in other cases, the enhancements are quite substantial, introducing rich UI elements that replace traditional HTML-style application concepts.

Regardless of the type of technology used to achieve these enhancements, they all focus on three major characteristics:

- They process much of the user interaction on the client without having to involve the server (such as field validation, state change of UI elements, and so on).

- They asynchronously communicate state changes to the server.

- They minimize page reloads by implementing partial page refresh.

Loads of Solutions for a Single Problem

Given the popularity of this new paradigm, it is natural that many different technologies and possible solutions have popped up from a variety of sources. With any new technology, to make its way into the enterprise, it must prove its viability and, more important, its potential to become a widespread platform or even a standard.

Most new technologies have one thing in common: They represent the application of existing, proven technologies such as JavaScript, XML, and such. Other technologies follow a different approach: Rather than using HTML and cascading style sheets (CSS) to render advanced UIs, they leverage the browser or the operating system itself to render the UIs. Most recently joining the circle of rich user interactions are technologies that draw on commonly used technologies—in particular, Adobe Flash—to render the UI. The biggest advantage here is the level of user interaction that can be achieved.

Before we dig deeper into those advanced technologies, let's take a look at the basics behind achieving the Web 2.0 user experience in existing applications.

Full Page Refresh: So '80s

When browsing the Web, the full page refresh is a common result for pretty much every action you take. Click a link, submit a form—no matter what you do—the whole page refreshes. This typical submit-response experience mentally transports us back more than two decades into mainframe and character mode ages.

The first order of the day is to eliminate those page reloads wherever possible, especially those that produce immediate responses in the good old client-server world, such as field validation, expand/collapse, or show/hide actions. Most of these can actually be performed before any data is sent back to the server by leveraging client-side processing via JavaScript.

Many page reloads can also be hidden by clever use of concepts such as frames and iFrames in HTML pages. If the area on the screen that needs to be refreshed is encapsulated in a frame, the page stays stable and only the affected frame is refreshed. The result is still a refresh, but the experience for the user is a partial refresh.

Quick Response Equals Quick Experience

If we look at the way users judge the subjective performance of an application, we can see that opinions deviate significantly from the numbers-based approach IT departments use to measure an application's performance. Page load and execution times don't really matter to an end user, as long as the actions happen in the amount of time they expect. In most cases, users' expectations are driven by client-side applications they use as reference. Simple operations, such as expanding and collapsing an area on the screen, are expected to happen instantly, while submitting data or performing a search can take some time—seconds, not minutes, however.

The goal of all RIA initiatives is to provide satisfactory application response by leveraging a combination of client-side and server-side processing.

RIA: The Best Thing?

Providing rich UIs for web applications has pros and cons. One important aspect of the Web 2.0 experience is that it is best used where and when it is called for. For example, not all websites benefit from applying Web 2.0 and RIA concepts. RIA is intended for application use, not for use on content-based websites.

Any RIA technology involves significant complexity, which makes development, testing, and maintenance more difficult and involved than performing those tasks on plain HTML pages. Another aspect that might hurt websites using RIA concepts is discoverability. Given that most content is dynamic on those sites, search engines do not yet take into account these new technologies and would have trouble indexing sites that rely heavily on RIA technology.

Given the asynchronous nature of RIA applications, measuring performance and response times becomes an issue in and of itself. The usual methods of measuring between request and response is no longer valid, as the requests are handled asynchronously and through concepts such as *Comet*, which keep an open channel to the client to push information back constantly; even page-load times become irrelevant as there is no measurable "end" of the page load.

Other approaches exist to enhance the rich experience users demand for this new generation of applications, which combine the interactivity with the discoverability of "normal" HTML pages. The following sections discuss these options in detail.

Dynamic DOM Manipulation

One of the most widely known terms when it comes to highly interactive web pages is *AJAX*—Asynchronous JavaScript and XML. AJAX is used to modify the document object model (DOM) of the page dynamically, either for the initial rendering or during runtime, to update areas of the page.

Traditionally, page assembly occurred on the server side. The whole document was then delivered to the browser and was rendered there. To get refreshed information, the new version needed to be assembled on the server, sent to the client, and refreshed there. With AJAX, the refresh can occur on a partial page level and is accomplished asynchronously. Parts of a page can be filled after the whole page has been sent to the client, which is a vital fact if we are talking about a collection of elements with different render times. In the past, the page was only as fast as its slowest component. Now the page skeleton can be rendered on the client and slower pieces can be filled in using AJAX as they become available.

The following example (excerpted from Wikipedia) shows a simple example for AJAX-based communication. The DOM object "`ajax_output`" of type DIV is used to facilitate the output coming from the AJAX call. Using the `innerHTML` method, the script can manipulate the content of a particular object in the DOM tree and replace its content, one of the fundamentals behind AJAX.

```
<div id="ajax_output">
Waiting to be replaced by Ajax Call
</div>

<script type="text/javascript">
```

```
<!-- // Required to be compliant with XHTML-->
var xmlHttp=null; // Defines that xmlHttp is a new variable.
// Try to get the right object for different browser
try {
    // Firefox, Opera 8.0+, Safari, IE7+
    xmlHttp = new XMLHttpRequest();
} catch (e) {
    // Internet Explorer
    try {
        xmlHttp=new ActiveXObject("Msxml2.XMLHTTP");
    } catch (e) {
        xmlHttp=new ActiveXObject("Microsoft.XMLHTTP");
    }
}
xmlHttp.onreadystatechange = function() {
    if (xmlHttp.readyState == 4)
        try { // In some instances, status cannot be retrieved and
              // will produce an error (e.g. Port is not responsive)
            if (xmlHttp.status == 200) {
                // Set the main HTML of the body to the info provided
                // by the AJAX Request
                document.getElementById("ajax_output").innerHTML
                    = xmlHttp.responseText;
            }
        } catch (e) {
            document.getElementById("ajax_output").innerHTML
                = "Error on Ajax return call : " + e.description;
        }

}
xmlHttp.open("get","pages/index.html");
xmlHttp.send(null); // Since there is no supplied form, null takes
                    // its place as a new form.
</script>
```

The nature of AJAX also causes some problems. Because all communication is asynchronous, it is difficult to measure the performance and page load. In addition, search engines will have problems locating content that is delivered asynchronously.

When studying AJAX examples, you might find similarities with Dynamic HTML (DHTML). The technique of manipulating the DOM to dynamically create content on pages is a central part of AJAX and is what DHTML is all about. DHTML doesn't get the attention AJAX is getting these days, and the reason for this is simple. Back when DHTML was gaining momentum, the browser environments and machines were still too limited to deal seriously with heavy dynamic generation and DOM manipulation. JavaScript is an interpreted language and hence puts a lot of load on the execution environment.

Yahoo! UI Library

The Yahoo! UI Library is a toolkit written in JavaScript to produce highly interactive Web UIs. It provides a set of APIs and style definitions that let you create a Web UI based on regular HTML markup, or you can dynamically instantiate the UI elements exclusively from JavaScript.

Here's an example of a UI based on HTML markup (from Yahoo! Developer Network's website):

```
<button type="button"
            id="pushbutton1"
            name="button1"
            value="Add">Add</button>
...
var oPushButton1 = new YAHOO.widget.Button("pushbutton1");
```

And here is an example on how to create a button based on scripting:

```
var oPushButton7 = new YAHOO.widget.Button(
{ label:"Add",  id:"pushbutton7", container:"pushbuttonsfrom
javascript" });
```

Through various methods (such as XMLHttpRequest [XHR], JavaScript Object Notation [JSON], and so on) Yahoo! UI Library also supports the connection to backend services and the binding to UI elements. You would contact a backend service that returns one of the supported return objects (such as JSON) and provide this object to the UI element (such as a dynamic table). The following example shows a dynamic table that contacts a backend service that returns a JSON object to provide the data for the table (from Yahoo! Developer Network's website):

```
<script type="text/javascript">
YAHOO.util.Event.addListener(window, "load", function() {
    YAHOO.example.XHR_JSON = new function() {
        this.formatUrl = function(elCell, oRecord, oColumn, sData)
```

```
{
        elCell.innerHTML = "<a href='" + oRecord.
    getData("ClickUrl") + "' target='_blank'>" + sData + "</a>";
     };

    var myColumnDefs = [
        {key:"Title", label:"Name", sortable:true,
         formatter:this.formatUrl},
        {key:"Phone"},
        {key:"City"},
        {key:"Rating.AverageRating", label:"Rating",
         formatter:YAHOO.widget.DataTable.formatNumber,
         sortable:true}
    ];

    this.myDataSource = new YAHOO.util.DataSource("assets/php/
     ylocal_proxy.php?");
    this.myDataSource.responseType = YAHOO.util.DataSource.
    TYPE_JSON;
    this.myDataSource.connXhrMode = "queueRequests";
    this.myDataSource.responseSchema = {
        resultsList: "ResultSet.Result",
        fields: ["Title","Phone","City",{key:"Rating.
        AverageRating",parser:YAHOO.util.DataSource.
        parseNumber},"ClickUrl"]
    };

    this.myDataTable = new YAHOO.widget.DataTable("json",
    myColumnDefs,
            this.myDataSource, {initialRequest:"query=pizza&zip
            =94089&results=10&output=json"});

    var callback1 = {
        success : this.myDataTable.onDataReturnAppendRows,
        failure : this.myDataTable.onDataReturnAppendRows,
        scope : this.myDataTable
    };
    this.myDataSource.sendRequest("query=mexican&zip=94089&
    results=10&output=json",
            callback1);

    var callback2 = {
```

```
        success : this.myDataTable.onDataReturnInsertRows,
        failure : this.myDataTable.onDataReturnInsertRows,
        scope : this.myDataTable
    };
    this.myDataSource.sendRequest("query=chinese&zip=94089&
    results=10&output=json",
            callback2);
  };
});
```

Ruby on Rails

Several new and evolving development frameworks/programming languages
provide new ways to create web applications that leverage AJAX to provide
highly interactive UIs. Without having to worry about the actual AJAX part of
development, you can create your application in a proper programming language
and the rendered application will leverage AJAX to enrich the user interface.

The focus of the Ruby on Rails applications is less about mimicking a
client-server experience and more about bringing greater responsiveness to
more traditional HTML UIs. Example applications include Basecamp (www.
basecamphq.com) project collaboration software, which, through a simple
interactive HTML UI, provides a useful and productive user interaction model.
Adding and removing elements produces immediate response to the user's actions,
regardless of the server roundtrip.

The biggest shortcoming of Ruby on Rails is its architecture as an interpreted
language, such as Python or Perl, and therefore it suffers all the disadvantages of
an interpreted language in terms of performance and effectiveness.

Here's an example of Ruby on Rails code used to print "Hello Ruby!" (from
www.tutorialspoint.com/ruby-on-rails/rails-introduction.htm):

```
# The Hello Class
class Hello
   def initialize( name )
      @name = name.capitalize
   end

   def salute
      puts "Hello #{@name}!"
   end
end
# Create a new object
```

```
h = Hello.new("Ruby")
# Output "Hello Ruby!"
h.salute
```

Adobe Flash–based Environments

Over the years, Flash has become a quasi-standard for creating rich Internet content on websites. Based on a common plug-in, developers can use Flash to create anything from simple animations to relatively complex games and other elements. Flash provides a means to create scenarios other than rich menus and animations and provides a natural progression to more dynamic websites.

At the beginning, creating applications in Flash was quite tricky and only a few brave souls attempted it. Creating Flash animations was a task for graphics designers with IT backgrounds. Scripting capabilities were limited and connectivity to backend services was nonexistent. Since then, Flash has evolved from a pure graphics and animation package into a scriptable application with the introduction of ActionScript and later with the move from ActionScript to ECMAScript. ECMAScript (ecma-262) is the vendor-neutral version of Netscape's JavaScript that allows anybody who knows JavaScript, with little to no learning curve, to script Flash applications.

Other additions to Flash, such as connectivity via HTTP, provided more push for Flash as an application platform; however, creating useful applications was difficult due to Flash's history as a cell-animation product, a concept that has nothing in common with application development.

Adobe Flex

With the introduction of Adobe Flex, an XML-based application language that provides a comfortable and developer-friendly way to describe applications, it was suddenly easy to create an application and leverage the Flash rendering technique on the client. Areas such as client-side validations and client-side scripting were as much a part of the results as were rich widgets and user interaction.

Here's an example of a Flex application used to create the Flickr custom component item renderer (from http://learn.adobe.com/wiki/display/Flex/1b.+ Code+Files):

```
<?xml version="1.0" encoding="utf-8"?>
<mx:VBox xmlns:mx="http://www.adobe.com/2006/mxml"
        width="125" height="125"
        horizontalAlign="center"
```

```
paddingBottom="5" paddingLeft="5" paddingRight="5"
paddingTop="5">

<mx:Image
        width="75" height="75"
        source="{data.thumbnail.url}" />

<mx:Text width="100" text="{data.credit}" />
```

`</mx:VBox>`

Using descriptive XML grammar, a developer can easily create an application definition or, alternatively, use Flex Builder, the integrated development environment (IDE) for Adobe Flex. These Flex applications can contain UI definitions and ECMAScript-based business logic that facilitates both client-side logic and communication with backend services. The application is deployed to the Flex server and, upon request by a client, translated into bytecode the Flash plug-in can understand and render. Because Flash was originally designed with graphics in mind, Flex applications can be skinned, adjusting their look and feel according to guidelines and standards, making it quite easy to produce sophisticated looking web applications.

In the example shown in Figure 6-1, a creative UI was added on top of data from Digg.com. As you can see, Flex can be used for endeavors more creative than simple

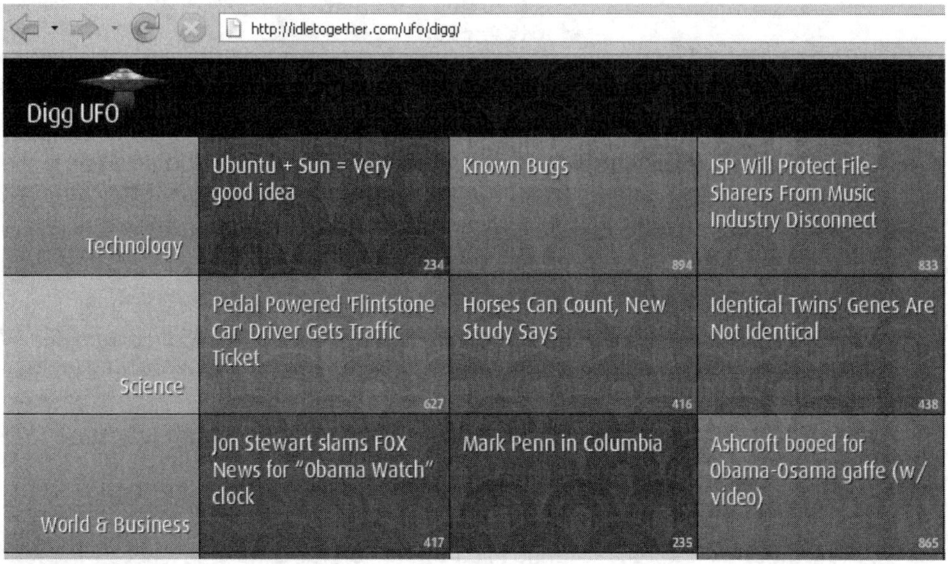

FIGURE 6-1   Alternative UI to access Digg.com postings

applications, but at the same time its history as an application development platform is apparent when you look at the elements available for creating those applications.

Flex can be very helpful in providing highly interactive front-end elements for Web 2.0 services.

OpenLaszlo

With OpenLaszlo, developers use a combination of XML and JavaScript (also called LZX code) to describe an application. The server infrastructure then translates the application into either Flash bytecode or DHTML. OpenLaszlo evolved from a Laszlo Systems product into this open source framework for building applications.

Through an XML grammar, an application developer describes the UI of the application and respective logic, independent of the resulting output technology. In the following example we simply create a radio group to select an option out of a list of three:

```
[...]
            <tabslider width="250" height="200">
                <tabelement text="Select one" selected="true">
                    <radiogroup>
                        <radiobutton text="my option 1"/>
                        <radiobutton text="my option 2"/>
                        <radiobutton text="my option 3"/>
                    </radiogroup>
                </tabelement>


            </tabslider>
[...]
```

Like Adobe Flex, OpenLaszlo is a development framework targeting proper applications, and not quite Web 2.0 scenarios that focus on web pages. Its ability to render DHTML, however, makes it a viable solution for application-like Web 2.0 scenarios. If your goal is to provide a non-weblike experience to your users, OpenLaszlo might be a viable solution.

Other Technologies

A few other technologies can be used to create Web 2.0 experiences for users. Most of them are either platform- or operating system–dependent.

Microsoft Silverlight

Microsoft Silverlight is technically a subset of the Windows Presentation
Foundation (WPF) that requires a small plug-in on the client to render Silverlight
applications. Using Extensible Application Markup Language (XAML),
developers can create applications that are executed through the Silverlight
plug-in. Currently the plug-in is available for Windows and Mac platforms, but
Microsoft has promised to widen the platform support for Silverlight.

One big advantage of Silverlight is that it is based on the Windows
infrastructure, so developers familiar with .NET and XAML programming can
easily create applications using Silverlight.

Here's an example of Silverlight source code used to create a web page (from
www.wynapse.com):

```
<Canvas
   xmlns="http://schemas.microsoft.com/client/2007"
   xmlns:x="http://schemas.microsoft.com/winfx/2006/xaml">

   <Canvas.Triggers>
      <EventTrigger RoutedEvent="Canvas.Loaded" >
         <BeginStoryboard>
            <Storyboard x:Name="animation" Storyboard.
             TargetProperty="(Canvas.Left)"
             RepeatBehavior="Forever" >
               <DoubleAnimation Storyboard.
                TargetName="ScrollingText" From="0" To="-820"
                Duration="0:0:10"  />
               <DoubleAnimation Storyboard.
                TargetName="ScrollingText2" From="820" To="0"
                Duration="0:0:10"  />
            </Storyboard>
         </BeginStoryboard>
      </EventTrigger>
   </Canvas.Triggers>


   <TextBlock x:Name="ScrollingText" FontFamily="Comic Sans MS"
FontSize="36" Foreground="Green"  Text="This is a medium-length
TextBlock scrolling left" />
   <TextBlock x:Name="ScrollingText2" FontFamily="Comic Sans MS"
```

```
FontSize="36" Foreground="Green" Text="This is a medium-length
TextBlock scrolling left" />
</Canvas>
```

Java Applets

Integrating Java applets within web pages has been the standard way of achieving highly responsive elements on a web page. Applets are downloaded and started within the context of the page and therefore provide the "zero-install concept" that users demand. The biggest shortcoming in the Web 2.0 context is the load applets put on the client and their overall limitation to integrate seamlessly into a web page. Like Flash or other plug-in–based concepts, Java applets can replace a certain area on the screen with dynamic content, but integrating the Java content with other elements on the page can be difficult and requires extra coding efforts.

Over time, applets have become more of a technology used to create web applications and less of a way to create dynamic elements on a web page.

ActiveX Controls

ActiveX controls have been used to enhance the functionality of websites for a long time. ActiveX, limited to Windows platforms and Internet Explorer, provides a way to enhance the UI as well as the functionality of a website. Lately, due to its ability to contact the world outside the browser's sandbox, ActiveX has become a prime target for virus developers. Security measures sometimes include disabling ActiveX as a whole and have resulted in serious discussion around the use of ActiveX on websites.

Especially within enterprise environments, the ability to execute ActiveX is usually restricted and requires, at least, a user's explicit approval. For Web 2.0 environments that deal with users of different levels, visiting a website can be a confusing experience, requiring the user to approve the execution of ActiveX controls. Furthermore, given the current environment, users might fail to approve a control, in fear that it might be a virus.

User Interface Languages

Instead of traditional HTML/XHTML, new UI languages have lately been introduced. Their common goal was to provide a descriptive UI layer that would rely on backend services for providing the processing logic for the application.

Examples such as Mozilla's XML User Interface Language (XUL) and Microsoft's WINForms show the main idea behind the UI languages: They basically use existing rendering environments such as a browser or the operating system to render rich interfaces for the benefit of the user's experience. So far, none of these languages has taken off as a standalone concept. XUL has had a head start over WINForms, but it is used only in the context of various Mozilla projects, including the Firefox browser, the Thunderbird e-mail client, and the calendaring application Sunbird. XUL is also used to create UIs for extensions to the Mozilla applications.

WINForms, part of the new Microsoft Windows Presentation Foundation, is included in the framework introduced with Windows Vista and might eventually gain traction as a way to create application front ends. WINForms will, however, likely have no major impact on Web 2.0 enabling applications, mainly due to their platform limitations of the associated browser or the associated operating system.

The following example for XUL syntax is from the Mozilla Developer Center (http://developer.mozilla.org/en/docs/XUL):

```
[...]
<groupbox>
  <caption label="These buttons tab oddly." />
  <hbox>
    <button flex="1" label="6" tabindex="6" oncommand="setText
    ('tab-text','6');" />
    <button flex="1" label="3" tabindex="3" oncommand="setText
    ('tab-text','3');" />
    <button flex="1" label="4" tabindex="4" oncommand="setText
    ('tab-text','4');" />
    <button flex="1" label="2" tabindex="2" oncommand="setText
    ('tab-text','2');" />
    <button flex="1" label="5" tabindex="5" oncommand="setText
    ('tab-text','5');" />
    <button flex="1" label="1" tabindex="1" oncommand="setText
    ('tab-text','1');" />
  </hbox>
  <hbox pack="center">
    <description  id="tab-text" value="(no input yet)" />
  </hbox>
</groupbox>

[...]
```

WINForms, or its associated XAML, has found its way into Microsoft Silverlight. These technologies will likely impact the ability to bring Web 2.0 services to the desktop and integrate them seamlessly into a user's environment.

Adobe AIR

Following on the idea behind Adobe Flex, Adobe AIR was introduced to allow Flex-based RIAs to be executed outside a browser environment, just like proper client-server applications. Given that Web 2.0 deals with websites, and not so much with standalone applications, Adobe AIR has not impacted Web 2.0.

Mozilla Prism

Mozilla Prism, formally known as WebRunner, is a project that provides a standalone environment to run XUL applications to execute them outside the scope of a Mozilla browser. Technically, Prism is an application-specific browser whose purpose is to execute an XUL application; it is not for normal web browsing, so it provides the execution environment for the XUL application.

AJAX with Active Update

The technologies discussed so far allow rich interaction and client-side business logic to create rich user experiences. Common across all of them is the delivery from the server to the client in a "pull" fashion. The client requests the application from the server or requests data later on in the execution. This model works well with data that does not update or information that does not grow over time and requires frequent updates; otherwise the inflow of data would have to be buffered until the next request comes in from the client to fetch the latest set of data.

The nature of the HTTP used in most cases that involve web applications is a *request/response model*, in which only a request can trigger a response, and does not involve a socket model, in which communication can be initiated from either peers involved and responses can be sent independent of requests. To provide the server with the ability to maintain a connection to the client to push data actively, AJAX was extended by another technique that leverages the concept—streaming or long polling (see Figure 6-2). Streaming leverages a persistent HTTP connection to communicate events back from the server to the client, which can then interpret the payload that was returned from the server and act accordingly. With long polling, a single persistent HTTP connection is responsible only for a single event. If more events are being handled in a single application, each one requires its own long poll.

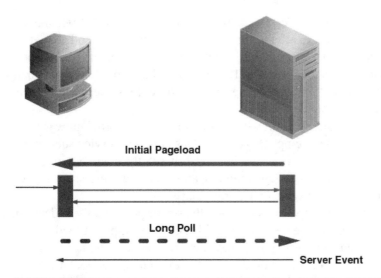

FIGURE 6-2   The concept of long polling to facilitate an active communication channel

A big disadvantage of this technique is the dramatic increase in required server resources. Most web servers or containers are not yet built with this model in mind, so the amount of threads required to deal with those requests and the associated memory requirements can increase by 15 to 20 times that of a Web 1.0 application. Nevertheless, allowing real-time updates via those channels is essential for some types of applications, where responses cannot be predicted and permanent polling for changes would increase the load on the server as well.

This kind of communication can be implemented in several ways, one being the infinite method whereby a request is created to be rendered in an iFrame on the page that is of 0 dimension or located off the actual render windows. The connections are established upon request of the client through the iFrame tag, but the connection is held until the server is ready to deliver the content. At that point, the server sends back JavaScript code, and since web pages are rendered incrementally, each script that is spooled back from the server is executed after it is delivered completely. This way, the server can send back multiple scripts that would then cause the actions required on the client machine.

Another method is to use XMLHttpRequest (XHR) to persist such a connection and process a multipart message or streams through JavaScript. In this case, a callback function would be executed each time a complete message was received. One downside of this technique is that, according to HTTP 1.1. specifications, a single user client should not maintain more than two connections back to the server, which could cause interference between Comet and AJAX when it comes to sending requests. A way around this is to separate the AJAX and Comet connections onto different hostnames and therefore fulfill the HTTP 1.1 specs. Because this technique relies on HTTP connections being held open for an unusual amount of time without any data being transferred, proxy servers and firewalls can actually cause this technique to fail.

The most obvious use case in which Comet is the most efficient was to go is a web-based instant messaging (IM) client. Consider a IM service such as Meebo (www.meebo.com). Its goal is to provide a web-based IM client environment. IM services are inherently a two-way communication channel—messages go between client and server and vice versa on a regular basis.

The simplest approach would be to poll the server periodically to determine whether new messages have been received. This, however, puts a load on the network, as the frequent polling uses some kind of message and hence creates network traffic. It also puts load on the client to execute some type of code permanently that facilitates the polling, and, last but not least, it creates load on the server to answer all the polling requests from all the clients. A much more straightforward approach would be to keep a channel open from the server, so the server can push new messages directly to the client, and that is exactly what happens in these cases to achieve the IM-style message transfer where information is not only submitted from the client but also pushed to the client from the server.

Other use cases, such as stock tickers, analytic applications, real-time analysis of transaction data, and system management information, are also supporting this important concept, such as Comet or other comparable technologies that effectively allow active communication from the server to the client.

One consideration when designing applications with a push mechanism should be how the clients are connected to the server. With HTTP being a stateless protocol, frequent connection drops can negate the benefits of the push mechanism as the permanent connection would have to be re-established if its breakdown was detected.

As you can see, quite a few technologies are available and can be leveraged to provide a beneficial user experience. In many cases, a combination of technologies can provide the best possible Web 2.0 experience for the user.

Especially with AJAX as the underlying technology, classical development frameworks are enriched by component libraries that allow application creation without considering AJAX or how it must be implemented.

When approaching a Web 2.0 project, or one that should eventually fall into that category, the decision for an implementation model and the respective technology stack can be a tricky one. First and foremost, the target audience and their access mechanisms to the resulting application or site should be considered.

If all users connect via broadband, mixing and matching HTML-based and other technologies is the way to go, since the main purpose—to provide a highly interactive UI—can be achieved without jeopardizing the overall performance of the system.

In scenarios in which the user population connects to the system via high-latency connections or with limited bandwidth, a pure HTML approach might be best. In this case, even such considerations as the traffic caused by AJAX traveling between the client and the server should be considered. If indeed the communication could end up being a problem, technologies such as applets or plug-in–based technologies could provide beneficial impacts, where the win of allowing a lot of client-side business logic could outweigh the cost of the initial download of the bytecode.

Once you have chosen an implementation concept, your next decision is determining whether your application can satisfy the requirements by using a simple push model or whether you need to employ concepts such as Comet or some other active data channel back to the client. In some cases, custom implementations based on socket communication might be necessary.

Chapter 7

The APIs: Interfaces and Ecosystems

By Philipp Weckerle

Having hundreds of millions of people globally connected together pervasively via one single high speed /two-way network (aka the Internet) will result in many of the things we're now seeing in the marketplace. It seems a fundamental new widespread focus on leveraging that two-way aspect of the network deeply in our online products, as well as increasingly playing to the fundamental strengths of the network that is the Web, is teaching us invaluable lesson after invaluable new lesson for our businesses. The result is that the living laboratory of the Web is now the source of the greater part of our innovation in business these days. Today's World Wide Web is a larger ecosystem and with far more brainpower and activity than any single organization could ever hope to match.

Dion Hinchcliffe, ZDNet

Now that you're familiar with the variety of aspects encompassed by Web 2.0 technology, it's time to put it all into the context of an enterprise environment. The preceding chapters covered the cornerstone services of Web 2.0 and the roles these services play in the public Internet. These services are usually exposed as part of a closed-box system that combines them into one experience for their users and members.

At an enterprise level, the goal is usually to enable these services as part of a larger application and within the scope of that application. For this purpose, integration layers are required to be in place between these services and applications, and in some cases integration is required across services.

Layer Integration

Integration possibilities exist at different layers. The most traditional route is to expose capabilities via Web services (in most cases, using Simple Object Access Protocol, SOAP, as the grammar for the payload). Web services can also be leveraged to bridge technology gaps between applications, such as .NET and Java applications.

A multitude of limitations can be associated with the use of Web services. First and foremost is the security aspect. Web services, or SOAP over HTTP, is implemented pretty much in clear text. Because of this, any confidential information could be accessed by unauthorized individuals, and it is difficult for the Web service to determine whether or not the requestor is actually an authorized party. To boost security, any communication between publisher and consumer needs to be encrypted; this is usually accomplished via the HTTPS protocol.

Encryption will prevent others from listening in on the SOAP communication between publisher and consumer, but it does not necessarily solve the issue of authenticating the consumer against the publisher. This could be accomplished via login operations, but since HTTP is a stateless protocol, keeping sessions logged in involves application-specific coding.

Session-based authentication is fine if the Web service is a single operation service, but Web 2.0 usually involves a series of interactions with a single service performing a task. In this case, it is easier to authenticate the consumer via a *shared secret concept*, where publisher and consumer share some certificate or a public-private key in order for the publisher to ensure the validity of the consumer.

Looking further into the way Web 2.0 services are integrated, two main approaches emerge:

- The integration happens on the backend, where the application connects to the backend service providers and its functionality surfaces via its own user interface.

- Services are integrated and aggregated on the client side using business logic in JavaScript.

In some cases, such as those in which all services are from the same vendor, integration might be feasible at the user interface (UI) level, but more often, services are already tightly integrated to begin with. The more common concept is a backend application that facilitates the aggregation simply because of the complexity usually involved with integration of disparate services, especially in a best of breed scenario.

Representational State Transfer

Representational State Transfer (REST) is a concept introduced in 2000 by computer scientist Roy Fielding, one of the authors of the HTTP specification. It focuses on more effective ways to communicate between Web front-end and backend services using regular HTTP-based communication. A basic concept of REST is how resources are defined and addressed directly from a URL; a different design is required when it comes to Web services. Here's an example of a product information Web service: Traditionally you would address a Web service with a URI and pass in a parameter to identify the resource—in this case a product (for example, *http://myURI.com/service/productInfo?id=12345*). With REST, you would address resources directly via a URI that could look something like this: *http://myURI.com/service/productInfo/12345*.

You might think that REST is a brand new type of Web service, but it's simply a new concept implemented like any other Web service. When designing a Web service the REST way, the main focus is on resources. For example, if we look at a simple people management application that would allow a developer to query, create, and delete entries from a repository, the classic remote procedure call (RPC) approach would provide different objects on the network for these operations:

```
createUser();
updateUser();
queryUser();
deleteUser();
```

In a REST scenario, the focus is on the resource:

```
http://example.com/users/
http://example.com/users/{user}
```

Each resource would be controlled by regular operations such as GET, POST, PUT, and DELETE:

```
Resource r = new Resource("http://example.com/users/001");
r.delete();
```

An example for REST-style APIs are the server-side integration points for Google's OpenSocial. For example, to query user information, you would use this:

```
http://domain/feeds/people/UserID
```

Or to get the "friends" of a particular user, you would submit this:

```
http://domain/feeds/people/UserID/friends
```

In this particular case, the service will return an XML document containing the requested information.

One of the issues with Web services is the transfer of payload. Traditionally, with RPC-style Web services, payloads are serialized using XML. While the XML can be deserialized easily when using regular programming languages, with JavaScript and its interpretive nature, deserializing large amounts of XML data can significantly decrease performance. In addition, the serialization of data can be complex, and creating the serialized XML can sometimes pose a challenge.

The ideal would be to have some mechanism that would let you easily create a serialized version of a data structure, send it via the response of the Web service, and deserialize it on the consuming end.

JavaScript Object Notation

JavaScript Object Notation (JSON) is a lightweight concept of describing hierarchical data in a format that can be easily read and written by both humans and applications by providing a serialized version of an array structure. Because it is lightweight, it is ideal as a basis for Asynchronous JavaScript and XML (AJAX) communication. Here's an example:

```
{
    "firstName": "John",
    "lastName": "Smith",
    "address": {
        "streetAddress": "21 2nd Street",
        "city": "New York",
        "state": "NY",
        "postalCode": "10021"
    },
    "phoneNumbers": [
        "212 555-1234",
        "646 555-4567"
    ]
}
```

Example: JSON Object

If you assume the JSON object is processed in a JavaScript application, you could use the `eval()` function. In the following example, the preceding JSON object would be stored in `JSON_array`:

```
var p = eval("(" + JSON_array + ")");
```

Example: eval() statement

`eval()` executes a string as if it were a script. In the JSON case, the result will be an array that could be further processed in the application. As you can see, this method of transmitting data is much easier to process on the client side than the traditional communication methods, such as SOAP-based Web services.

When implementing the service, the main consideration should be the target consumer. If the focus is on another application, SOAP might be the way to go, as it will simplify the communication with the service. If, however, the client is supposed to be an AJAX front end, JSON is much easier to evaluate and process due to the somewhat limiting capabilities of JavaScript.

Other more service-specific implementation approaches would be at the respective protocol level, such as the Session Initiation Protocol (SIP) for communication and presence, Internet Message Access Protocol (IMAP) for messaging, and so on. Although these approaches are service-independent, they are also generic and require that you implement your own abstraction layer to expose meaningful APIs to your applications to integrate those services.

More Specialized Approaches

In addition to the low-level APIs described so far, you can use more specialized methods for connecting your Web 2.0 ecosystem. The term *ecosystem* implies a set of services that are loosely coupled to create the infrastructure upon which your Web 2.0 experience is built.

Today, although relatively new, Web 2.0 is on the verge of becoming more than a collection of commonly used services; it is evolving into a platform that can be leveraged to deliver services to users and applications. To become that platform, however, Web 2.0 delivery and access need to be standardized.

As with any platform, vendors initially tried to provide their own sets of services as closed-box solutions users could leverage online. Consider Facebook, for example, which was intended to provide a social networking platform on which people could connect and share. Eventually, connecting with others and sharing assets proved to be only a part of the growing demand for networking capabilities. The requirements for enhancing the platform grew, and eventually Facebook decided to introduce an API that would allow developers to create applications that could leverage certain aspects of Facebook (such as the list of friends of a user) to integrate into their own flow and link back to the Facebook system by triggering events, such as updates or news. In this way, external applications could be integrated and could leverage the social networking capabilities of Facebook.

The biggest drawback is that these applications really aren't external to Facebook but have to run within the scope of Facebook on its canvas page (Figure 7-1) for a variety of reasons. They therefore have become an extension of Facebook more than anything else.

In 2007, Google started the OpenSocial initiative, with the goal of providing an open, common API for social networking. Rather than creating yet another social networking platform, Google tried to convince partners, such as Plaxo, Friendster, Oracle, and others, to provide their services via this open API so other application vendors could integrate with them. OpenSocial is based on the Google Gadget framework and consists of a set of JavaScript and REST APIs that provide access to data from within the social network.

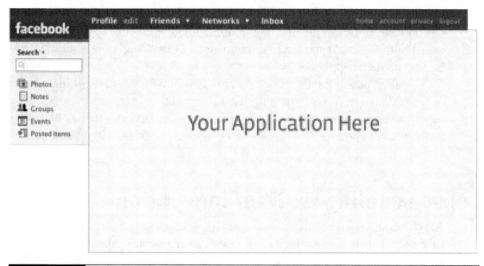

FIGURE 7-1   The Facebook canvas page

The following example shows how easy it is to send a request to an OpenSocial platform. The `onLoadFriends` class would contain the data returned from the service and expose it to the application.

```
/**
 * Request for friend information when the page loads.
 */
function getData() {
  var req = opensocial.newDataRequest();
  req.add(req.newFetchPersonRequest(opensocial.DataRequest.
    PersonId.VIEWER), 'viewer');
  req.add(req.newFetchPeopleRequest(opensocial.DataRequest.Group.
    VIEWER_FRIENDS), 'viewerFriends');
  req.send(onLoadFriends);
};
```

Example: OpenSocial "Retrieve Friends"

By using this common API, developers can create applications independent of the actual hosting framework. These applications can integrate with any environment that supports OpenSocial. Social applications that are based on OpenSocial connect to the backend social networking service using the OpenSocial services provider interface (SPI) and provide gadgets to expose their functionality.

A number of hosted service providers have committed to supporting OpenSocial. For example, in conjunction with OpenSocial, a new Apache project called Shindig was launched to implement an OpenSocial container to allow the hosting of social applications.

OpenSocial and the Facebook API are tied in with the networking aspect of Web 2.0 and used for managing friends and activity streams, but they do not supply a means of integrating the different Web 2.0 services themselves. When it comes to integrating different services, traditional integration methods are still required.

Loose Coupling vs. Tight Integration

Another interesting consideration is the loose coupling of services that otherwise have no connection to each other. Loose coupling occurs when an overarching service takes over the orchestration and connection between the underlying services. In a way, this can be done using the OpenSocial approach, where the scope would be the social network and the integration would be the container (platform) on which the social applications are running.

The central characteristics of loose coupling are the connections between artifacts of disparate services that form relationships and the semantics that might otherwise have been overlooked. These connection services are usually custom to whatever application implements them. An example of a generic approach to this would be Oracle's WebCenter links service. WebCenter is Oracle's Web 2.0 platform consisting of various disparate services that are connected using the open-links service. Any service that is added to the framework can join the links services and by that become part of the bigger picture.

Enterprise 2.0 Challenges in a Web 2.0 World

When we take a closer look at the services integrated into applications, we discover that many services do not satisfy the requirements an enterprise deployment imposes on them. With all the services out there on the Internet, requirements for reliability and availability, as well as security, are not quite up to the standards usually defined by many corporations for their internal systems.

This can be easily explained by the heritage of those services on the Internet. Like Web 1.0, these brave new services were conceived through personal requirements and ideas and with only those in mind. No business aspects and "what-if-when" scenario considerations were required to be in the picture. Level of service was only a secondary concern and usually only in systems that were created for the commercial market. When it comes to enterprise deployments, however, those "afterthoughts" often become the first and foremost criteria that determine the feasibility of implementing these services. Today, however, the list of service types that can be considered "enterprise ready" is steadily growing.

When considering individual services for implementation in the enterprise, several aspects are important to include: First and foremost, with the fast-moving industry in mind, any service you integrate should provide either standardized methods for integration or prebuilt integration components so that your system is open to changes and enhancements in the future. Usually a number of different flavors of a particular service are available. Consider instant messaging (IM) as an example. Over time, a number of systems have evolved to enterprise grade and a number of protocols are being used—while some are proprietary, such as the YMSG protocol used by Yahoo!, others are standardized, such as Extensible Messaging and Presence Protocol (XMPP) or the Session Initiation Protocol (SIP). Looking at this from another angle, multipurpose protocols, such as SIP, that can cover more than one service or capability, are certainly favorable.

Another aspect to consider when implementing these services is whether your company wants to invest in creating the necessary infrastructure to host these services or whether it should go with a hosted solution. For less traditional services, this might not even be an option, as no hosting offerings may be available. More traditional services, however, can often be hosted, which can lower the total cost of ownership (TCO) and therefore make them more affordable.

In addition, when choosing certain services, your company must comply with any rules and regulations that might apply. For example, your company might be required to keep records of any type of conversation that occurs between its employees and external parties. While e-mail archiving is a fairly common capability, other types of communication, such as IM or messages via social networking platforms, might not be auditable and could cause your company to violate these regulations.

Another important aspect in enterprise deployments is security. While a lot of enterprises have standardized on a certain authentication and identity management topology, integrating those new services into existing infrastructures is usually a huge undertaking. In some cases, a direct integration might not even be possible. In these cases, the concept of external application integration should be considered, where credentials of the individual services are securely managed with the user's identity in the corporate identity management system.

Choosing Services

Any ecosystem's key to survival is the coexistence of different species—in our case, that means different services. This coexistence is controlled by various factors—first and foremost, individuality. To survive and contribute, each service needs to have distinct characteristics and its own unique purpose. For this reason, when it comes to choosing what services to implement, you should first inventory the services that have already been deployed internally. The goal is to ensure that none of the new services overlap significantly with existing ones. An analysis might reveal that service overlap exists; in such a case, you could perform a controlled replacement or postpone the introduction of the new system.

The second consideration should focus on the integration and commonality that exists between those services (old and new), and also through what channels and what places the services should be exposed to the users. Last, but not least, you should consider to what degree these services should be integrated or whether it is more beneficial to keep certain services on their own, resulting in higher value and productivity for the user.

Chapter 8

Security and Compliance: Maintaining Control While Providing Flexibility

By Vince Casarez

Since Web 2.0 platforms enable anyone to upload content, these sites are easily susceptible to hackers wishing to upload malicious content. Once the malicious content has been uploaded, innocent visitors to these sites can also be infected, and the site owners could be potentially responsible for damages incurred.

Yuval Ben-Itzhak, *SC Magazine*

With businesses investing in and adopting applications leveraging Web 2.0 technologies, it is imperative that applications be designed to address not only the same security issues and regulations as any other enterprise-class application, but also the new security concerns specific to Web 2.0 technologies.

Applications consuming Web 2.0 technologies are being adopted in the enterprise at a faster than expected pace. In this rush to adopt, architects and designers sometimes overlook security aspects that can hurt their businesses and leave them noncompliant with the tight regulatory and governance laws in force today. It is important to be aware of the security vulnerabilities and gaps that Web 2.0 applications can expose.

In addition, collaborative applications are stretching the boundaries of the enterprise. Web 2.0 services such as wikis and blogs have gained popularity and are being adopted at a feverish pace, because they can provide significant productivity for the knowledge worker who is constantly in need of subject matter expertise and information in general. Publishing and sharing content via blogs and wikis can get the quick attention of an audience that could not be reached before these technologies were available.

Some corporations are encouraging their employees to contribute to public blogs—whether to create brand awareness or simply to evangelize their products. In doing so, however, these companies risk losing proprietary and confidential information. In some cases, employees have inadvertently disclosed information about products that have not yet been released and put their employers in a difficult position in the marketplace. Information leaks can cost companies a lot of money. To prevent such issues from occurring, companies must draft strict blogging policies for their employees and must constantly police employee blogs to make sure that sensitive information is not being released to the public.

Corporations that deal with customer, financial, or healthcare data must identify potential threats and vulnerabilities to which they could be exposed by the adoption of Web 2.0 technologies or services into the enterprise. Financial institutions are bound by legal and regulatory compliance guidelines by entities such as the US Securities and Exchange Commission (SEC) in terms of sharing and timing of availability of data. The task of making these services compliant is especially difficult since the compliance policies themselves are still evolving.

The following considerations and measures must be taken into account when adopting Web 2.0 technologies into an enterprise to maintain the current level of security, compliance, and regulatory needs.

Mature Application Frameworks

Enterprise Web 2.0 applications use the same rich UI technologies used by their counterpart applications in the consumer space. Using technologies such as AJAX, developers can create a rich UI experiences by leveraging the XMLHttpRequest (XHR) API to request a URL without refreshing the browser page as discussed in Chapters 6 and 7. Such highly dynamic applications pose greater security risks than typical web applications, in which the interaction between the presentation layer and the backend server(s) is controlled to some extent. In the same way, applications built using technologies such as JavaScript Object Notation (JSON) are prone to JSON hijacking, which builds on cross-site request forgery (CSRF) to allow a malicious "service" to intercept data. In an application with a lot of functionality built into the presentation layer, it is typical for designers to implement security checks on the client side without adding access control checks on the server side.

To address these concerns, developers should consider using mature UI frameworks such as those based on JavaServer Faces (JSF). Oracle ADF Faces, based on JSF, provides numerous rich, reusable UI components. Partial page rendering functionality allows defined areas of a page to refresh without refreshing the entire browser page. Such rich UI functionality comes with a security framework built upon a pluggable architecture using Java Authentication and Authorization Service (JAAS). The framework comes with "security-aware" model layer objects and predefined component-specific permissions. ADF security also includes authorization editors, which let developers manage security policies while developing applications.

Figure 8-1 shows Oracle ADF security in action, depicting a use case in which a user attempts to execute an action against an ADF Faces page (a protected resource) that has a defined grant. If the user is not yet authenticated, the application displays the login page or form. If the user has been authenticated, Oracle ADF security checks to see whether the user is a principal defined in the grant. If the user does not have the appropriate permissions, a security error is displayed.

Application development frameworks can provide authorization provisioning editors with resources such as a JSF page that can be leveraged in placing

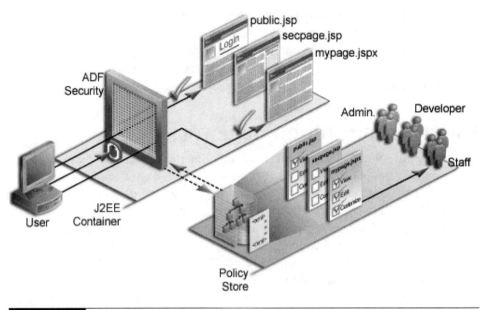

FIGURE 8-1   Oracle ADF security authorization

permissions while developing the application. Figure 8-2 shows an Authorization Editor that helps the developer place permissions for editing, customizing, personalizing, and viewing a page.

Many Web 2.0 applications leverage capabilities to consume web feeds, such as Really Simple Syndication (RSS), to keep track of the changes occurring in the system. Applications need to be careful to guard against vulnerabilities exposed by the feeds. A feed can often find ways to steal cookies, execute programs, and log keyboard clicks that can be played back at a later time for nefarious purposes. Schemes such as injecting an `<img src>` tag can make an unsuspecting user connect to a malicious site.

Service Layer Security and Compliance Policy

A conventional enterprise application can benefit by leveraging Web 2.0 services. For example, to resolve a trouble ticket, a customer service representative can use a Web 2.0–style application to create an ad hoc community and invite the necessary participants to collaborate and resolve the issue. This type of community could use a multitude of services including discussion forums and wikis in which

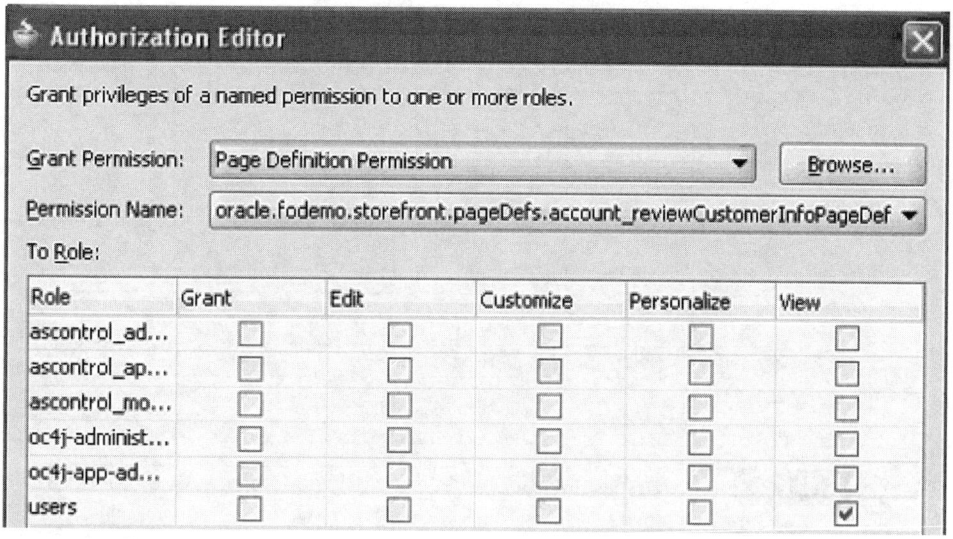

FIGURE 8-2 Authorization Editor for an ADF page (based on JSF)

participants can share ideas and provide feedback; content services that enable sharing and publishing documents; and tagging services that help classify, share, and find information. Each service should be responsible for protecting the resources and information it exposes; thus it is important that security be enforced at the service layer.

Unfortunately, security enforcement in Web 2.0 applications often takes place in the presentation layer, because these applications integrate content from different sources (both inside and outside the firewall) within the presentation layer (commonly referred to as a *mashup*). It is recommended that developers leverage frameworks that help build and assemble the services and the content they expose on the server side, thereby providing server-side components that act as a proxy to the various services. Placing policy enforcement on the server side frees the UI developer from putting authorization calls in the UI layer, and, more important, it lets developers use the various server-side frameworks for security enforcement.

Figure 8-3 shows the security extension mechanism for Oracle's WebCenter Framework. The Web 2.0 services can leverage this extension mechanism to implement their own security checks and security provisioning. Each service defines the security model in a declarative fashion in its security extension. For example, the service will annotate the implementation class that the framework should call when the security provisioning or checks are to be made. The

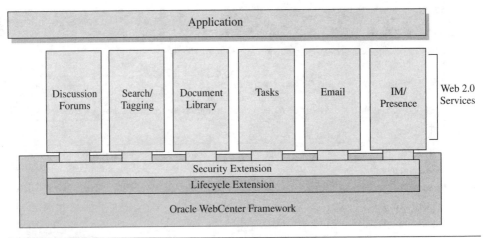

FIGURE 8-3   Extensible security model for easily adding new Web 2.0 services

implementation class dictates how to execute permission checks based on its backend store and specific needs in general. Therefore, the application is relieved of the responsibility of performing authorization checks on each service's behalf.

Just as each service takes the responsibility of enforcing security, each may also support mechanisms for the purposes of complying with the regulations and policies set forth by the business. This translates to the application adding schemes for digital signatures and having secure audit logs based on the required granularity. This is important for nonrepudiation purposes. Therefore, it is important that frameworks that inherently support auditing be considered when building a Web 2.0 application.

Communication Data Security

Web services have provided the means for interoperability between distributed and disparate applications and services. Web services are highly leveraged by the Web 2.0 enterprise applications in general since they provide a model that lends itself very well to loosely coupled service endpoints.

Messages exchanged between an application and the service over the wire usually contain sensitive data. In fact, most applications consuming these services need to propagate the identity of the user accessing the application. This scheme of propagating user information over the wire using Simple Object Access Protocol (SOAP), a protocol used at the core of the Web services technology, is known as *identity propagation*. Identity propagation helps the service make an authorization decision about whether to surface sensitive data or not. This identity information sent in the SOAP header/message can be prone to tampering. It is therefore important to ensure that the messages, including the identity information flowing between the consuming application and services, be protected.

Attacks such as parameter manipulation, in which the parameters in the SOAP message are manipulated to inject different kinds of programming constructs such as SQL, XPath, and shell scripts, are common. A lot of collaboration Web 2.0 applications interactively let users search data across services. For example, a user using a collaborative application can search across many backend systems such as corporate Lightweight Directory Access Protocol (LDAP), e-mail, discussion forums, and content repositories. Mechanisms such as XPath are used to query data exchanged between the application and the service backends. This means that the user entering a search string triggers a data query. If the application or service does not perform proper input validation, the system can be prone to XPath injection.

Schemes used by attackers can result in extraction of more information than a typical search would provide, so it is important that the application and service developers enforce input validation at both their levels. Input validation schemes should be designed in such a way that only known good input is accepted. Other techniques that can mitigate the risks of XPath injection include parameterized queries that are precompiled and passed parameters instead of user input.

In addition to preventing attacks such as parameter manipulation, you need to ensure that the confidentiality and integrity of the SOAP message is maintained. Two levels of security can be enforced to secure messages—transport-level and message-level security. Both security levels should be used between the application and services in case sensitive data is being exchanged.

Transport-level security is typically achieved by enabling SSL/TLS (Secure Sockets Layer/Transport Layer Security) between the two endpoints: the consuming application and the service. Message-level security is achieved using Web Services Security (WS-Security). A message is considered secure only if the data being passed is confidential and has not been tampered with. XML encryption must be leveraged to maintain data confidentiality and the service's authenticity and integrity ensured using the XML signature. The enterprise application should ensure the kind of token profile (username with optional password digest, Security Assertion Markup Language token, and so on) supported by the service and include it as part of the SOAP header.

Figure 8-4 shows various stages of a SOAP message being processed both on the client and server sides. The client-side interceptor signs, encrypts, and adds a token to the request, which is verified by the service. The response from the service is also securely sent after signing and encrypting the message.

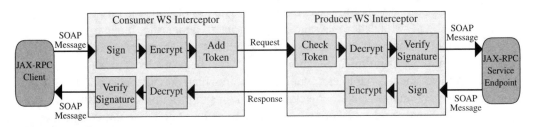

FIGURE 8-4 Message-level security using WS-Security

Web Services Trust (WS-Trust)–based solutions can also be used when trust must be brokered between partner applications. Developers can use mature frameworks such as Oracle Web Services Manager (OWSM) to implement agents (serving as policy enforcement points) that can execute against inbound and outbound Web service calls without affecting the logic of the service. Such frameworks can provide a decentralized platform for configuring policies across services and proactively managing the services being consumed by the application.

One of the difficult tasks in setting up WS-Security is configuring keystores with certificates obtained from a certificate authority (CA) for signing and keys for encryption. Frameworks such as OWSM allow a service to advertise its security requirements in the Web Services Description Language (WSDL) itself, which helps simplify the security configuration.

In addition to SOAP, Web 2.0 services also expose Representational State Transfer (REST)–based interfaces. Unlike SOAP, REST exposes each resource as a URI. REST style is becoming prevalent because it has many advantages. Among other advantages, a REST service's endpoints can be bookmarked like any other URI. Search engines can easily discover these URIs. It is expected that an enterprise application using REST-based services will interact using an HTTP construct such as GET, DELETE, POST, or PUT. Ideally, GET is used to retrieve resource(s), DELETE is used to delete a resource, POST is used to create a resource, and PUT is used to update a resource. Practically speaking, a lot of REST-based implementations use GETs for performing operations such as delete, create, and update as well. Hence, to ensure that the communication is secure, you cannot make any assumptions for securing REST-based services. A simple access control list (ACL)–based enforcement on REST methods may therefore not be enough for REST services that overload the GET construct mentioned. It is important that checks against SQL injection be in place, as REST usage includes parameters being passed in the query string. Appropriate validation in terms of the size and contents of the parameters should also be performed.

Web 2.0 applications use services that help users collaborate in new ways by providing rich collaboration services using technologies such as instant messaging (IM), presence information, and Voice over IP (VoIP). With such services exposed directly into the application (see Figure 8-5 for an example of such an application), users can interact with others seamlessly and in real time. For example, in a collaborative call center application, a sales representative can quickly detect whether her manager is online and send an IM or make a VoIP call to inquire about information she needs to complete a call.

One of the protocols that ties together presence information from all possible channels of communication is the Session Initiation Protocol (SIP). Like any other

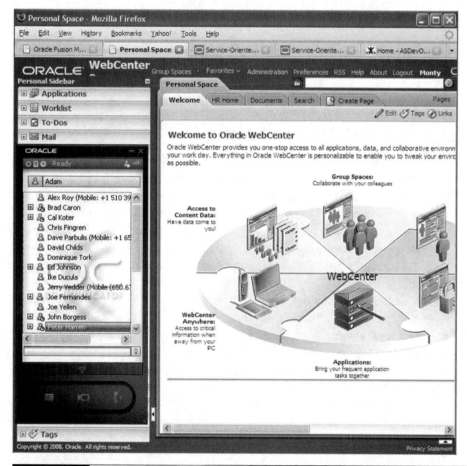

FIGURE 8-5   Application utilizing Web 2.0 services such as IM, presence information, and VoIP

communication, information exchanged to provide the functionality of real-time messaging and presence is prone to security breaches. It is important to ensure that the IMs and presence information being exchanged between the application and the IM server be confidential and tamper-proof. The Web 2.0 services that provide this functionality must ensure that all aspects of security are addressed. The user's identity from the application should be propagated in a secure way. This identity propagation is used to identify the user and make presence information available to others on the system. The messages exchanged should be encrypted for confidentiality and digitally signed for integrity.

Web 2.0 services backends using SIP in general are also prone to security vulnerabilities such as Denial-of-Service (DoS) and "session tear-down" attacks. A DoS attack can occur when the SIP server is swamped with a flood of subscription requests that prevents the server from responding to legitimate requests. A session tear-down attack typically occurs when an unauthenticated user is able to terminate a SIP session. Various hardware and software solutions are designed to counter these attacks and can prevent them when employed.

Identities and Access Control

The role-based access control (RBAC) model is designed to protect privileged resources based on a user's role in the enterprise. Because it reduces the complexity and cost of security provisioning, RBAC is the most prevalent permission model used in enterprise applications today. The "resources" protected using RBAC are mostly created and managed by the administrator of the enterprise application. However, enterprise applications also have to deal with the access control models and implementations of various participating services.

The roles and policy definitions of these services may conform to various schemas and can be different from those of the enterprise application. For example, if an enterprise application consumes a service that provides content management features, a user with a "viewer" role in the application will have a "reader" role in the content management backend. The implementer would thus need to create a new permission model that maps application roles to service roles, so that any user who is granted a "viewer" role in the application is given the corresponding "reader" role on the content management system. Therefore, a contract–service provider interface (SPI) and API, as illustrated in Figure 8-6, needs to be established between the application and participating services to facilitate this new permission model, so that the user has all the access control privileges needed to use the application in a coherent way.

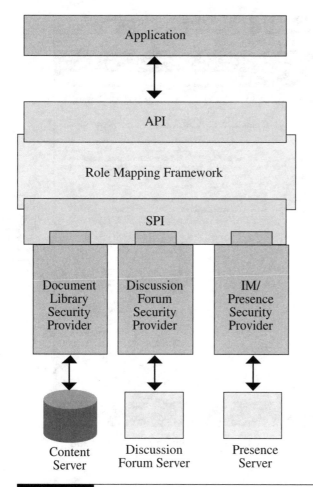

FIGURE 8-6   Architecture for role mapping from one application or service to another

The SPI defines the interfaces that each individual service needs to implement. For example, the *document library* (the service providing content management capabilities) implements a security provider that encapsulates operations to manage permission in its backend policy store.

Provisioning UIs like the one shown in Figure 8-7 can be developed based on the provisioning abilities supplied by the service provider where the administrator of the application can map the application role to the service role.

The distributed nature of services consumed by Web 2.0 applications imposes further requirements on existing identity management solutions. A service may

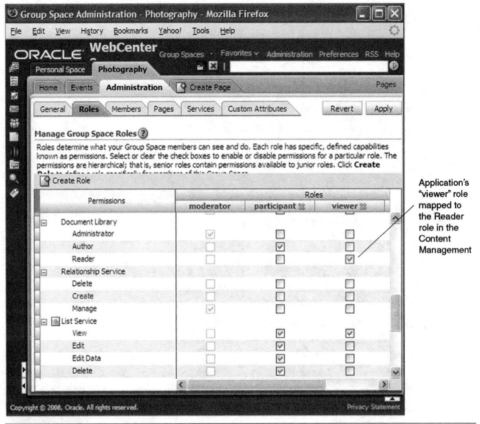

Application's "viewer" role mapped to the Reader role in the Content Management

FIGURE 8-7   Provisioning security for services with a remote backend

house its own identity management store and use an authentication model that's totally different from that of the fronting application. A user may have different identities and credentials in the application's identity store and the service's backend identity store. Credentials for identities need to be mapped using secure credential stores, or identities should be asserted using WS-Security token profiles in case the services expose Web service interfaces.

Administrators must keep all the services' disparate identity and policy stores in sync to avoid security holes and policy proliferation. In addition, it is important to avoid "orphan" policies, or outdated policies for roles that no longer exist, which can cause unintended privileges to be granted to a user. For example, if an orphan policy grants a privilege to a nonexistent role, and an administrator creates a new role with the same name as that in the policy and assigns the role to a user, the user now has privileges to the resources without the administrator explicitly granting those privileges. For such reasons, the application's security provisioning interfaces must be designed in such a way that they proactively manage and maintain the referential integrity between all the service stores.

Figure 8-8 shows a scenario of the security stores (including identity store, policy store, and credential store) with which an application may be interacting. All this related information must be kept in sync.

Managing identities and access control across application and services can be a complicated and error-prone task. Solutions that provide identity management capabilities along with access control services can help in providing a centralized security solution that consists of authentication, policy-based authorization, auditing, and advanced administration functionality such as delegated administration. A solution such as Oracle Access Manager (OAM) that combines identity and access management administration can greatly help in managing applications and services running in a heterogeneous environment.

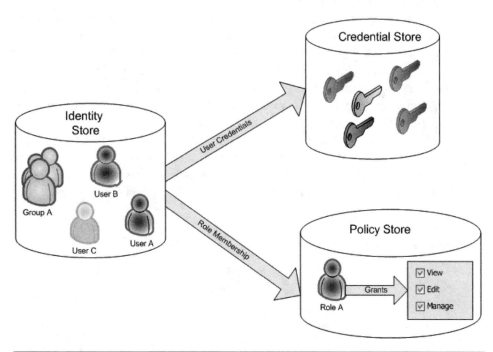

FIGURE 8-8   Users and groups, often managed in a central store, continually update and synchronize their information with credential stores and policy stores.

Proliferation of Identities

Enterprises are building applications that facilitate collaboration with their business partners. To enable this participation, administrators or moderators of the collaborative enterprise application can require an external partner's user to create an account (an identity) in the system before the collaboration begins. Typically, this results in creation of a user account in a corporate identity store. Applications build custom self-registration functionality to enable users to create identities for themselves. This functionality should be carefully designed to consider security issues related to identity creation. Adequate measures should be taken to prevent unintended users from entering a site and creating an identity, thereby causing a proliferation of identities. And, more important, checks should be in place to prevent automated bots or spammers from creating identities repeatedly. You must consider schemes such as CAPTCHA (Completely Automated Public Turing test to tell Computers and Humans Apart) that use a "challenge-response" test to determine whether the user is human. A common CAPTCHA requires that a user identify text from a distorted image and enter it before successfully completing registration, as shown in Figure 8-9.

Explicit targeted invites (via e-mail) should be sent, inviting people to self-register. Usually, this digital invitation should have enough built-in smarts to prevent uninvited users from registering on your site. The URL sent as part of the e-mail can include a token such as a Hash Message Authentication Code (HMAC) key that embeds information, including the e-mail address to which the invite was originally sent, the time of expiry of the token, and context information such as the name of the collaborative community for which the invite is being generated. Other measures, such as having time-based or one-time-use-only tokens, can also be in place. A time-based token expires after a set period of time and can be used one time only. This can prevent automated bots from reusing the token again and again and registering multiple dummy identities into the identity store.

Word Verification: Type the characters you see in the picture below.

Letters are not case-sensitive

FIGURE 8-9   CAPTCHA used on a self-registration form to insure huma confirmation

To control identity creation, introducing a workflow or an explicit business process to approve identity creation can help the administrator maintain total control over who can self-register. Ideally, the identities created by self-registration should be segmented in the identity store. This separates them from the identities created explicitly by the administrator.

Authorization

Since most Web 2.0–based applications are collaborative in nature and involve user-generated content, access control should sometimes be based on user profile attributes rather than just user roles. Based on the use case, the authorization checks can also consider the context in which the request to access a resource is being made.

Services such as *tagging* require finer control if privileged resources are being tagged. For example, if a person tagged a page that only people in his digital community can view, the authorization framework should support functionality that will allow filtering of the tags when a person from another digital community performs a search. In this case, the authorization decision will include the scope or the identifier for the digital community in which the request to access is being made.

One of the widely used features of Web 2.0 applications is social networking. Various security issues must be kept in mind when using the power of social networking within the enterprise. In case of professional social networks, a user within the enterprise must be careful when allowing another person to "join her network," since in doing so, the user may be implicitly allowing another person to access information about the cherished relationships that she has built up with other colleagues. This means that while you may not mind adding someone to your network, your associates may prefer that their personal contact information not be shared with others. Access to such information poses a real threat regarding some forms of identity theft.

It is therefore important to weigh the pros and cons of enabling a social network within the enterprise. If the benefits are in favor of such a network, it will be prudent to use a fine-grained authorization mechanism to limit sharing of user information. The problem can be solved if your security framework supports fine-grained authorization policies that let the user define which of his profile attributes can be shared with his immediate connection versus a connection that is two or more degrees away, for example.

Compliance Policies for Your Business Domain

Organizations face a long list of regulations based on the industry segment to which they belong. For example, the US Health Insurance Portability and Accountability Act (HIPAA) regulation is applicable to institutions that deal with patient information. Some of the other well-known regulations in the United States include Sarbanes-Oxley (SOX) and Gramm-Leach-Bliley Act (GLBA). Regulations such as SOX are broad in scope and do not necessarily enforce a mandate on how enterprise applications per se should deal with protection of financial data. Web 2.0 applications bring new challenges in governance and compliance management. It is important to understand these compliance laws and interpret them into the security requirements they impose on your application.

In today's world, it is a given that almost all of the data is processed and maintained by one or more enterprise IT applications. So, by default, these applications must be secure and must comply with corresponding industry regulations. The compliance becomes especially challenging when the applications leverage and consume Web 2.0 services such as discussion forums or content services that inherently allow users to share and publish content. Architects and designers of enterprise applications leveraging Web 2.0 services must therefore consider development frameworks that will help them not only enforce access control policies but also log and audit any authentication, authorization, or access events. Security frameworks can provide automatic configuration of audit trails that can help ensure and demonstrate that a company is compliant with the regulations.

Security frameworks such as those offered by Oracle provide out-of-the-box support for data privacy by leveraging the support for encryption and secure search, among other things (Figure 8-10).

Although not explicitly called out in SOX restrictions, application security is the most important factor in SOX compliance. Application security involves securing data handled by the application at all stages—from creation to the time it is purged. All along the way, access events on the data must be audited and logged. To achieve complete application security, you need to consider all the approaches detailed in this chapter—from building applications on frameworks with coherent security models to approaches to protect data and identity and enforce fine-grained access control. You must also constantly monitor any security vulnerabilities and new threats that can put the data you protect at risk.

Various Web 2.0 services have made their way into the applications being used in the healthcare industry by doctors, patients, and providers. Huge amounts of patient data are being stored and transmitted digitally. Many doctors' offices

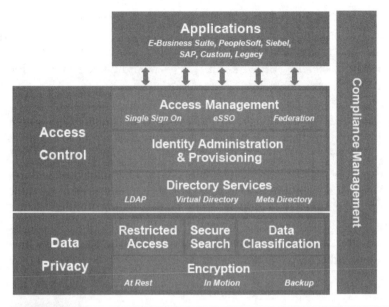

FIGURE 8-10 Oracle security architecture (figure courtesy of Oracle Corporation; see References at the end of this book for more information)

are now digitally transmitting prescription data to pharmacies and foregoing the archaic paper-based systems. The security standards set forth under the HIPAA details specific technical safeguards for the guidance of regulated entities in implementing security for protecting Electronic Protected Health Information (EPHI). The technical safeguards are the technology, policies, and procedures for its use in protecting EPHI and controlling access to it.

The people who put together these technical safeguards clearly understood the penetration of technology solutions in the healthcare industry. These safeguards are careful in not suggesting any specific implementation technologies or approaches, as such suggestions would place a high financial and technical burden on the industry. The regulated entities have been given flexibility in determining which technical solutions they choose to enforce the recommended safeguards.

Some of the standards set forth in HIPAA for compliance directly map to the Web 2.0 services being consumed by doctors, pharmacies, and health insurance companies. Consider the case of a Web 2.0 application that empowers a doctor to send a newly written prescription directly to the pharmacy, which then sends that information to the health insurance provider to determine the patient's coverage. In this scenario, strict HIPAA security rules need to be fulfilled that require transmission integrity controls and encryption.

Web 2.0 applications also provide a means for doctors to participate in discussion forums or use other collaborative services in which they can discuss a particular patient's case to seek advice from colleagues. This use case, for instance, will need to address specific HIPAA security rules regarding person or entity authentication and access control.

Doctors and healthcare professionals are using Web 2.0 applications that require the advanced capabilities of searches that may execute across multiple backends, such as a discussion forum store, content repository, or a data store belonging to another external application. For such a use case, several HIPAA rules regarding audit and access controls must be considered and addressed.

While Web 2.0 technologies aren't inherently secure or insecure, taking a critical look at existing security systems and how they interact with new Web 2.0 deployments is key to protecting any organization. By setting clear guidelines for developers and users, organizations will be able to adhere to new and emerging regulations to provide compliance.

Part III

Best Practices

Chapter 9

Putting Web 2.0 to Use in the Enterprise: Higher Value from Greater Participation

By Jean Sini

When you scale animals you can't just keep everything in proportion. For example, volume grows as the cube of linear dimension, but surface area only as the square. So as animals get bigger they have trouble radiating heat. That's why mice and rabbits are furry and elephants and hippos aren't. You can't make a mouse by scaling down an elephant.

Paul Graham, "A New Venture Animal"

Under its various guises, the Web 2.0 phenomenon has been at the forefront of mindshare in consumer application development and has embodied the revival of the World Wide Web as the ubiquitous computing platform, post bubble, for what qualifies in Internet terms as an eternity. Tim O'Reilly not only helped pioneer and define the Web 2.0 movement, but he also organized the first Web 2.0 conference back in 2004. Whether we focus on its enabling technologies or on its social characteristics and the participatory culture it encourages, Web 2.0 has been the pervasive driving force behind much of the innovation released online, in its trademark state of perpetual beta, since 2004. Yet for all its reach and omnipresence in the consumer space, the read-write Web, and with it all the benefits of rich user experience and social computing, Web 2.0 has been slow to mutate and make deep inroads in the enterprise.

Scale Matters

In venturing to weave key Web 2.0 elements into the cultural fabric of the workplace, we must acknowledge the qualitative differences between the corporate and public spheres, understand how these differences impact the distribution of tools and best practices, and be prepared with countermeasures to palliate the shortcomings of merely transposing from one environment to the other.

Many of the pitfalls encountered when deploying Web 2.0 applications in the enterprise have to do with culture rather than technology. This is not to say that technical and architectural choices don't matter, and important traits to look for in that regard are covered in this chapter. But what is truly going to make or break the value proposition of a solution has to do with adoption. Why? Web 2.0 is all about The Long Tail—it's about participation, about the wisdom of the crowd. It's about harnessing the intelligence diffused throughout the network and bringing it into focus for everyone's benefit. As such, it needs a critical mass to take shape, and, just as important, it needs those forming that mass to become, as famous blogger Kathy Sierra coined it, "passionate users" (see References at the end of the book for source information).

Scale matters. We can't simply deploy the same tools and promote the same behaviors found in the wild and hope that they'll thrive in the scaled-down enterprise ecosystem. Given the typical rate with which people participate, that would pretty much exclude any but the largest corporations from getting anyone to blog, author a wiki article, or otherwise contribute. The transposition is imperfect at best across these two environments, and to survive behind the firewall, Web 2.0 needs to be even better at eliciting involvement. The virtuous feedback loop at play in the most effective contributory services starts with individuals extracting value from their own submissions. Their publicly sharing these contributions yields value to observers, who are then moved to participate, adding to the original contributor's value (see Figure 9-1). It's critical to tend to each step of this cycle as it translates into the workplace, to ensure that it goes on uninterrupted, allowing network effects to develop.

Because enterprise Web 2.0 initiatives need not only match but must exceed, in terms of participation, the levels seen in the consumer space, we must take stock of the fundamental differences in motivation and barriers driving and limiting deployment and adoption to achieve critical mass. And when it comes to driving usage, at least some of the consumer web applications have catered to the thirst for entertainment manifest in the public: Whether watching and voting on popular YouTube videos, reading and commenting on friends' LiveJournal diaries, or

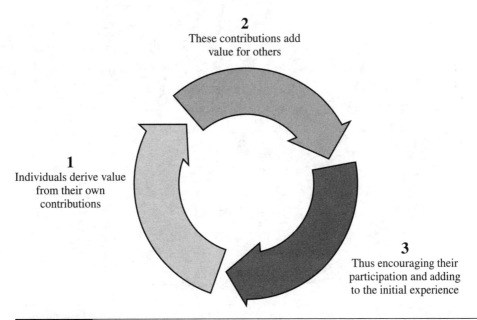

2
These contributions add
value for others

1
Individuals derive value
from their own
contributions

3
Thus encouraging their
participation and adding
to the initial experience

FIGURE 9-1   Contributory feedback loop

socializing on Facebook (see Figure 9-2), certain demographics use the Web to such an extent that it is practically displacing television as the primary source of entertainment (Figure 9-3). This does not mean that Web 2.0 should be reduced to a new form of entertainment or that it has no place at work: Instead, this is about setting realistic expectations and identifying alternative drivers.

This chapter elaborates on the importance of articulating clear goals, at the enterprise level, for any Web 2.0 initiative. But for success to take hold at the level of the individuals fueling the system, a few key factors must be addressed, and some fundamental fears must be assuaged.

Participatory Systems

How do we satisfy self-interest? Successful participatory systems need to reward contribution as, first and foremost, useful to the individual. Gains in productivity

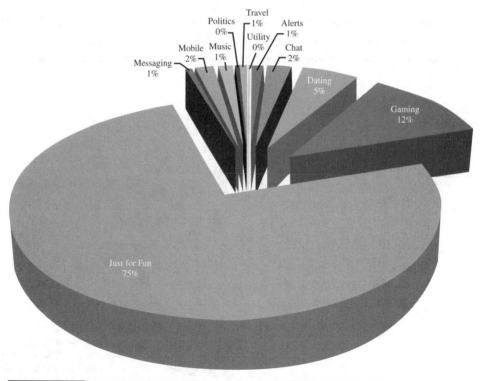

FIGURE 9-2   Consumers seeking entertainment value: Popularity of Facebook applications by category

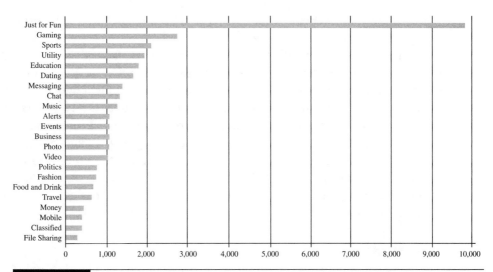

FIGURE 9-3   Consumers seeking entertainment: Number of Facebook applications

need to be made obvious, whether they stem from sharing information on a wiki page instead of sending e-mail messages to each employee, or revamping the system to identify more accurate expertise than indicated via traditional mailing lists.

Companies can achieve great returns from rewarding their contributors by highlighting their participation. For instance, by featuring the most popular employee blog posts on the front page of the company's internal or customer-facing website, a corporation leverages its own footprint and visibility to create avenues and extend opportunities for individuals to attain exposure as a direct result of their contribution. Just as consumers on social networks engage in identity-building activities, employees can cultivate, through participation, expertise and credibility, a currency valuable both inside and outside the company. Given that hoarding information to achieve success within an organization, at the cost of much higher overall performance for the company and all its employees, still remains a widespread behavior, it is important that the company facilitate any mechanism likely to lead to the free flow of key knowledge.

Articulating and broadcasting incentives for all to participate in building these incentives into the corporate culture is crucial: As Nick Carr explains in a 2006 essay (see References), without detracting from the seemingly egalitarian dimension of contributions, the ultimate quality of what the beehive produces (whether a Wikipedia entry or an internal wiki) isn't merely determined by the quantity of contributors but by their quality, their level of competence. If only mediocre output is produced, the system will fail to gather momentum and interest.

To put it simply, the company elite, the experts, must be on board and must be willing to spend cycles in the system.

Other barriers exist specific to the enterprise. Privacy, for one, is a key concern, given the amount of information typically floating around on social networks: The perception that a blog allows your employer to be aware of the intimate details of your thoughts and deeds might be too close for comfort. Conversely, the need to ensure the safety of data that may be deemed proprietary by the company is just as important. Earlier chapters talked about the blogging policies and guidelines implemented by companies to help employees supplement common sense when in doubt. With the variety of tools, channels, and modalities becoming vehicles for potentially sensitive information, it's important to decouple those guidelines from specific tools, to have medium-independent policies in place.

Search Links

The importance of scale reappears when considering another defining trait of the Web to the enterprise: search. More specifically, the scale issue is partly at play when considering the role of links in establishing the relevance of search results. It's no mystery that Google and other search engines took search results to a high level when their algorithms started leveraging links as a key measure of relevance. The more inbound links into a given document, with surrounding text related to a given query, the higher the rank of the page in the results.

Incidentally, this approach isn't without side effects. Scientist and author Tom Slee (see References) likens the approach to the one in favor at some universities when it comes to laying down footpaths across campus: At first, let everyone walk around the campus any way they choose. Then, lay paving stones where the most natural traffic is observed. The catch is that after the initial phase emerges from natural behavior, the paths are frozen, making it difficult for new patterns to emerge, and each step merely reinforces the existing pattern. The same is true of linking: Once discovery is mostly derived from linking, it becomes difficult for new content to achieve high visibility.

Still, enterprise search, paramount to enable the discovery-driven behaviors prevalent on the Web, will likely fall short in terms of relevance until it can derive authority from links. And fostering the emergence of links in the enterprise currently hits two obstacles: First, the smaller amount of content making up the corpus of internal enterprise documents makes it difficult to derive authority. Even if the density of links were comparable to those of the Web at large, the potential for error would be greater. Second, we need to deal with the link-poor characteristics of the content. Documents themselves still are largely produced with office productivity applications or industry-specific software that until recently didn't emphasize linking. Furthermore, these documents were largely transported by e-mail, as opposed to being posted to an intranet and linked to.

With search and discovery being such key aspects of facilitating Web 2.0, it is essential to consider means to increase link density. As much content as possible should be web-addressable, and as many applications as possible should be link-aware. And if necessary, links should be derived from implicit behaviors.

Tapping into Existing Flows

Along with creating opportunities for users to access content so they can bookmark, vote, blog, wiki, or e-mail links to it, the enterprise can supplement that explicit data stream by offering applications and content management systems and by measuring actual traffic for each document. This allows the inference not only of overall or local popularity but also of taxonomies, of recommendations about similar content. Potential privacy issues are associated with collecting fine-grained clickstream information: Not only must the anonymity of the data be secure, but it must be used only in aggregate. Ultimately, the goal isn't to replace explicit behaviors, but to supplement them in particular in the initial phases when only a few links are explicitly promoted by users. The distinction between *implicit* and *explicit* signals is akin to the distinction between *data* and *metadata* when it comes to content online: How content is characterized, classified, and organized eventually blends with the content being described, to augment and modify it based on the additional discovery entailed.

Just as critical to bootstrapping and ensuring the ongoing success of any Web 2.0 initiative is the need to maximize *in-the-flow* as opposed to *above-the-flow* interactions. Andrew McAfee coined the terminology in a January 2008 blog post about wikis, as summarized here:

■ *In-the-flow wikis* let people do their day-to-day work in the wiki itself. These wikis are typically replacing e-mail, virtual team rooms, and project management systems.

■ *Above-the-flow wikis* invite users to step out of the daily flow of work and reflect, codify, and share something about what they do. These wikis are typically replacing knowledge management (KM) systems (or creating knowledge management systems for the first time).

The underlying concept extends well outside the realm of wikis. And the issue with above-the-flow collaboration is generic: Contribution means interruption and translates into context switches, and as such it is far less likely to prevail naturally due to the overhead costs. However, tools can be wedged into existing tasks and functions to create opportunities for sharing and participation, instead on relying on employees to undertake a new set of additional tasks to kick start collaboration. Many of the woes of formal KM systems stem from their reliance on out-of-band requirements for updates to capture and maintain information, and as a consequence, KM databases end up both sparse and outdated.

It's worth considering the bottom-up dimension of Web 2.0 infrastructure and adoption patterns, and the consequences in terms of deployment, oversight, and formal involvement from the IT organization. As BBC long-timer and blogging enthusiast Euan Semple explained in a March 2007 post (see References), Web 2.0 will happen in the enterprise with or without IT assistance, and the best way to foster its spread within rather that outside of the firewall is to tread lightly: Sprinkle a few basic tools onto the infrastructure, stay out of the way, and engage those employees already involved in Web 2.0 activities on the greater Web to participate on the inside. At the very least, the grassroots nature needs to be seeded with the proper tools to facilitate the flow to enable integration with legacy tools and to power discovery features such as search. In other words, while Web 2.0 may just happen by itself, it won't be of much use and won't prove productive unless contributions are visible and integrated with the rest of the intranet cloud. The path Semple highlights allows for a progressive, iterative approach in which benefits can be reaped at little cost, allowing engagement to ramp up and participation to yield early yet significant benefits—from plain wikis, blogs, and bookmarking services—before necessitating deeper integration into legacy stacks and applications.

Know Your Goals

The guidelines outlined so far are generic and address typical pitfalls, fears, and risks associated with just about any endeavor pertaining to bringing Web 2.0 into the enterprise. Let's get more specific. Many flavors and possible angles and potential goals are present in such initiatives. One of the first steps involved is to make a clear assessment of scope and its implications.

The goal is not merely to scale down the greater Web into the firewall. Instead, deploying each initiative requires answering a few questions: Where does this service naturally live, and who are its users? Is it meant exclusively for the intranet? Is it meant as an outbound or outreach medium? Or, with a majority of services, does it really belong at the intersection where internal and external concerns mesh?

While it might be tempting to try and bypass several iterations in one go and lay out a sophisticated, fine-grained access control model that accommodates a wide set of participants, with visibility into various documents and with various permissions, it might also be daunting enough to derail the effort. It's interesting to note that, even in the case of public social networks, the learning curve has been progressive. Successful networking services have started with simple models that gained traction and ramped up the complexity of their privacy and sharing controls, all along educating their users and allowing them ample time to pick up the new features. And even then, defaults widely prevail, with most users not bothering to tweak the access controls they enforce on their information or going with all-or-nothing approaches.

Consider internal efforts, such as intranet wikis or blogs. At the highest level, the goal of rolling out such tools is to improve productivity through better information sharing. Setting up an internal environment is easy, even if the organization takes steps to ensure that the newly introduced platform plays nice with existing single-sign-on schemes, company directories, or social networks. But eliciting participation takes more than simply stating that switching from e-mail or shared file systems to wikis will help achieve productivity gains. It's important that the enterprise articulate those expected gains in terms that relate to the specific "pain points" in the company. That means surveying and understanding the perceived needs for better information sharing, recognizing factors that prevent its smooth dissemination, and identifying who are the likely early adopters, the likely champions of an initiative aimed at streamlining those flows. These are the people who will be willing to change their current toolsets to eliminate friction and replication. The strongest advocates are likely those who have been exposed to and are users of streamlined and social tools, who perceive being confined to e-mail as a step back. This is why McAfee claims that one of the characteristics of successful deployment of Web 2.0 in the enterprise is to engage lots of young people who consider sharing on social networks to be the norm.

For projects aimed at outreach, such as participation in the blogosphere or social networking sites, the key point is simultaneously to nurture an authentic voice and to engage with an existing community of customers. This combined with the need to establish clear, tool-agnostic policies in terms of authoring will help employees feel empowered and informed when it comes to contributing.

Web 2.0 Culture: Success Enablers

Long-term sustainability for the competitive enterprise implies an evolution toward pull-based business models, in which customers aren't merely consumers of products but are participants in a community involved in designing the products. This means the enterprise must ensure an open, porous environment, where actors inside and out are loosely but frequently connecting and collaborating. It pays to ensure that, even in the early stages of rolling out outbound Web 2.0 efforts such as blogs, employees are aware that they are not merely writing, but starting conversations with their users.

When it comes to choosing and implementing the various solutions, Dion Hinchcliffe at ZDNet coined a useful acronym of desired characteristics in a Web 2.0 solution: *FLATNESSES*, derived from an earlier version by McAfee, *SLATES*. What does the revised mnemonic stand for?

- **Free-form** Emphasizing ease of use and egalitarian permissions, free-form tools not only foster participation but also enable users who were not originally anticipated to participate when rolling them out.

- **Links** Promoting links is crucial as the unit of exchange and are of value in helping create connections and enabling structure to appear.

- **Authorship** The premise in Web 2.0 is to be inclusive, to provide access to every employee to easy publishing tools that facilitate participation.

- **Tagging** As opposed to folder hierarchies, tags allow folksonomies to evolve naturally and let users slice information along multiple dimensions.

- **Network-oriented** Corollary to the promotion of links, it is critical to make as much content as possible web-addressable, to have web-centric applications mediate as many exchanges as possible. This not only allows users to discover content through links, but supports the reuse of information without a need to replicate it, e-mail–style.

- **Extensions** McAfee refers to extensions of knowledge by extracting patterns, by mining activity to derive implicit behaviors. You can also interpret extensions as the ability for the system to mutate from having mashups and widgets interoperate, reusing data under different guises and perspectives, extending its reach and value.

- **Search** Search is the key to discovery and thus to augmented value for the information held in the system, to accelerated circulation, and to lower replication.

- **Social** At least some of the tools in the ecosystem need to allow weak ties to thrive beyond the static group of the organization chart. Along with fomenting discovery of ad hoc connections and similarity in interests, they enable low-key interactions, push-based status updates (Twitter-style), and profiles, and thus foster a climate of trust, collaboration, and participation.

■ **Emergence**   Emergence supports organic structures to build over time from the content—as opposed to predefined, rigid categories—by leveraging taxonomies, implicit behaviors, votes, bookmarks, tags, and other linking patterns.

■ **Signals**   No longer solely dependent on e-mail, tools use subscription-based signals such as RSS feeds and mobile devices to update interested parties about new or modified materials.

These characteristics constitute powerful and helpful guidelines for assessing the quality and appropriateness of a service or tool for a collaborative initiative, and for determining how well it complements and integrates with existing solutions. But even more generic principles are worth considering. These straddle both technology and culture and are early indicators of success. In particular, one need is to emphasize ease of use above feature-richness, especially early on. It might be possible to roll out new features over time, but a steep and time-consuming learning curve is a deterrent to significant adoption.

In addition, executive support is important—beyond merely paying lip-service to the initiative or lecturing the rank-and-file about the need to embrace this or that tool. A cultural change is required of everyone in the company, and executives must lead by example and illustrate what it means to open up and participate, whether by spending time contributing to blogs or otherwise breaking the boundaries of the targeted information silos. The executives' own actions and continued support will be more telling and more beneficial to any Web 2.0 initiative than their original stamp of approval on a product rollout.

Cultural hurdles are also encountered when fostering participation through establishing an environment of trust and openness. This is also driven by example. A key success factor is to make sure at least some of the tools deployed are explicitly social, allowing the organic social fabric to be exposed and thrive, and ultimately to be leveraged, as contributors gain more confidence sharing with their collaborators.

Finally, in addition to champions and early adopters, an early set of users willing to spend the cycles needed to tend to the new space should be identified. These users will be available to iterate over versions of the evolving knowledge being built, similar to how Wikipedia has dedicated volunteers who tend to its content.

Beyond the Basics

When considering advanced Web 2.0 tools, be sure that they integrate within the existing environment. Wikis, blogs, and to a lesser extent social networks can be rolled out without much interference—from a strict tool-centric perspective—with existing legacy applications such as e-mail. Ideally, single-sign-on schemes and integration with preexisting search infrastructures can help smooth any barrier to adoption. There are many creative ways to start meshing legacy and new systems. Granted, Ross Mayfield, chairman of startup SocialText, a leading provider of enterprise wiki solutions, is far from unbiased in his embrace of wikis, but here's how he deals with e-mail overload (see References for source information): When he leaves for a vacation, instead of sending the customary automated response listing a few emergency contacts and reassuring senders that their messages were received and will be read, he asks senders to post their questions to his "away" page on the company wiki! Conversations continue while he's away, and he also contributes to reinforcing the mental shift from e-mail-centric to wiki-centric conversations.

The productivity tools of choice for nondevelopers in the enterprise, until now, have been e-mail and Microsoft Excel. So migrating as many e-mail conversations as possible onto a blog or wiki medium represents a great step toward a collaborative ecosystem. In particular, wikis interact well with e-mail and news readers to signal recent updates and allow users to subscribe to specific topic areas, or tags. Of course, there's more to Web 2.0 than blogs, wikis, and social networks. But an incremental approach that leverages those well-known services to reap benefits both internally and with customer and partner communities allows for the culture of participation to grow and develop in the organization with little technical learning curve involved.

What's next? How can you take users even further, by empowering them beyond Excel and breaking free of e-mail? That's where mashups and application-centric wikis come into play. JotSpot, acquired in 2006 by Google, offered its enterprise customers a powerful development metaphor under the guise of a wiki. In addition to WYSIWYG and concurrent page editing, JotSpot's environment supported advanced features such as embedding spreadsheets, calendar, forms, galleries, or forums. In early 2008, Google relaunched the product as Google Sites, which integrates with Google's word processor, spreadsheets, and calendar. What distinguishes these services from a regular wiki, or from a developer-centric approach, is that they make it possible for users to harness powerful application models without any programming skills in a natively collaborative setting.

To open the architecture further to mashups, companies need to start micro-chunking their content and exposing APIs to the applications from which they want their employees to build. This eventually will lead to a model in which application and data fragments are dynamically chained together to achieve the desired functionality. It implies an adequate infrastructure that is flexible enough to adapt on demand to the needs, in terms of storage, processing power, and networking, of contributors piping the applications together. This translates into setting up a computing grid as a commodity, either within the corporation or, if possible given the potential data-sensitivity issues, by leveraging outside grids such as Amazon's EC2, S3, and SimpleDB. Finally, heterogeneous applications can also integrate software as a service (SaaS) components from outside vendors.

Ultimately, through this incremental approach, we can achieve a collectively intelligent organization that is read-write in nature, that supports emergent structure, with powerful discovery fueled by explicit and implicit signals and mediated by search. As participation reaches critical mass, network effects kick in, making the organization smarter with each new user.

Chapter 10

The Semantic Web:
New Paradigms and the Future

By Billy Cripe

Interactive and collaborative systems have changed the way people work on the web, moving from a read-only environment to a social one. Layering Semantic Web technologies on top of these new networks of people and content has the potential to integrate this distributed data in ways that will revolutionize the way information is accessed, presented, and used.

Dr. Jennifer Golbeck, University of Maryland

Web 2.0 technologies and paradigms hold great promise for reshaping any business organization. As people are able to collaborate with greater ease and better access to relevant information, business efficiencies grow as risk is reduced. Yet despite all the capabilities of Web 2.0 and the process-evolving effects that these may have on a business, little changes have occurred in the way computers understand people and the information we produce and consume. This is where the Semantic Web comes in. Like Web 2.0, the Semantic Web is not a single piece of technology or software. It is the collections of ways in which information is made understandable to our computers.

As mentioned in earlier chapters, relevancy is in the mind and mashup of the user. But what if the machine could understand relevancy: *what* a person *is* in the context of a document or a metadata attribute? Today computers understand protocol and syntax. The Internet consists of protocols for identifying and reaching the location of information as well as the syntax for displaying that information. Computers do not understand the difference between a funny website and a serious website—there is no syntax for humor or irony. The Semantic Web is a way of describing information such that computers can start to understand the relationships among concepts, topics, and objects.

For example, *Gibson is a guitar* describes a relationship. *Billy knows Kellie* describes another relationship. When these kinds of descriptors are added to web pages (for example, as micro formats), computers are able to read the relationships while displaying the information to us humans. With this kind of information in place, we can expect much richer interaction between ourselves and our machine counterparts. Searching for everyone Billy knows becomes possible if and only if there is a way to identify the relationship inferred by *knows* and the people assumed by *everyone*.

This is all interesting for the public Internet, but it becomes wonderfully pregnant with potential when considered within the bounds of the enterprise. After all, businesses run on information. Employees interact with others to produce information. Workers step through processes that process, you guessed it, information. Semantic Web frameworks can be applied throughout the enterprise by using the means afforded by Web 2.0 technology. Where Web 2.0 brings people closer together with information through machines, the Semantic Web brings machines closer together with the information. The result of this deeper three-way unity of people, machines, and information is a business that can operate smarter, quicker, with more agility, and with greater success than ever before. By tracing the path from Web 2.0 in the public spaces through its adoption and implementation within the enterprise, we can anticipate the next steps of semantically enabling business information.

Web 2.0 paradigms, technologies, and practices hold immense promise and more than a few challenges for the enterprise. While businesses cannot be successful by simply scaling down the public Web's strategies for Web 2.0, they can be successful by using proven technologies and leveraging the pervasive mindsets as a starting point for their behind-the-firewall implementations. Though faced with challenges such as achievement of critical mass and adoption momentum of Web 2.0 in the enterprise, businesses also benefit from great advantages over the public Web. The fact that most business work occurs behind the firewall means that we can safely make several key assumptions about the content and the creators. We start by focusing on two of the most important factors: users and information.

Business Users

In the enterprise, it is usually safe to assume that the creators of data and information, whether humans or applications, are supposed to be present and supposed to be creating that data. However, even that generic assumption is not safe to make regarding the public Web. Trolls, lurkers, and competitors can and do pollute information simply because they can. They engage in undesirable actions and post undesirable or irrelevant materials simply because they want to. In March 2008, for example, some mischief-makers on the Web actually posted potentially seizure-inducing (through rapid light pulsing) images on an epilepsy discussion board (as featured in articles on Wired, Digg, and other sources; see References at the end of the book).

Similar behavior is not tolerated within the enterprise, however, and, in some cases, it is grounds for dismissal. The expectation is that the community of corporate users is made up of people who belong there. The firewall limits participation to people and systems that are part of the organization. While exceptions exist to any general rule, the fact of the general rule allows for some useful assumptions and shortcuts when considering strategies and tactics for the future of Web 2.0 paradigms and technologies within the enterprise.

For example, identity management becomes less an exercise in validating users and more about tapping into already existing identity systems. Most businesses have corporate Lightweight Directory Access Protocol (LDAP), identity management (IdM), or Active Directory systems in place to provide basic authentication and authorization access to network resources. Because of this, any business activities undertaken by employees are trackable, traceable, and able to be aggregated.

While privacy concerns are a hot issue on the public Web, most corporate IT policies stipulate that little to no expectation of privacy exists within the enterprise. This is not to say that Big Business should be Big Brother. But barriers to certain technologies, such as tracking user behavior, that are distasteful, cumbersome, or threatening in public Web environments largely dissolve in the enterprise setting. For example, because of the "closed-web microcosm" of the enterprise, businesses can track and trace those parts of the corporate intranet users are accessing most often. If, for example, usage within the human resources department spikes on the internal job-postings system, you could predict that new hiring is in the works. Actions based on such predictions become more meaningful. A job transfer or recruiting bonus message could be posted on the home page of the corporate intranet to tap the power and social networks of company employees to help find the right candidate for a new position. If marketing department employees start hitting the internal R&D discussion forum for a new product, it probably indicates that a new marketing campaign is underway. Armed with such information, enterprise R&D product managers can get some of the newest and sexiest screen shots, product photos, or early beta-test information to marketing to help with promotion of a new product.

This kind of aggregate tracking and reporting becomes much easier within the enterprise when you start off knowing who's who: Betsy is in Human Resources and William, Seth, and Monique are in Marketing. When information download requests are logged and tracked by enterprise content management systems, aggregations are performed that allow intelligence to bubble up and out of the raw numbers. If you see, for instance, that between January and April, a spike occurred in downloads and information access of product data by people who work in marketing, you can leverage this micro trend for better and more efficient product-to-marketing communication and project coordination. Such information is possible only if the systems know that the product download spike results largely from employees in the marketing group. And the only way you would know that is if you are tracking both downloads as well as who is downloading. The only way you can know who is downloading is if an identity system exists for those users.

While it is possible but difficult to glean individuals' identity information from the public Web, identity information within the enterprise is much more readily available. Consequently, businesses have a unique advantage over the public Web in this regard. In Chapter 9 you read that Web 2.0 success within the enterprise starts when users are able to gain advantages from their own actions, information footprint, or data usage. Tapping into the latent information of the enterprise to augment business processes and daily activity is the best and least risky way to start. Realizing that your employees are people who have an inherent level of trust and expertise, they describe their needs and trends simply by accessing, creating, and requesting enterprise data they require can give your company a substantial and significant competitive advantage—provided you can identify those needs and tap the trends.

Business Information

Within the enterprise's internal web, we can assume that the information posted there is supposed to be there. We can reasonably expect that e-mails, memos, reports, documents, blog posts, wiki entries, discussion threads, and so on are all at least basically relevant to the business. Some of you are undoubtedly scoffing right now as you remember the e-mail with the collection of drunken Facebook photos your buddy across the office sent you last week. Of course, there are exceptions. However, think about what even that friendly e-mail says: It establishes or bolsters an informal social network and says that you have a relationship with that person, and that relationship is probably good for more than just swapping humor.

Here's an example: I have a friend who works in the documentation group. The bulk of our e-mail correspondence revolves around trading links to *Star Wars* geek websites, blog posts, and eBay items. That's usually what we talk about. However, if I have a question about product documentation, you can guess who I go to first. When he has a product question, you can guess who he asks. Our loose and informal e-mail link establishes two nodes in a social network that is relevant to the way we do business. So the presumption that the e-mail content belongs in the office still holds true.

Similarly, corporate compliance officers have recently been championing the need to save every e-mail, every piece of data or information the company generates, because it is considered *discoverable*—legalese for "likely relevant." We must presume that the information belongs, even the trivial, anecdotal, or temporary stuff. This does not mean that every portion of a content item or information artifact is of paramount importance. Where my friend from documentation is concerned, the body of the e-mails we trade is largely irrelevant. But the information artifact, the e-mail itself, includes the FROM and TO data and a timestamp. Aggregate the timestamps on several of our e-mails and a frequency pattern emerges. The strength of our social network can be inferred from that frequency. Such information is highly relevant and extremely valuable.

When the frequency of our social interaction, as evidenced by our e-mails, is plotted against product release schedules, training programs, or even travel schedules, a pattern emerges. This pattern transcends the simple e-mail frequency graph and indicates a time of increased interaction that corresponds with the activities related to launching a new product. When this meta pattern is understood, the organization can take steps to facilitate, focus, and coordinate the activities around product launch. Because one worker's interaction pattern is repeated among other groups when their products launch, the enterprise can gain efficiencies by formalizing and facilitating the work between R&D and documentation teams. Previously this work was informal and ad hoc; the enterprise was unaware of the trend, or at least the regularity with which it occurred. By understanding the kinds of interaction patterns that define the social networks within the organization, the enterprise can set aside several days of face-to-face R&D and documentation work time and overcome the operational delays that might have taken days to work through. In this way, organizational intelligence is gleaned from the aggregate of day-to-day interactions among workers. To be sure, trends and aggregates matter only when numbers are substantial enough to overcome standard deviation margins of error.

The reality, aside from the humorous e-mails and scanned cartoons, is that most information and data produced within a business is directly relevant to business processes. Product teams produce market research documents. Services and consulting teams produce project plans and statements of work. Quality assurance teams produce spreadsheets with performance benchmarks and bug reports. Retail and merchandising teams produce floor plans, order forms, invoices, and catalogs. Shift managers produce employee schedules. Employees produce status reports, and shift workers create timestamps as they punch in and out. At a high level, all this information pertains to the business. At a more granular level, the information is relevant to processes, departments, teams, and individuals. Those people and groups of people are tied together by the threads of the business processes, tasks, and responsibilities they have and perform for the organization.

This presumption of relevancy may not seem earth-shattering. Obviously, businesses create business information. But this simple presumption is unique to businesses and does not necessarily hold true in the wilds of the public Web.

Within the business ecosystem, the overarching presumption of relevancy leads to a foundation of trust and authority. On the public Web, trust systems are still a tough nut to crack, though some promising efforts are underway. Within the enterprise, trust, and by extension the relevancy of information, are able to be assumed. This does not mean that layers of quality do not exist within information aggregates. Certainly some information is better or more authoritative than other data within the enterprise, but all of it shares a common basic relevance to the business.

The shared basis of information pertinence and relevancy is a thread that runs through all enterprise information. If the information from disparate groups, teams, departments, and individuals across the enterprise can be drawn together in ad hoc, on-demand, and novel ways, then the collective impact can bubble up new intelligence, trends, needs, competitive advantages, and opportunities. As with the presumption that users belong, the presumption that information belongs allows the enterprise to tap nascent links between and create inferences from diverse and heterogeneous stores of information.

Web 2.0 vs. Semantic Web

Web 2.0 is uniquely centered on the human element in the human–machine–information triumvirate. Web 2.0 makes human interaction with the machine (application) more convenient, easier, richer, more entertaining, and more useful. What it does not do is fundamentally understand or improve the data. Wikis may allow the rapid correction or supplementation of information. Blogs make creating and distributing information convenient and accessible. Social networks foster relationships and reveal hidden avenues for problem-solving. Tags help describe information. AJAX technology streamlines the interaction experience. The information—the data—is still interpreted by people. The context of information and its meaning is still imported by the human agent. In the human–machine–information interaction, meaning is elusive until the human gets involved.

In some ways, the ascendancy of Google as an advertising and keyword engine exemplifies this point. What Google did for persuasive advertising was to turn the *meaning is relevant* axiom on its head. Rather than cataloging layers and nuances of meaning from keywords and web pages and links, Google brought a raw statistical analysis to bear on the relevancy challenges posed by the massive amounts of information available on the Web. With its complicated algorithms, Google has leveraged the massive amount of data on the Web to yield finely tuned statistical analysis, which in turn drives advertising and suggested link displays. To Google ads, the axiom has become *statistical similarity is relevant*. This is how Google's popular Gmail application can suggest links and ads that pertain to what your eccentric Uncle Bergeson wrote in his last e-mail without actually understanding the meaning of what he wrote. Given enough statistical similarity and small enough statistical deviation, relevancy is presumed (Anderson, 2008; see References at the end of this book for source information). Yet meaning is still absent until a human participates in the display. The statistical approach makes an asset out of the pile of data we know as the Web, but the algorithms still do not *understand*. Consequently, and despite its advantages, the mathematical approach will ultimately take second seat to a semantics-based relevancy approach.

The various projects and research underway that fall generally under the heading of the *Semantic Web* all strive to remedy this. According to Tim Berners-Lee, father of the World Wide Web and the Semantic Web projects overseen by the World Wide Web Consortium (W3C), the Semantic Web is where "information is given well-defined meaning" and "machines become much better able to process and 'understand' the data that they merely display at present" (Lee, Hendler, Lassila, 2001). If Web 2.0 is about enabling the display and interaction of information for and with people, the Semantic Web is about enabling the interpretation of information by applications so that they (the machines, programs, and applications) can create linkages across disparate information sources rather than simply reporting on linkages that already exist.

Consider some examples. The word *plant* and the phrase *rubber plant* are easily understood in context. The meaning of the sentences *Caelin works at a rubber plant* and *Kessie watered her rubber plant* are clearly different and nonambiguous. However, to a machine, the use of *plant* or even the phrase *rubber plant* is ambiguous. Try performing an Internet search for *plant* and *rubber plant*, and your results will include information about both factories and botanical life forms.

If I want to send a greeting card to all women who are aunts in my county, I could certainly do that if I have demographic information that provides an *aunt* attribute. But what if I do not have that information? What if I have only birth certificates and marriage records listed in my system? If my mail merge application knows that any female with a sibling who has a child or any female who is a wife of a sibling with a child is considered an aunt, then I'm set. If I can create that rule and then use it as a lens through which my application parses the available demographic data, then concepts such as *aunt* are brought to my system without needing the attribute of *aunt* being applied in a brute-force approach to each appropriate individual.

Within a business context, consider the 401K savings plan for retirement. To you and me, *401K* is the same as *401-K* and *401 k* and *"four-oh-one-kay."* An application has no simple way to establish such equivalence, however. The computer evaluates the string literal *401K*, which means that *401K* is *not* the same thing as *401k* or *401-K*. Now suppose a company's benefits application has details on the official *Corporate 401K Program*, and a human resources staffer named Kaity wants to answer all the questions people have posted in the corporate discussion forum regarding corporate benefits. Kaity could look through all the forum postings and try to answer each one individually. That, however, would not be very efficient. She could write a single post telling people to review the packets they received when they were newly hired. That would not be very useful either, and it certainly wouldn't answer any specific questions. She could write a program that would create an FAQ based on the questions people ask and the information available in the benefits system. This starts to approach a better solution. But how can she write a program that understands that *401-K* is the same as *401K* (and all the other variants)?

Thesauri were used early on as brute-force attempts to deal with equivalence and ambiguity issues. But the brute-force approach itself suffers from efficiency drags and the enormity of the task of cataloging every synonym that could possibly be relevant. Thesauri and other "knowledge management systems" suffer because they are centralized systems that require not only centralized maintenance, but also an enforced and shared vocabulary of understanding. In the massively distributed environment of the public Web, brute-force approaches are simply unworkable. Enterprise IT ecosystems are only slightly less distributed, especially when you consider the extended networks of partners, service providers, and branch offices or franchises.

At their core, the various Semantic Web projects seek to provide a way to describe both information as well as the relationships between those descriptions and, in so doing, provide a means for applications to reason or create programmatic inferences about that information. In our examples, semantic meaning is needed to programmatically disambiguate the *rubber plant* factory from the *rubber plant* in my garden. Semantic meaning is needed to programmatically infer that females whose siblings have children or who are married to someone whose siblings have children are *aunts*. Semantic meaning is needed to programmatically establish the conceptual equivalence of *401K* with *401-K*. Without a means to programmatically infer, disambiguate, or equate concepts, applications are stuck playing catch-up with the data that they are helping to create.

In many ways, Web 2.0 and the Semantic Web are complete opposites. If Web 2.0 is fundamentally about connections among people, the Semantic Web is fundamentally about connections among data. More specifically, it's about the relationships among data—lots of data, large sets of heterogeneous, distributed data. Fortunately, the oppositeness of these two web paradigms has moved them so far away from each other that they are curving back upon themselves. We are now seeing them meeting and even overlapping; the early results are exciting and the opportunity for business is amazing.

Web 2.0 is technology-agnostic and people-centered. To be blunt, it is sexy but stupid. The human is still the primary interpretive engine for Web 2.0 applications. Conversely, the Semantic Web is structural- or descriptive-centric. It is not yet sexy or pretty. It is still very much the realm of taxonomists, linguists, and post-structuralist semioticians. But it is very, very smart. There is not much to look at but the machine and the network, and the Web becomes the interpretive engine for applications. Combine smart systems with pretty, useful, efficient applications and the world is immediately at your feet.

In terms of similarities, both Web 2.0 and the Semantic Web aggregate and share information—or, at the least, they describe the rules and logic and provide the interfaces to do so. However, the focus on immediacy and user experience so prevalent in Web 2.0 is absent from the Semantic Web. Semantic Web–enabled systems look for patterns in diverse data sets, silo-bound data sets, data sets unrelated or unavailable to the human interpretive engine. Semantic Web systems find these patterns, inferences, dependencies, and relationships and then bubble them up to the human via some user interface, which may very well be Web 2.0–enabled.

While Semantic Web systems and Web 2.0 workplaces may share some commonalities, they also have some important differences in their starting points and endpoints. Because Web 2.0 is primarily interested in human-to-data and human-to-human interaction, you and I as human beings figure prominently in the Web 2.0 endeavor. Semantic Web–enabled systems are primarily interested in data and information—specifically the relationships among data sets, how information is described, and by what rules it is described. The end goals are machine-interpretable rules and structures by which coded systems can understand data and information that is second nature to humans. In many ways, Semantic Web projects are about bringing structure to unstructured data sets and interpretative power to loosely structured or lightly structured data. Where Web 2.0 relies on people to provide context to information, whether through tagging, social networks, or enabling feedback on blogs or wikis, the Semantic Web endeavors to find, discover, and infer context from the descriptions attributed to information and the defined relationships between concepts.

The structural requirements of the Semantic Web give it power and brains. However, they are also its biggest weakness and, so far, the primary barrier to broad-based implementation. Because systems and applications can only semantically understand information that they can parse, semantic systems are only as good as three interrelated resources. The first resource is the relationship defining map (called *ontologies*) available to the system. The second resource is the degree and granularity to which the information is labeled according to a schema that conforms to at least one of the available ontology maps. The third is the information artifact itself—the thing that is being queried, aggregated, parsed, included, or referenced for consumption by a person or application. These prerequisites, along with several other infrastructure-related necessities, put implementation and adoption patterns into a classic "which comes first, the chicken or the egg" quandary. Do businesses invest in promising technology that is not widely available, or do they wait until technology becomes available to start adoption?

Semantic Web–evangelist Jim Hendler recognizes the inherent challenges when he admits that "motivating companies or governments to release data, ontology designers to build and share domain descriptions, and Web application developers to explore Semantic-Web–based applications all hinge on one another" (see References). However, the news is not all paradoxes. Hendler also points out that some such as Friend of a Friend (FOAF) ontologies are seeing an increase in uptake. What is not mentioned explicitly (but taken for granted) is that the uptake in these early available FOAF ontologies is almost exclusively in, around, and among Web 2.0 sites and applications.

Social networks and graphs such as those described in Chapter 4 are both consumers and producers of information that fit nicely in a FOAF ontology. When semantically enabled applications get hold of a FOAF ontology and have social network data available to them, the result is a convergence of social networks into a massive metagraph that spans systems. This is one of the first practically realized, "Web 2.0-ified," publicly available, though not widely implemented as of this writing, semantic technology examples. Remember that the goals of Semantic Web projects are to enable applications to associate, deduce, and infer information and meaning from heterogeneous and distributed data sets. My LinkedIn profile data is different from my Gmail data, which is different from my del.icio.us profile, which is different from my internal employee profile data and my OpenID profile. However, a large amount of data overlap exists between these systems and can serve to link my identity with my social connections with my professional interests as well as my casual browsing interests. It requires a structured vocabulary of terms and rules to link my identity with my relationships and my interests.

You should now be starting to see how the goals of Web 2.0 technologies and paradigms are intersecting with the goals of Semantic Web technologies and mindsets. With a FOAF ontology in hand and information precipitated out of my social graph and the Web 2.0 sites and applications I use, you could create a powerful inference engine to suggest people or websites to my colleagues that they do not know about but might find interesting.

Within the business setting, the ability to percolate up information to people of which they are unaware but will nevertheless find persuasive or useful is a holy grail of marketing, advertising, business intelligence, training, and legal groups. This goes far beyond simple "top-10 requested items" lists or FAQ pages, which are only basic tallies of single-dimensional behavior. It taps the latent information that already exists in the enterprise to expand the footprint of actions and information that has already been accomplished or produced, to add value both to the information originators and others. Proofs of these kinds of concepts are still located primarily in the academic realm. However, conclusions by leading researchers, such as Jennifer Golbeck of the University of Maryland, are promising and should spur enterprises into tapping into the latent information and connections they have to create semantically enabled, rich Web 2.0 applications. "The integration of social networks, semantics and content has the potential to revolutionize web interaction" (Hendler and Golbeck, 2008).

Semantic Web Structures

The Semantic Web tools and frameworks such as Resource Description Format (RDF) and Web Ontology Language (OWL) establish, define, and evolve the relationships among information artifacts. For example, symptoms exhibited by a patient coming into an urgent care clinic with chest pains may be logged in a semantics-enabled application. The application could immediately search with and match those symptoms against a structured database of heart and lung diseases maintained by the Centers for Disease Control (CDC), the patient's genetic profile or family history maintained by his family physician's system, and clinical drug trial profiles maintained by a consortium of pharmaceutical companies. Rather than performing a "dumb" query across a number of databases and then normalizing the results, Semantic Web–enabled applications and data are able to match disparate and non–exact-matching data from different data sources and make inferences based on structured vocabularies. In this example, the symptom of chest pains can be automatically related to heart and lung diseases, narrowed by a family genetic history of heart disease, and queried against a list of possible drugs for treatment.

In short, Semantic Web–enabled applications solve the problem inherent in all self-service applications. While the information available on any topic has grown exponentially, the ability to access the right information at the right time has become exponentially more difficult. The fact is, the right information is out there, but it is of no use if it cannot be found at the right time or in the desired context.

The spin-meisters in PR and marketing have put a band-aid on an open artery and called it good when they invented the term "self-service application." This is simply a euphemism for "the information is in there somewhere but we don't know where, so good luck!" The intrinsic problem with self-service applications is that they all presume that you know what you're looking for. Imagine you are in a mega-mall that offers those small 2-by-2 lockers in which you can store your coat or excess bags for easier shopping. Now imagine that instead of stores and restaurants, the entire mall is made up of those 2-by-2 lockers. Self-service applications are akin to that mall. You can tell your employees with absolute certainty that what they're looking for is in the mall, but beyond that, they're on their own. Sure, they might get lucky—once. Most people get frustrated and give up in such a situation. No matter how pretty the mall looks or how easy the lockers are to operate, if the information is buried in a mall-sized vault of lockers it may as well not exist. Now realize that the amount of data within the enterprise dwarfs any physical mall metaphor. The Semantic Web effectively takes a generic request and reasons through the structure applied to the terms provided and the rules available to it to narrow the probable locations of your information to a map of a small segment of that mall.

For any semantic processing to occur or for any data to be related or linked, however, that information must exist in an infrastructure that allows for such linking. Our human brains are one such infrastructure, but, unfortunately, our brains are not accessible to applications for processing cycles. RDF schemas and OWL-described ontologies contained in specialized databases (such as Oracle's Spatial database) or simply available through Universal Resource Identifier (URI) references are also examples of available infrastructures. Data that is not labeled in a way that can be found or recognized as a member of an OWL structure or that does not participate in an RDF schema is not semantic, it is just data. It may be useful, and it may be important. It may be included in easy, compelling, and productive UIs. But at the end of the day it is not available as a resource with which a machine can reason.

If it can be labeled, however, it can participate in a semantically enabled structure. If labels can originate organically, evolve, morph, grow and shrink, and be aggregated, the semantic structure in which they participate is made that much richer. As a result, inferences are stronger and more accurate, and results are made more relevant. This is where the meeting of the data-centric Semantic Web efforts and human-centric Web 2.0 efforts start to come together.

The challenges should not be minimized. Simple labeling alone is not necessarily semantic attribution. Tagging and annotation of content is easy and accessible because the barrier to participation is low. No expertise is required beyond the ability to operate a computer. On one hand, tagging is little more than the creative application of condensed opinion to an information artifact. Some applications restrict tags or types of tags for different purposes such as to enrich the tag set rather than duplicate data that exists already. Researchers have attempted to percolate out semantic hierarchies from tagging or labeling data and clouds. Results, so far, have been mixed. While folksonomic tag clouds (like those described in Chapter 3) are reasonably successful at producing flat thesauri-like conceptual synonyms, they are not as good at revealing hierarchical relationships. While thesauri are properly within the realm of semantic ontologies, the primary inference power of the Semantic Web lies in hierarchies such as *parent of*, *subclass*, *instance of*.

Nevertheless, tapping the nascent power of the conceptual clusters encased in tag clouds and other folksonomic implementations remains to be fully exploited. In this there remains great business opportunity for leading-edge entrepreneurs in either crafting products to sell or crafting solutions within businesses that offer a competitive advantage. Even where hierarchical exploitation is required for full Semantic Web power to be brought to bear, the existing Web 2.0 structures and paradigms in place have much to offer. For example, while some remain skeptical about the ability to tap hidden relationships automatically in existing folksonomic clusters, they largely critique on the grounds that the tags, keywords, or metadata labels are contained in a flat or single-dimensional orientation to one another. This is true for most tagging implementations. Even for those where it is entirely true, it is true only in the relationship of the tags to other tags within the same aggregate or aggregate space. Yet Web 2.0 tagging, labeling, and attribution interfaces are not presented in a vacuum. Those user interfaces always exist in a larger context. Tagging interfaces appear as forms, browser plug-ins, or input devices that have an important and often overlooked presentational, and therefore relevant, data context. The information and data artifacts being tagged provide an important context that as yet is largely untapped, but is inherently hierarchical.

Web applications contain information artifacts that have tags or labels applied to them. Consider a catalog-building application in a marketing department. The application creates a catalog object (a semantic parent container). The catalog has certain attributes: It is an outdoor sporting goods catalog that contains images, descriptions, pricing, and ordering information. Each piece of information is a discrete artifact, a content item—images are one type of artifact, product descriptions are another. Images can be tagged as part of an enterprise digital asset management system with descriptors and attributes that customers and company employees think about when interacting either with previous versions of the catalog or in the internal image-management system. Description text is also able to be folksonomically tagged by users, consumers, and employees. Because the catalog-building application "understands" that an image of a blue kayak and the description text of the "Arctic Adventure Series Two Seater Kayak" belong together in a layout, the application is programmatically able to update image and description metadata, add RDF-formatted triples (Blue Kayak *is-a* Catalog Image), or even add a tag to the image; we start to be able to capture inherent hierarchical relationships without relying on one-dimensional tag clouds. Combined with a folksonomy tag cloud that includes the tag *boat*, not unlikely for a picture of a kayak, it becomes possible to find all images and descriptions of boats in corporate catalogs. Going a step further and combining those kinds of semantic queries with information from the informal networks of people who receive the catalog, we can leverage FOAF and other demographic data about users to find customers who are likely and have the means to buy a kayak. Such business intelligence can drive real-time decisions to present persuasive advertising or special offers to visitors to the corporate catalog website.

The point is that latent semantic information exists that we humans can intuitively understand but that is much more difficult for machines to interpret. The advances and wide-ranging adoption of Web 2.0 practices such as tagging and social networking interaction mean that those practices can be tapped for information that is, at first, one-dimensional, but when combined with presentation or usage contextual information, it becomes multidimensional and hierarchical. Businesses, much more so than public Web applications, have better access to and likelihood of quality data and analytics of these kinds. Remember that while the enterprise acts as a microcosm of the public Web in many ways, the smaller nature of the enterprise means that data, information, systems, and users are more tightly controlled and therefore better known. Success is simply a matter of tapping the information that exists but is latent, enriching it with Web 2.0 patterns and paradigms for input and interaction, and then mixing it up the right ways to apply semantic reasoning rules to it.

Folksonomies as Seeds of Semantic Ontologies

A brief but deeper digression on the distinctions between the meaning and purpose of information captured in folksonomies and Semantic Web ontologies may be in order. At the risk of oversimplifying the issue, an information meaning or ontology (small *o*) is a way of microdescribing the concepts contained by and held in an information artifact. A metadata model does this to some extent. But an information ontology also contains the relationship of those concepts to other concepts in the artifact and other similar artifacts. A metadata model does not do this usually. Simplistically, an information ontology is what the content is, is about, or contains. Consider images of a sunset, like those shown in Figure 10-1.

If we're asked to tag the images, we might easily imagine a set of labels that include *picture*, *sunset*, *sun*, *clouds*, *photograph*, *ship*, *bird*, and *pink*. As more people view and use the sunset pictures, certain terms or tags are applied more often. In this way, the semantic strength or suitability of each tag is indicated. If the folksonomy of the sunset images is taken as a whole, what emerges is a *conceptual thesaurus*: a semantic network of concepts that are similar or synonymous when understood in the context of this image. With a sunset picture at the center of a Semantic Web of related terms, enough of a descriptive schema is supplied to allow for formal Semantic Web Ontology querying. Each of the terms is inherently related to the artifact in a loose *is-a*, thesaurus equivalence. The picture is a sunset. The picture is a ship. The picture is pink. The collection, rather than any individual triple statement, completes the semantic picture. When combined with the network of relationships that spurred the tagging in the first place and the context in which the tagging took place, even more semantically rich information about the meaning of the artifact is able to be captured and then analyzed.

In addition to meaning—what an information artifact is, is about, or contains—an artifact also has purpose or utility. This is what is meant by the concept of *information teleology*. It answers the questions *What is the information or data used for? Why is it here or there? What is its purpose? What is/was its intent?* This information may also be captured as part of a folksonomy but is able to be programmatically gathered from the contexts in which the artifact is used, presented, leveraged, or implemented.

Consider the images of sunsets again. If asked to label the purpose of the images, dramatically different tags might emerge: *demonstration*, *presentation*, *gallery*, *showcase*, and *display* might be some appropriate tags. If such purpose-centered tags were combined with the meaning-signifying tags, it would be

FIGURE 10-1   Many different images of types of sunsets

difficult to identify any individual tag as purpose-centered rather that meaning-signifying. Strategies could be devised that create separate UIs for meaning-type tags and purpose-type tags. In some Web 2.0 applications, that might be appropriate. However, it is much more convenient for end users and far more powerful to glean the usage information programmatically based on how people are implementing and leveraging the image. If it is included on a web page, that usage information is tracked and available through an enterprise digital asset management system, presumably. If it is used in a print publication, that usage information should be captured either by the application creating the print artifact or at request time when the image is selected for inclusion. Leveraging analytics that, for the most part, exist today on how information artifacts are used is critical for accurate aggregation and parsing of content teleologies. The *is-a* relationships still hold. The image is a presentation, the image is a display, and the ontology remains valid and is enriched to the degree to which purpose-based or teleological semantic data is made available.

The Semantic Web project and various standards bodies are focused on enabling and defining content ontologies and the structures that support them (such as RDF and OWL) to allow machines to make "reasoned" inferences about the information and the subsets or supersets to which it is related. These inferences provide users with additional relevant, though perhaps initially unrealized or un-asked-for, information. An information teleology is a way of describing the purposes of or for a data artifact as well as the network-style relationship of those purposes to other purposes for those information artifacts. While the two concepts of information ontology and information teleology may be easily blend together as *Semantic Web Ontologies*, they are in fact different and distinct. When identified and leveraged distinctly, they each hold great potential for answering, solving, or at least mitigating the relevancy problems presented in our exponential times—if not in the vast and wild expanses of the World Wide Web's universe, then certainly in the more tamed and manageable backyards of our enterprise systems.

Keywords and tags are provided by a small set of individuals when compared to the much larger volume of information consumers. The intent is that the tags and keywords act as signs of the information artifacts they describe. As such, they are carriers of the seeds of an organic Semantic Ontology but are not, in themselves, a Semantic Ontology. Remember that a Semantic Ontology is a structured way of talking about a topic or conceptual space. Tags and keywords taken in the context of the information artifact they describe indicate the social and democratic consensus about what a set of data means, what it is for, and what it is about. As such, they contribute to and jumpstart a formal Semantic Ontology that is fleshed out with other formal metadata structures including RDF and OWL attributes and rules.

Keywords as Information Ontology

Information ontology is a concept that is vital to the goal of a Semantic Web. It is also a goal that a top-down metadata model or corporate taxonomy achieves only halfway. Remember that an information ontology is a way of describing the concepts in a piece of content as well as the relationship of those concepts to other concepts in the content items. When keyword attributes are included in a metadata model, they represent aggregates of components of an information ontology. As such, they are able to do a decent job of flavoring or providing nuance to the ontology. But they suffer from a myopic view inevitably imported from the author-originator. We cannot think ourselves outside our own heads—that is, we cannot escape our own conceptual baggage. Consequently, author-originator keywords represent a "what the content might mean, to whom" rather than a formal specification of "what the content is." Insofar as the audience shares the intent and context of the author-originator, keywords as helper-carriers of an information ontology may be enough to provide a glimpse of what is actually in there.

However, Web 2.0 practice, theory, and implementation increasingly realize a divorce between the audience and any shared intent and context with the author-originator. Indeed, you need only think on the proliferation of mashups to grasp the scope of this divorce. There is a growing realization of the randomness of author-originator keywords as signifiers of meaning. Although these keywords are a necessary component of a semantic relevancy strategy, they are no longer sufficient to guarantee relevance. What is required is a complementary strategy that encourages author-originator keywords while democratizing and socializing content tagging. Furthermore, author-originator keyword application should be implemented differently from social tagging schemas. To tap the latent power of keywords as ontological signifiers while simultaneously enabling a democratic approach that will rank and display keywords over time, two principles are suggested. It should be noted, however, that these principles are not solutions to the problems of the author-originator's own baggag but rather prerequisites for implementation of this necessary but insufficient part of a semantic relevancy strategy. First, keywords should be managed but extensible artifact sets. Second, keywords should be predictable or at least anticipatable by applications.

Keywords as managed but extensible artifact sets would solve a critical semantic problem inherent to a freeform keyword input paradigm: the synonym problem. While thesauri and stemming rules have been implemented with varying success on the computer-interpretation side, the user-input side remains open to the problem. A computer system attempting to tally and aggregate keywords for ranking and relevancy purposes will miss the synonyms or misspelling and therefore the relevancy signified by the set of similar but not identical keywords. Stemming rules and thesauri lookups cannot keep pace with a social or democratically oriented organic solution and consequently have a limited utility in such contexts. Keywords applied thusly will contribute to rather than alleviate the problem of info-glut.

As managed artifact sets, however, author-originators may be presented with a select list or semantic taxonomy tree of keywords from which to choose. An author-originator is relieved of the burden of having to pick the "right" synonym. The keyword artifacts (lists or trees, for example) should be extensible, however, to allow author-originators to submit new keywords for consideration. Corporate librarians and keepers of the corporate semantic schemas would meet regularly to consider, validate, and implement new offerings. In this way, the management of artifact (that is, keyword) sets is not completely a top-down approach typical of standardized corporate taxonomies. Rather it is a managed approach that enables input from across the organization and allows the artifact sets to be organic and evolve with the needs and requirements of the enterprise.

This management approach to keyword artifact sets is critical if the artifact sets are to be accessible to machine systems. A keyword list or semantic taxonomy tree (or OWL branch of an enterprise taxonomy) may be exposed as a computer-readable object such as a JavaScript object for AJAX manipulation and evaluation. The ability to expose a keyword artifact set is necessary if computers and code are going to be able to anticipate terms and evaluate keywords in relationship to other keywords as well as their place in a set. The more structured the exposed keyword set, the greater the potential an algorithm has to make relevancy determination and inferences about the keyword. Relevancy may be determined by the "distance" of a keyword from a search term in a taxonomic hierarchy. An inference engine is an easy step from a relevancy algorithm as, in its most basic form, it may be little more than polling for other keywords "near" a specified keyword or pulling keyword sets higher up a taxonomic chain.

Finally, if keyword artifact sets are managed sets and exposed to computer APIs, then convenience factors for end users (author-originators in this case) may be more easily implemented. Type-ahead capability, keyword suggestions, or automatic keyword labeling applications may all leverage such a set. While these capabilities and conveniences may be implemented as standalone functionalities, what cannot be missed is that although they are necessary parts of a semantic strategy, they lack sufficiency as a semantic strategy. They must be integrated into a larger semantic discipline.

Tags as Information Teleology

Information purpose or teleology is another goal vital to the realization of a Semantic Web. It describes the purpose of a piece of data or information. While corporate taxonomies and application metadata models may allow for a keyword or two related to purpose, there is little flexibility after a purpose attribute has been assigned. After all, purpose is in the mind of the user.

The reusability of information in ways unforeseen and unanticipated by the author is a hallmark of Web 2.0. The ability to find and interpret what that information is and what it is doing is a hallmark of the Semantic Web. Consequently, the ability to anticipate what a content item might be used for is nigh on impossible. Nevertheless, the ability to catalog and visualize what an item is doing and what it is being used for holds strong promise. Let's start by defining the meaning of the term *information teleology*. For example, tags or metadata attributes such as *press release*, *website item*, or *for print* indicate purpose rather than meaning. Unfortunately, in an owner-administrator attribution context (that is, where only content owners or administrators are provisioned to add, modify, and remove attributes), the ability to keep these kinds of attributes up to date and relevant to now is substantially diminished. Combined with mashup and other repurposing/compositing abilities that are becoming more commonplace, these purpose-indicating attributes become increasingly incomplete with the passage of time. Incompleteness risks irrelevancy. The solution is to allow purpose-signifying tags to evolve organically and grow from the source of their changing purpose: the consumers. This is an inherently social approach; when combined with programmatic analytics, social tagging enables end users and consumers to indicate how an information artifact is used.

Semantic Business Intelligence

If, as analysts state, 80 percent or more of business data is unstructured (it is), and if the pace of information creation is growing exponentially (it is), then unstructured information is the dark matter of the business intelligence (BI) universe. We continue to be blissfully unaware of the majority of information spreading through our business ecosystem. This unstructured information does not just nuance and flavor bottom-line calculations and logarithmic charts: Just like the dark matter sought and studied by particle physicists and cosmologists, unstructured information potentially holds the vast majority of intelligence's gravitational force. In short, traditional analysis of pure structured data for BI purposes is accurate but constitutes the palest tip of the informational iceberg, and organizations relying only on quantitative BI to steer their entrepreneurial ships will soon leverage these sematic web contexts to provide a more efficient rudder.

Consider another example: A sick patient instant messages (IMs) his doctor to tell her that he has a fever, body aches, stomach pains, and nausea. He thinks he has the flu. The doctor prescribes flu medication. Ten days later, the patient dies. What happened? Unfortunately, the information, while accurate, was incomplete. The doctor made the diagnosis without some important contextual information— the patient neglected to mention the ring-shaped rash under his arm. The doctor also didn't have access to information about a possible life-threatening plague outbreak in the patient's neighborhood, because that information was buried in the CDC's e-mail system. Information about possible local plague outbreaks was available in other area physicians' offices, along with successful ways to treat the plague, but this information was not available to the doctor in the *context* of her chat with the patient. The patient was accurately descriptive, but the resulting diagnosis was incorrect with dire consequences.

The patient represents current BI systems, able quickly and accurately to assess information and present it to the user (the doctor in our example), who then makes decisions based on the analysis of that information. The patient's message was *descriptive* but not *predictive*. Important contextual information buried in unstructured information sources, such as documents, e-mails, web pages, and videos, was missed, with devastating results.

Nearly 80 percent of the information an organization produces is unstructured. A huge body of data, context, and information is being overlooked or ignored by intelligence systems. In our Web 2.0 world, information is created with utmost simplicity. Distribution of information is facilitated by a near ubiquitous network of Internet-enabled applications and infrastructures. But consuming that information *meaningfully* is difficult. Relevant information must rise up through a swamp of info-glut. The e-mails to the CDC about a possible plague outbreak could have been sitting in a system with other e-mails about erectile dysfunction drugs and get-rich-quick schemes. Even if the patient could access the CDC system, finding the relevant plague information would have been a daunting quest.

The wealth of information in unstructured data sources, such as documents, web pages, e-mails, or other file types, is simply too great to ignore. Uncovering that data for BI analysis has been challenging, but emerging solutions can enable BI engines to utilize semistructured and unstructured information. Analysts have been writing about enterprise information management (EIM) systems for some time. Tapping semistructured and unstructured information in enterprise systems such as content management systems is an important and emerging capability. Now, unstructured data can be analyzed to provide vital, enriching context for traditional BI results. The gap between analyst conceptualization of what *should* happen and what *is possible* is finally closing.

Many organizations already own the ingredients for an EIM system. BI capabilities are built into most modern customer relationship management (CRM), sales force automation, and data warehouse systems. Additionally, most of these modern systems are built on and with service-oriented architecture. This means that BI capabilities can be invoked and consumed in a manner that is delinked from, or loosely linked to, the housing applications. On the other hand, enterprise content management systems (CMS) are common infrastructure assets within an organization. These unstructured information stores have not only information management capabilities but also information transformation and description capabilities. Combined with advances in enterprise searches around entity extraction, topic clustering and mapping, and sentiment analysis, the raw capability for rich BI analysis and predictive analytics of unstructured information exists today. All the pieces to the puzzle are laid out, but the picture is not yet known.

Bringing the unique capabilities of Web 2.0 paradigms, semantic analysis, and inference technology together with enterprise applications is a necessary though not trivial step to moving from an information-reactive organization to an information-driven and intelligence-predictive organization. To be sure, raw capability does not necessitate desirability. Two factors, tactical utility and strategic vision, need to be taken into account to determine and target initial steps. The decision calculus for tactical utility is very different from strategic vision considerations. Both play important roles in outlining a plan from initial working proof to critical enterprise strategy.

Tactical Utility

Tactically speaking, two important permutations of the semantic business intelligence combination must be considered. The first is the exposure of information management transactions within the enterprise to traditional BI engines. The second is the BI-enabling of information management systems and content-enabled vertical applications (CEVAs). Several compelling scenarios emerge when we look at CEVAs and how BI can be applied to them.

Critical to understanding the value of exposing information management transactions to BI engines is acceptance that information management systems such as ECM are more than sophisticated "buckets of stuff." Therefore, they are candidates for traditional BI analysis. Most information management systems employ sophisticated taxonomic, classification, and metadata schemas to content objects, information access structures, content distribution channels, and users. They track and keep records of what happens to each content item—from versioning to transformation, access requests, workflow events, and a host of specialized transactions related to the artifacts. These records are kept in a database or other structured organization system such as serialized result sets in files on the file system, or in XML data islands in dynamic content objects.

As a result, the content metadata, user transactions, system usage, and patterns of access reflect several key aspects of the unstructured information managed by the system. Metadata profiles of individual content items or subsets of items, or even the entire corpus of unstructured information in the system, can be leveraged by the BI systems in the same way as any other system. BI analysis of metadata patterns can precipitate out high-level topic clouds. Beyond simple tallies of metadata attributes, BI systems bring intelligent weighting and aggregation of multivariate metadata attributes. Intelligent segmentation of metadata based on factors available to the BI engine but not to the information management system allows crucial external factors to slice and parse the raw data sets. For example, BI services can query for the aggregates of download requests for all whitepapers about a particular topic. Uninteresting in itself, whitepaper download requests become very interesting when the BI engine also brings that information into analysis against sales leads and then to opportunity closures. To achieve this, the combined BI and information management system must also understand the following:

- What a whitepaper is—this information is available from metadata classifications.

- What the download request is—this information is available from service tracking and web server access logs.

- That the download requester is either sales staff or not someone from your company—this information is available from the web delivery components of the system and your corporate IdM systems.

- That the download requester is from an organization to which you are trying to sell—this information is available from sales force automation (SFA), web delivery, and CRM systems.

- How successful you are at selling into that organization—this information is available from CRM and SFA systems.

Adding in tracking information about how the whitepaper requester actually made the request and tracking what else she did during the session in which the request was made adds even more rich data to the set for the BI engine to analyze. Folksonomic navigation and relevancy clouding (as described in Chapter 3) provide the ability to find information hidden away in systems of which the requestor may not be aware. Furthermore, semantic technologies such as text mining and semantically enabled enterprise searches can be displayed to the requestor to facilitate the discovery of relevant information. Those extracted entities such as people, locations, and topics come direct from each individual content object. As such, they can be incorporated into the data set evaluated by the BI engine.

There's more to the process than download request transactions being tracked by information management systems. Other transactions are also ripe for BI analysis. Revision (upload, edit, review cycles) tracking against a set timeframe provides an organization with important internal views into the dynamic areas of its business. Distribution transaction analysis in and with other applications provides an organization with an understanding of how its content is being reused. Information reuse rather than re-creation is an important factor for maximizing efficiency. Analysis of the quantity of user interactions with certain types of content against the types of users accessing that content provides important internal trend-spotting and organizational efficiency. If, in a month, 40 percent of the marketing users access technical engineering documents, that might indicate to R&D that marketing is readying for a big technical push. It would behoove R&D to help out. Or, if an existing group's charter is technical marketing, such a result might indicate the need for better organizational communication so that job duties do not overlap. If sales staff from a global organization start hitting automotive aftermarket solution briefs at levels greater than a "normal" baseline, this would indicate to corporate leadership that a trend may be emerging within the automotive aftermarket industry. A quick but coordinated marketing blast and sales enablement campaign around those solutions can tap emerging trends or exploit micro trends before competition is even aware that such a trend exists.

This alphabet soup of systems and programs leads inextricably to the CEVAs. The transactional nature of information management systems is rich with information that is relevant to a more complete view of the business scene in which critical decisions are being made. Once the transactional aspects of information management systems are recognized, the power of the BI engine can be used to work on the business scenarios that matter most. At one end of the spectrum, these scenarios may be simple imaging or document management applications, such as check processing, accounts payable, purchase orders, or image capture and automation, which have a fairly simple one-to-one relationship between the content object and the transaction. Much more common and interesting is when the content transaction is a case or event scenario with a lifecycle all its own. A case will often contain various disparate content items linked together by the case object—the aggregate of those related items. As the case moves through a series of stages, a number of important transactions occur. The case may have additional content items added to, removed from, or modified in it as it progresses.

Cases are often driven by processes, but many of these governing processes only move the case and its aggregated content items from state to state such as create case, add supporting materials, review, approve, close, archive. Rarely does one overall, end-to-end process encompass the states through which the case moves, handling the ways in which disparate content items relate to the case and recognizing the transactions that occur to items and the case aggregate as a whole. When the information management system is the de facto content store under a case management system, and when information, metadata, and transaction data are housed in heterogeneous locations but associated with a case (such as the data is being reused rather than re-created, which is good ECM practice), the BI system becomes the only way to gather full-spectrum intelligence about what is going on inside the CEVAs.

To the detriment of business, BI systems are rarely used in this way. Instead, first-generation reporting tools and basic database queries are the norm for gathering information about unstructured information. These basic reporting tools cannot span the cross-system structured and unstructured context of the CEVAs and are unable to bring interesting and leading business trends and analyses to light. Conversely, when BI and information management systems are combined into composite EIM systems, the information management transactions that occur because or in the context of the application scenario are selected, analyzed separately, and composited with application transactions. This yields a unique, rich BI report (or dashboard or XML output) that provides a vastly more comprehensive picture of what is going on than a simple reporting or application-centric BI tool alone. This structured information provides the basis for inference-aware systems. Those semantic analysis systems are able to ingest the structured relationships defined in the BI output and consume them as the inference trails followed by predictive systems.

Consider several examples of information management applications:

- Court case management
- Accounts payable/administration
- ISO 9000 quality assurance
- Bid management
- Marketing extranet management
- Manufacturing process management
- New hire induction/education
- New product development
- Policies and procedure creation
- Project collaboration

- Government publications management
- Vendor communications

The applications fall into a number of information management styles:

- Case management
- Transaction processing
- Customer relationship management
- Document-enabling enterprise resource planning
- Team support/collaboration
- Filing and archiving management
- Electronic records management
- Project and technical document management
- Publishing
- Library and knowledge services management

Each of these application styles has a defined structure. Defined structures have predictable needs and markers, against which progress, success, and effectiveness can be programmatically measured provided the data is collected and integrated in a system that understands the structure. As soon as we start to think of information management systems as case management or information handling applications, BI becomes an obvious necessity. Furthermore, if a pervasive BI perspective is adopted, all sources of BI data must be included. The dark matter of the information universe matters immensely.

Strategic Vision

At its core, the strategic vision of semantically enabled information management systems is to move from the highly accurate but reflectively descriptive analyses of BI systems to highly accurate, persuasive, and forward-looking predictive systems. Such systems move beyond today's hyper-accurate and granular online analytical processing reports and dashboards. They start to make semantic reasoning inferences based on organically and automatically generated thesauri, taxonomies, and ontologies. Those inferences drive real-world, automated decisions that affect the bottom line.

Oracle's Real-Time Decisioning (RTD) is an example of currently available BI technology that tracks user or application behavior and determines what information is most likely to benefit, persuade, or be useful to the user. Consider this example: An employee searches your internal systems for the term *snibbling griblious*. Several results are returned and include not only links to assets but also organically extracted keyword concepts, people, and locations. The employee selects the top result, which links him to the web page of the SG department. The page is not a simple, static HTML brochure; it is built by the company's web delivery system. This is, in turn, part of a larger EIM strategic infrastructure and therefore BI-enabled. As the information management web delivery system starts building the page, it sends the referring URL, search string, extracted keywords/entities, landing page, and cookie ID to the RTD server. The RTD service maintains a session for each visitor, which is started when the web delivery system provides the initial information about the visitor. The visitor is keyed by a cookie or a login/user ID that includes information on the referrer, landing page, and search string. Then the web delivery system indicates to the RTD services the user's page visits. When constructing a page that includes implicit personalization, marketing, or a test, the web delivery system asks the RTD service to select specific content out of the information management system.

The RTD service retrieves the information it has stored to see if this particular user has previously visited the page. The web delivery system asks the RTD service to select an appropriate, persuasive banner advertisement or other information asset for this user. To determine what content is eligible for each decision, the RTD service consults the information management system directly through Web Services or another API. This ensures that the RTD service has an up-to-date view of the content options. Whenever new content is presented and active, the RTD service starts using it. As the web delivery system is building the landing page for the user, the RTD service retrieves from its memory cache all the possible IDs for the information asset in the home page. These results were previously cached in the RTD service, so it was not necessary to retrieve them again from the information management system. The RTD service computes the likelihood of a click-through for each information asset, based on previous BI analysis, heuristics, and semantic profile data. It then selects the most relevant asset to return to the web page. The user views the landing page, is intrigued by the banner ad or promoted content item, and accesses it. As soon as he clicks, that "success" information is returned to the RTD service, which stores the information in its own schema to use in further RTD analyses. The system self-tunes for the set of conditions that triggered the response.

Advanced BI analysis is performed in real time to generate persuasive and personalized results for the user automatically. In addition, every action taken by the user is registered with the RTD service, which allows the EIM system to learn what is persuasive to particular users. This is just one example of how off-the-shelf software that is available today can be brought together in rich business intelligence contexts to impact internal operations with semantically enabled persuasive user experiences.

EIM goals may be different for various stakeholders within an organization. It is important that organizations are able to leverage strategic investments rather than always creating one-off solutions for different constituencies. A rich Web 2.0–enabled platform for application compositing, user interaction, and intelligence is a necessity. Consider, for example, a judicial case management system. A judge, court administrator, and a lawyer may each have different perspectives on what constitutes a performance improvement in the case management system. Once these distinct goals are identified, the metrics used to monitor and optimize the case processes for each goal can be utilized. For a judge, key goals might include consistency and correctness of sentencing. The metrics used to track these goals are key performance indicators about sentencing rates for certain crimes, appeals won, and so on. For a court administrator, a key goal could be the efficient use of resources, such as time and courtroom space. The metrics used to track this goal might include court usage rates, cycle time from charge to verdict, and so forth.

Compositing disparate systems into an EIM platform is important to enable this kind of view of cases and the processes that intersect the data and transition their states. In this scenario, the BI analytics application would source the data from transactional (such as ERP and CRM) as well as traditional enterprise information management systems. Information management systems often have full-text indexing capabilities built in. The index is a pre-aggregated set of unstructured data that is ripe for semantically oriented text mining. Such text mining can, at the least, produce a set of topical thesauri that represent the conceptual topography of the enterprise. Those conceptual maps become indispensable inputs for additional, more traditional BI analyses as well as emerging semantic inference analysis and restructuring into OWLs. They become the baselines and benchmarks against which other analyses are measured, compared, or inferred. Within such a mapped conceptual topography, the judge in our example can determine whether her sentencing (unstructured writing) is consistent with published sentencing guidelines (structured data), as well as how consistent her decision is with previous cases (unstructured to unstructured content analysis). The judge or lawyers can run the published but unstructured judicial ruling document through the EIM-enabled information management system. The decision is full-text indexed, and the index is then analyzed by the BI engine against the EIM conceptual topography for cases with similar characteristics.

The results are predictions and percentages of consistency in concepts, keywords, and emphasis. Based on the results, the losing lawyer can decide if he wishes to pursue an appeal—a good bet if the ruling misses on a "precedent compatibility score." All this is available from a fairly simple thesaurus-styled conceptual topography analysis. This is descriptive BI evolving into a predictive EIM system. And this is, quite simply, what businesses need to do in order to become proactive rather than reactive organizations.

Parsing and relating concepts to a morass of unstructured data is a key capability made possible with semantic technology in a Web 2.0 platform. The challenge heretofore has been to uncover the information in a document, e-mail, video, or other source. However, the transformation and full-text index capabilities of many information management systems provide a view into the content that BI engines require to start the interpretive process. Transformation and templating capabilities can change an unstructured memo into a semi-structured XML document. Rather than forcing an extract transform load (ETL) process to push "square" unstructured information into the "round hole" of a data warehouse application, the native capabilities of information management systems should be leveraged to glean data programmatically as part of the normal flow of the user experience. Contribution is uninterrupted. Transformation occurs with leading conversion capabilities built into enterprise software systems to convert unstructured information, on demand, into human consumption formats such as HTML, PDF, or TIF as well as BI consumption formats such as XML or comma-separated values (CSVs). The appropriately converted content is then made accessible to the distribution channel appropriate for it: the Web for HTML, PDF, and humans; search, BI, and Web Services for XML semi-structured content. Entity extraction by semantics-aware natural language–processing technologies can create a concept map based on term frequencies, proximities, usage, and heuristics. When combined with metadata classifications and transactional data, an organic classification structure begins to surface. Mapped against topics, groups, or classifications, specific semantic ontologies begin to emerge. These organic ontologies can then be used as the basis for further BI inferences that produce predictions for users and that enable inference-based querying, suggestion engines, and sentiment analysis–based next-best-step recommenders.

Assumptions and the Physician's Redux

Returning to our physician/patient chat example from earlier in the chapter, a semantically enabled, predictive EIM system demonstrates five key improvements over either a standalone BI or information management system:

- When the doctor hears the patient's symptoms, she is able to extract the patient's location automatically. (The system is smarter.)

- Based on his location, she securely obtains similar topical information from other doctors in the patient's area. (The system uses intelligent aggregation of information.)

- In real time, she realizes that she should ask him if any unusual rashes appear on his body (an example of predictive intelligence).

- The patient tells the doctor that he has noticed a red ring-shaped rash under his arm. When he reports this symptom, the doctor runs an analysis against the CDC, which has a pathology ontology for bubonic plague published and updated automatically on the basis of several e-mails in their medical messaging ECM system. (The system uses a semantic structure grown organically from unstructured information concept mining.)

- Based on the conceptual matches between the patient's symptoms, local pathologies, and CDC verifications, the doctor prescribes the appropriate medication and quarantine. The patient's information is uploaded to the doctor's system, the RTD system is notified of the accurate diagnosis, and the CDC is informed of another plague case. The patient's life is saved and further outbreak is averted. (The system uses a feedback loop and self-learning, organic modification of conceptual topographies.)

Challenges still exist in combining semantic technology with BI and information management capabilities into true EIM systems. Composite systems, by their nature, are multifaceted and therefore require infrastructure resources as well as a critical mass of usage and data before the benefits are realized. Fortunately, with the exponential growth in the creation of information, organizations are rarely lacking for that critical mass of data. The importance of the immediate and the tactical will continue to trump the more deliberate pace of strategic implementations. Yet with a strategic vision firmly in place, progress is inevitable. As tactical needs breed strategic opportunities and as strategic pilots prove themselves in tactical situations, the blending of tactical BI capabilities with information management infrastructure augmented with predictive analytics and intelligent enterprise searches will yield a strategic EIM framework.

Thinking Semantically

Though still evolving, most current Semantic Web approaches are akin to developing and publishing a centrally defined taxonomy. They are centrally planned, brute-force approaches that suffer from the massive scope of the task as well as from technology that has not quite caught up to the vision. They struggle in the ability to implement and maintain schemas across enterprises as well as in the ability to process massive amounts of data within timeframes end users find acceptable. However, as we start thinking according to Semantic Web principles, it is evident that the content item is no longer the fundamental building block of the Web. Rather, discrete data becomes the fundamental building block, and ideas and concepts become more building blocks.

Ideas and concepts are malleable rather than static and hyper-personal; while denoting the same thing, the two terms may connote different things to different people. This is one of the reasons why the emerging mashup paradigm of Web 2.0 is so inherently exciting. At a deep level, we get it: This is how we think and infer and reason. Concepts and ideas should be emancipated from the prisons of documents and web pages and the data should be made available. But as Shakespeare's Hamlet would say, "Aye, there's the rub": To make the data available to applications, it must reside in some structure or format that applications can understand. Welcome RDF.

Still there is no inherent reason why the creation of RDF artifacts cannot be socialized or socializable. Each constituent of an RDF triple (subject, predicate, object) may be aggregated into a cloud. Conversely, automatic ingestion of social tags into an RDF schema will both facilitate the creation of a truly organic and evolving Semantic Web and greatly increase the richness of inferences that can be made. Computers would have the RDF schema to make rich and nonstatic programmatic inferences about the content while human consumers would have cloud aggregates from which to make inferences about the content.

Integrated Relevancy Discipline

A discipline is an ongoing activity, not a commodity. To be disciplined, one must have the necessary prerequisites in place. Organizations' production of information is outstripping their ability to effectively find it, let alone utilize it. While Semantic

Web strategies will eventually help automate parts of the relevancy discipline, the sheer scope and size of the Semantic Web project means that progress noticeable by the layperson may be some time in the coming. Organizations can ill afford to continue to gasp and struggle under the tidal wave of information while waiting for a relevancy discipline to surface.

References

Chapter 1

Gunkel, David. *Thinking Otherwise: Philosophy, Communication, Technology.* Purdue University Press, 2007.

Hempel, Jessi. www.businessweek.com/print/magazine/content/06_39/b4002422.htm?chan=gl. "Crowdsourcing, Milk the Masses for Inspiration." *Business Week*, September 25, 2006.

Little Green Footballs blog. http://littlegreenfootballs.com/weblog/?entry=12526&only. "Bush Guard Documents: Forged."

Reynolds, Glenn Harlan. www.instapundit.com. "Libel in the Blogosphere: Some Preliminary Thoughts." 2007.

Sifry, David. www.sifry.com/alerts/archives/000493.html. "The State of the Live Web, April 2007."

Surowiecki, James. *The Wisdom of Crowds.* Anchor, 2005.

Winchester, Simon. *The Professor and the Madman: A Tale of Murder, Insanity, and the Making of the Oxford English Dictionary.* Harper Perennial, 1999.

Chapter 2

Aldred, Jessica, Amanda Astell, Rafael Behr, Lauren Cochrane, John Hind, Anna Pickard, Laura Potter, Alice Wignall, and Eva Wiseman. www.guardian.co.uk/technology/2008/mar/09/blogs. "The world's 50 most powerful blogs." *The Guardian*, March 2008.

Anderson, Nate. http://arstechnica.com/news.ars/post/20061127-8296.html. "Experts rate Wikipedia's accuracy higher than non-experts."

Borges, Jorge Luis. *The Total Library* (Penguin Classics, 2001).

Cohen, Noam. www.nytimes.com/2008/02/25/business/media/25marshall. html. "Blogger, Sans Pajamas, Rakes Muck and a Prize." *New York Times*, February 2008.

comScore. www.comscore.com/press/release.asp?press=1524. "comScore Releases Worldwide Rankings of Top Web Properties: 772 Million People Online Worldwide in May." 2007.

Fisher, Ken. http://arstechnica.com/news.ars/post/20051214-5768.html. "Wikipedia founder: 'don't cite'."

Giles, Jim. www.nature.com/nature/journal/v438/n7070/full/438900a.html. "Special Report Internet encyclopaedias go head to head." *Nature*, December 2005.

Hansen, Evan. www.news.com/Google-blogger-I-was-terminated/2100-1038_3-5572936.html. "Google blogger: 'I was terminated.'."

Hodson, Steven. www.winextra.com/2008/02/17/a-golden-opportunity-for-bloggers/. "A Golden Opportunity for Bloggers."

Ingram, Mathew. www.mathewingram.com/work/2008/02/17/bloggers-need-to-try-even-harder/. "Bloggers need to try even harder."

Kelly, Kevin. www.kk.org/thetechnium/archives/2008/02/the_bottom_is_n.php. "The Bottom is Not Enough."

Li, Charlene. http://video.google.com/videoplay?docid=-2736790538945773557&hl=en. Lecture at Palo Alto Research Center, December 2007. And http://www.parc.com/cms/get_article.php?id=701 "Strategies for Winning in a World Transformed by Social Technologies."

Long Bet. www.longbets.org/2. Dave Winer vs. Martin Nisenholtz on relative importance of blogs vs. mainstream media.

Maher, Vincent. www.vincentmaher.com/?p=400. "Citizen Journalism Is Dead."

———. www.vincentmaher.com/mit/papers/VMO-01.pdf. "Towards a Critical Media Studies Approach to the Blogosphere."

Rose, Alexander. http://blog.longnow.org/2008/02/01/decision-blogs-vs-new-york-times/. "Decision: Blogs vs. *New York Times*."

Rose, Charlie. http://video.google.com/videoplay?docid=-1951879923858017460. Charlie Rose interview with Chris Anderson and Michael Arrington about the future of technology.

Sifry, Dave. http://technorati.com/weblog/2007/04/328.html. "The State of the Live Web, April 2007."

Simonetti, Ellen. www.news.com/I-was-fired-for-blogging/2010-1030_3-5490836.html. "Perspective: I was fired for blogging."

Tapscott, Don, and Anthony D. Williams. *Wikinomics: How Mass Collaboration Changes Everything.* Portfolio Hardcover, 2006.

Tech 4D. www.tech4d.com/blog/2007/07/11/wikipedia-contributor-math/. "Wikipedia Contributor Map."

Timmer, John. http://arstechnica.com/news.ars/post/20060323-6442.html. "Britannica begs to differ on Wikipedia's accuracy."

Wikipedia. http://en.wikipedia.org/wiki/Reliability_of_Wikipedia#Assessment. Wikipedia's own statement on reliability assessment: "Reliability of Wikipedia."

Wilson, Fred. http://avc.blogs.com/a_vc/2008/02/journabloggers.html. "Journabloggers Should Do Their Work Too."

Chapter 3

Cripe, Billy. http://blogs.oracle.com/fusionecm/2008/05/16#a379. "Aggregation." Fusion ECM Blog, May 16, 2008.

Elworthy, David. http://googleenterprise.blogspot.com/2006/03/enterprise-search-relevancy-in-eye-of_15.html. "Enterprise search relevancy—in the eye of the user." Official Google Enterprise Blog, March 15, 2006.

Facebook Developers. http://developer.facebook.com/documentation.php?v=1.0&method=photos.addTag. "facebook.photos.addTag." API reference.

Moulton, Ryan, and Kendra Carattini. http://googlewebmastercentral.blogspot.com/2007/01/quick-word-about-googlebombs.html. "A quick word about Googlebombs." Google Webmaster Central Blog, January 25, 2007.

Chapter 4

Apophenia. www.zephoria.org/thoughts/archives/2007/01/07/pew_data_on_ soc.html. "PEW data on social networking site use."

———. www.zephoria.org/thoughts/archives/2007/04/02/relationship_pe.html. "Relationship performance in networked publics."

Boase, Jeffrey, John B. Horrigan, Barry Wellman, and Lee Rainie. www. pewinternet.org/PPF/r/172/report_display.asp. "The strength of Internet ties: The Internet and e-mail aid users in maintaining their social networks and provide pathways to help when people face big decisions."

Boyd, Danah. www.danah.org/SNSResearch.html. "Research on Social Network Sites."

———. www.danah.org/papers/KnowledgeTree.pdf. "Social Networks: Private, Public, or What?"

Boyd, Danah M., and Nicole B. Ellison. http://jcmc.indiana.edu/vol13/ issue1/boyd.ellison.html. "Social Network Sites: Definition, History, and Scholarship."

Carfi, Christopher. www.webpronews.com/blogtalk/2006/09/26/ways-businesses-can-use-social-networking. "Ways Businesses Can Use Social Networking."

———. www.socialcustomer.com/2006/12/executive_brief.html. "Executive Briefing: Social Networking for Businesses and Associations."

ComScore. www.comscore.com/press/release.asp?press=1555. "Social Networking Goes Global: Major Social Networking Sites Substantially Expanded Their Global Visitor Base During Past Year."

Granovetter, Mark S. www.stanford.edu/dept/soc/people/mgranovetter/ documents/granstrengthweakties.pdf. "The strength of weak ties."

Hicks, Matthew. www.eweek.com/c/a/Messaging-and-Collaboration/Social-Networking-Vendors-Aim-for-the-Enterprise. "Social Networking Vendors Aim for the Enterprise."

Hinchcliffe, Dion. http://blogs.zdnet.com/Hinchcliffe/?cat=44. "openid: The once and future enterprise Single Sign-on?" ZDNet, February 4, 2008.

Horrigan, John, and Lee Rainie. www.pewinternet.org/PPF/r/181/report_display.asp. "The Internet's Growing Role in Life's Major Moments."

Lenhart, Amanda, and Mary Madden. www.pewinternet.org/PPF/r/198/report_display.asp. "Social networking and teens: An overview."

McAfee, Andrew. http://blog.hbs.edu/faculty/amcafee/. "The Impact of Information Technology (IT) on Businesses and Their Leaders."

McManus, Richard. www.readwriteweb.com/archives/ibm_enterprise_social_networking.php. "IBM Launches Enterprise Social Networking Suite; Microsoft Helpfully Offers to Migrate IBM Customers off It."

Mendelson, Jason. www.feld.com/blog/archives/2007/10/undergraduate_v.html. "Undergraduate viewpoints on social networks and music."

Patel, Bhavisha. www.crcconnection.com. "Social Networking Sites Cause Distraction for College Students." May 1, 2008.

Rosenbush, Steve. www.businessweek.com/technology/content/apr2006/tc20060418_044277.htm. "MySpace for the office: Venture giant Kleiner Perkins is backing Visible Path in its bid to take social networking corporate." *BusinessWeek* online, April 18, 2006.

Schwartz, Ephraim. www.infoworld.com/article/03/12/15/49NNsocial_1.html. "Social networking targets the enterprise."

Sevastopulo, Demetri. www.ft.com/cms/s/0/6e2648ea-5014-11dc-a6b0-0000779fd2ac.html?nclick_check=1. "US Launches 'MySpace for Spies.'" *Financial Times* online, August 21, 2007.

Taylor, William C. www.nytimes.com/2006/03/26/business/yourmoney/26mgmt.html?ex=1301029200&en=0d90ed5116e769d0&ei=5090&partner=rssuserland&emc=rss. "Here's an Idea: Let Everyone Have Ideas." *New York Times* online, March 26, 2006.

Venture Capital and Technology blog. http://avc.blogs.com/a_vc/2007/11/my-facebook-ad.html. "My Facebook Ad."

Young Adult Library Services Association. www.leonline.com/yalsa/positive_uses.pdf. "Social Networking and DOPA." 30 positive uses of social networks.

Chapter 6

Ezzy, Ebrahim. www.readwriteweb.com/archives/webified_desktop_apps_vs_browser_apps.php. "Webified Desktop Apps vs. Browser-based Apps." ReadWriteWeb, September 7, 2006.

Tutorials Point. www.tutorialspoint.com/ruby-on-rails/rails-introduction.htm. "Ruby on Rails Introduction."

Yahoo! Developer Network. http://developer.yahoo.com/yui/examples/button/btn_example01.html#buildingfromdatasource. "YUI Library Examples: Button Control: Push Buttons."

———. http://developer.yahoo.com/yui/examples/datatable/dt_xhrjson.html. "YUI Library Examples: DataTable Control (beta): JSON Data Over XHR."

Chapter 7

Hinchcliffe, Dion. http://blogs.zdnet.com/Hinchcliffe/?p=130. "A Checkpoint on Web 2.0 in the Enterprise." ZDnet, July 26, 2007.

Chapter 8

Ben-Itzhak, Yuval. www.scmagazineus.com/Tackling-the-security-issues-of-Web-20/article/35609/. "Tackling the security issues of Web 2.0." *SC Magazine*, September 10, 2007.

IBM and Microsoft. www.ibm.com/developerworks/library/specification/ws-secmap/. "Security in a Web Services World: A Proposed Architecture and Roadmap."

Oracle Corporation. www.oracle.com/security/docs/securitybrochure.pdf. "Security Inside Out—Oracle Security Solutions."

Chapter 9

Arrington, Michael. www.techcrunch.com/2006/07/24/jotspot-20-launches/. "JotSpot 2.0 Launches."

———. www.techcrunch.com/2008/02/27/it-took-16-months-but-google-relaunches-jotspot/. "It Took 16 Months, But Google Relaunches JotSpot."

Bernoff, Josh. http://blogs.forrester.com/charleneli/2008/03/where-are-you-o. html. "Where are you on the Purist-Corporatist scale?"

Broache, Anne. www.news.com/8301-10784_3-9903070-7.html. "Corporate employee blogs: Lawsuits waiting to happen?"

Carr, Nick. www.roughtype.com/archives/2006/04/web_20s_numbsku.php. "Web 2.0's numbskull factor."

Graham, Paul. www.paulgraham.com/ycombinator.html. "A New Venture Animal."

Hickins, Michael. www.internetnews.com/ec-news/article.php/3601356. "Social Networking Comes to the Enterprise."

Hinchcliffe, Dion. http://blogs.zdnet.com/Hinchcliffe/?p=143. "The state of Enterprise 2.0."

———. http://blogs.zdnet.com/Hinchcliffe/?p=107. "The story of Web 2.0 and SOA continues—Part 1."

———. http://blogs.zdnet.com/Hinchcliffe/?p=41. "A round of Web 2.0 reductionism."

———. http://hinchcliffe.org/archive/2007/01/20/12675.aspx. "Eleven Emerging Ideas for SOA Architects in 2007."

Howlett, Dennis. http://blogs.zdnet.com/Howlett/?p=347. "Google for enterprise: my $500 bet."

IBM. http://services.alphaworks.ibm.com/qedwiki/. "What is QEDWiki?"

Idinopulos, Michael. http://michaeli.typepad.com/my_weblog/2008/03/enterprise-adop.html. "Enterprise Adoption: Why wikis aren't like other IT."

Israel, Shel. http://redcouch.typepad.com/weblog/2008/02/two-social-medi. html. "Two Social Media Camps in the Enterprise."

JotSpot. www.jot.com/learn/. "Why you should try JotSpot."

Malik, Om. http://gigaom.com/2006/05/13/the-myth-reality-future-of-web-20/. "The Myth, Reality & Future of Web 2.0."

Mayfield, Ross. http://ross.typepad.com/blog/2006/04/manage_knowledg.html. "Manage Knowledgement [sic] (MK)."

McAfee, Andrew. http://blog.hbs.edu/faculty/amcafee/index.php/faculty_amcafee_v3/explaining_my_fondness_for_explicit_content/. "Explaining My Fondness for Explicit Content."

———. http://blog.hbs.edu/faculty/amcafee/index.php/faculty_amcafee_v3/comments/whats_most_important_for_success_with_enterprise_20/. "What's Most Important for Success with Enterprise 2.0?"

———. http://blog.hbs.edu/faculty/amcafee/index.php/faculty_amcafee_v3/the_mechanisms_of_online_emergence/. "The Impact of Information Technology (IT) on Businesses and Their Leaders."

Needleman, Rafe. www.webware.com/8301-1_109-9883496-2.html?part=rss&tag=feed&subj=Webware. "Google Sites: Not so pretty in the morning."

O'Reilly, Tim. www.flickr.com/photos/36521959321@N01/44349798. "Web2MemeMap."

Perez, Sarah. www.readwriteweb.com/archives/google_sites_the_next_sharepoint_maybe_notwhy_google_apps_could_lose_the_enterprise_market.php. "Google Sites the Next Sharepoint? Maybe Not…. Why Google Apps Could Lose the Enterprise Market."

Semple, Euan. http://theobvious.typepad.com/blog/2007/03/the_100_guarant.html. "The 100% guaranteed easiest way to do Enterprise 2.0?"

Sierra, Kathy. http://headrush.typepad.com/about.html. "Creating passionate users."

Slee, Tom. http://whimsley.typepad.com/whimsley/2008/03/mr-googles-guid.html. "Mr. Google's Guidebook."

Suarez, Luis. www.elsua.net/?s=work+e-mail. "Nexto8: Giving up on Work e-mail—Status Report on Week 14."

Wikipedia. http://en.wikipedia.org/wiki/The_Long_Tail. "The Long Tail."

Winer, Dave. www.scripting.com/2006/05/15.html#isWeb20ABubble. "Is Web 2.0 a bubble?"

Chapter 10

Anderson, Chris. www.wired.com/science/discoveries/magazine/16-07/pb_ theory. "The End of Theory: The Data Deluge Makes the Scientific Method Obsolete." *Wired Magazine*, July 2008.

Berners-Lee, Tim, James Hendler, and Ora Lassila. www.sciam.com/article. cfm?id=the-semantic-web. "The Semantic Web: A new form of Web content that is meaningful to computers will unleash a revolution of new possibilities." Scientific American.com, May 17, 2001.

Hendler, James, and Jennifer Golbeck. www.cs.umd.edu/~golbeck/downloads/ Web20-SW-JWS-webVersion.pdf. "Metcalfe's Law, Web 2.0, and the Semantic Web."

Hendler, Jim. "Web 3.0: Chicken Farms on the Semantic Web." IEEE Computer Society, *Computer* magazine, January 2008.

Poulsen, Kevin. www.wired.com/politics/security/news/2008/03/epilepsy. "Hackers Assault Epilepsy Patients via Computer."

Index

GET YOUR FREE SUBSCRIPTION
TO *ORACLE MAGAZINE*

Oracle Magazine is essential gear for today's information technology professionals. Stay informed and increase your productivity with every issue of *Oracle Magazine*. Inside each free bimonthly issue you'll get:

- Up-to-date information on Oracle Database, Oracle Application Server, Web development, enterprise grid computing, database technology, and business trends
- Third-party news and announcements
- Technical articles on Oracle and partner products, technologies, and operating environments
- Development and administration tips
- Real-world customer stories

If there are other Oracle users at your location who would like to receive their own subscription to *Oracle Magazine*, please photo-copy this form and pass it along.

Three easy ways to subscribe:

① **Web**
Visit our Web site at **oracle.com/oraclemagazine**
You'll find a subscription form there, plus much more

② **Fax**
Complete the questionnaire on the back of this card and fax the questionnaire side only to **+1.847.763.9638**

③ **Mail**
Complete the questionnaire on the back of this card and mail it to **P.O. Box 1263, Skokie, IL 60076-8263**

ORACLE®

Want your own FREE subscription?

To receive a free subscription to *Oracle Magazine*, you must fill out the entire card, sign it, and date it (incomplete cards cannot be processed or acknowledged). You can also fax your application to +1.847.763.9638. **Or subscribe at our Web site at oracle.com/oraclemagazine**

⬭ **Yes, please send me a FREE subscription** *Oracle Magazine*. ⬭ No.

⬭ From time to time, Oracle Publishing allows our partners exclusive access to our e-mail addresses for special promotions and announcements. To be included in this program, please check this circle. If you do not wish to be included, you will only receive notices about your subscription via e-mail.

⬭ Oracle Publishing allows sharing of our postal mailing list with selected third parties. If you prefer your mailing address not to be included in this program, please check this circle.

If at any time you would like to be removed from either mailing list, please contact Customer Service at +1.847.763.9635 or send an e-mail to oracle@halldata.com. If you opt in to the sharing of information, Oracle may also provide you with e-mail related to Oracle products, services, and events. If you want to completely unsubscribe from any e-mail communication from Oracle, please send an e-mail to: unsubscribe@oracle-mail.com with the following in the subject line: REMOVE [your e-mail address]. For complete information on Oracle Publishing's privacy practices, please visit oracle.com/html/privacy/html

X _____
signature (required)   date

name   title

company   e-mail address

street/p.o. box

city/state/zip or postal code   telephone

country   fax

Would you like to receive your free subscription in digital format instead of print if it becomes available? ⬭ Yes ⬭ No

---

YOU MUST ANSWER ALL 10 QUESTIONS BELOW.

① WHAT IS THE PRIMARY BUSINESS ACTIVITY OF YOUR FIRM AT THIS LOCATION? (check one only)

- ☐ 01 Aerospace and Defense Manufacturing
- ☐ 02 Application Service Provider
- ☐ 03 Automotive Manufacturing
- ☐ 04 Chemicals
- ☐ 05 Media and Entertainment
- ☐ 06 Construction/Engineering
- ☐ 07 Consumer Sector/Consumer Packaged Goods
- ☐ 08 Education
- ☐ 09 Financial Services/Insurance
- ☐ 10 Health Care
- ☐ 11 High Technology Manufacturing, OEM
- ☐ 12 Industrial Manufacturing
- ☐ 13 Independent Software Vendor
- ☐ 14 Life Sciences (biotech, pharmaceuticals)
- ☐ 15 Natural Resources
- ☐ 16 Oil and Gas
- ☐ 17 Professional Services
- ☐ 18 Public Sector (government)
- ☐ 19 Research
- ☐ 20 Retail/Wholesale/Distribution
- ☐ 21 Systems Integrator, VAR/VAD
- ☐ 22 Telecommunications
- ☐ 23 Travel and Transportation
- ☐ 24 Utilities (electric, gas, sanitation, water)
- ☐ 98 Other Business and Services _____

② WHICH OF THE FOLLOWING BEST DESCRIBES YOUR PRIMARY JOB FUNCTION? (check one only)

CORPORATE MANAGEMENT/STAFF
- ☐ 01 Executive Management (President, Chair, CEO, CFO, Owner, Partner, Principal)
- ☐ 02 Finance/Administrative Management (VP/Director/ Manager/Controller, Purchasing, Administration)
- ☐ 03 Sales/Marketing Management (VP/Director/Manager)
- ☐ 04 Computer Systems/Operations Management (CIO/VP/Director/Manager MIS/IS/IT, Ops)

IS/IT STAFF
- ☐ 05 Application Development/Programming Management
- ☐ 06 Application Development/Programming Staff
- ☐ 07 Consulting
- ☐ 08 DBA/Systems Administrator
- ☐ 09 Education/Training
- ☐ 10 Technical Support Director/Manager
- ☐ 11 Other Technical Management/Staff
- ☐ 98 Other

③ WHAT IS YOUR CURRENT PRIMARY OPERATING PLATFORM (check all that apply)

- ☐ 01 Digital Equipment Corp UNIX/VAX/VMS
- ☐ 02 HP UNIX
- ☐ 03 IBM AIX
- ☐ 04 IBM UNIX
- ☐ 05 Linux (Red Hat)
- ☐ 06 Linux (SUSE)
- ☐ 07 Linux (Oracle Enterprise)
- ☐ 08 Linux (other)
- ☐ 09 Macintosh
- ☐ 10 MVS
- ☐ 11 Netware
- ☐ 12 Network Computing
- ☐ 13 SCO UNIX
- ☐ 14 Sun Solaris/SunOS
- ☐ 15 Windows
- ☐ 16 Other UNIX
- ☐ 98 Other
- ☐ 99 None of the Above

④ DO YOU EVALUATE, SPECIFY, RECOMMEND, OR AUTHORIZE THE PURCHASE OF ANY OF THE FOLLOWING? (check all that apply)

- ☐ 01 Hardware
- ☐ 02 Business Applications (ERP, CRM, etc.)
- ☐ 03 Application Development Tools
- ☐ 04 Database Products
- ☐ 05 Internet or Intranet Products
- ☐ 06 Other Software
- ☐ 07 Middleware Products
- ☐ 99 None of the Above

⑤ IN YOUR JOB, DO YOU USE OR PLAN TO PURCHASE ANY OF THE FOLLOWING PRODUCTS? (check all that apply)

SOFTWARE
- ☐ 01 CAD/CAE/CAM
- ☐ 02 Collaboration Software
- ☐ 03 Communications
- ☐ 04 Database Management
- ☐ 05 File Management
- ☐ 06 Finance
- ☐ 07 Java
- ☐ 08 Multimedia Authoring
- ☐ 09 Networking
- ☐ 10 Programming
- ☐ 11 Project Management
- ☐ 12 Scientific and Engineering
- ☐ 13 Systems Management
- ☐ 14 Workflow

HARDWARE
- ☐ 15 Macintosh
- ☐ 16 Mainframe
- ☐ 17 Massively Parallel Processing
- ☐ 18 Minicomputer
- ☐ 19 Intel x86(32)
- ☐ 20 Intel x86(64)
- ☐ 21 Network Computer
- ☐ 22 Symmetric Multiprocessing
- ☐ 23 Workstation Services

SERVICES
- ☐ 24 Consulting
- ☐ 25 Education/Training
- ☐ 26 Maintenance
- ☐ 27 Online Database
- ☐ 28 Support
- ☐ 29 Technology-Based Training
- ☐ 30 Other
- ☐ 99 None of the Above

⑥ WHAT IS YOUR COMPANY'S SIZE? (check one only)

- ☐ 01 More than 25,000 Employees
- ☐ 02 10,001 to 25,000 Employees
- ☐ 03 5,001 to 10,000 Employees
- ☐ 04 1,001 to 5,000 Employees
- ☐ 05 101 to 1,000 Employees
- ☐ 06 Fewer than 100 Employees

⑦ DURING THE NEXT 12 MONTHS, HOW MUCH DO YOU ANTICIPATE YOUR ORGANIZATION WILL SPEND ON COMPUTER HARDWARE, SOFTWARE, PERIPHERALS, AND SERVICES FOR YOUR LOCATION? (check one only)

- ☐ 01 Less than $10,000
- ☐ 02 $10,000 to $49,999
- ☐ 03 $50,000 to $99,999
- ☐ 04 $100,000 to $499,999
- ☐ 05 $500,000 to $999,999
- ☐ 06 $1,000,000 and Over

⑧ WHAT IS YOUR COMPANY'S YEARLY SALES REVENUE? (check one only)

- ☐ 01 $500, 000, 000 and above
- ☐ 02 $100, 000, 000 to $500, 000, 000
- ☐ 03 $50, 000, 000 to $100, 000, 000
- ☐ 04 $5, 000, 000 to $50, 000, 000
- ☐ 05 $1, 000, 000 to $5, 000, 000

⑨ WHAT LANGUAGES AND FRAMEWORKS DO YOU USE? (check all that apply)

- ☐ 01 Ajax
- ☐ 02 C
- ☐ 03 C++
- ☐ 04 C#
- ☐ 05 Hibernate
- ☐ 06 J++/J#
- ☐ 07 Java
- ☐ 08 JSP
- ☐ 09 .NET
- ☐ 10 Perl
- ☐ 11 PHP
- ☐ 12 PL/SQL
- ☐ 13 Python
- ☐ 14 Ruby/Rails
- ☐ 15 Spring
- ☐ 16 Struts
- ☐ 17 SQL
- ☐ 18 Visual Basic
- ☐ 98 Other

⑩ WHAT ORACLE PRODUCTS ARE IN USE AT YOUR SITE? (check all that apply)

ORACLE DATABASE
- ☐ 01 Oracle Database 11*g*
- ☐ 02 Oracle Database 10*g*
- ☐ 03 Oracle9*i* Database
- ☐ 04 Oracle Embedded Database (Oracle Lite, Times Ten, Berkeley DB)
- ☐ 05 Other Oracle Database Release

ORACLE FUSION MIDDLEWARE
- ☐ 06 Oracle Application Server
- ☐ 07 Oracle Portal
- ☐ 08 Oracle Enterprise Manager
- ☐ 09 Oracle BPEL Process Manager
- ☐ 10 Oracle Identity Management
- ☐ 11 Oracle SOA Suite
- ☐ 12 Oracle Data Hubs

ORACLE DEVELOPMENT TOOLS
- ☐ 13 Oracle JDeveloper
- ☐ 14 Oracle Forms
- ☐ 15 Oracle Reports
- ☐ 16 Oracle Designer
- ☐ 17 Oracle Discoverer
- ☐ 18 Oracle BI Beans
- ☐ 19 Oracle Warehouse Builder
- ☐ 20 Oracle WebCenter
- ☐ 21 Oracle Application Express

ORACLE APPLICATIONS
- ☐ 22 Oracle E-Business Suite
- ☐ 23 PeopleSoft Enterprise
- ☐ 24 JD Edwards EnterpriseOne
- ☐ 25 JD Edwards World
- ☐ 26 Oracle Fusion
- ☐ 27 Hyperion
- ☐ 28 Siebel CRM

ORACLE SERVICES
- ☐ 28 Oracle E-Business Suite On Demand
- ☐ 29 Oracle Technology On Demand
- ☐ 30 Siebel CRM On Demand
- ☐ 31 Oracle Consulting
- ☐ 32 Oracle Education
- ☐ 33 Oracle Support
- ☐ 98 Other
- ☐ 99 None of the Above

0801400